IF THE GODS
HAD MEANT
US TO VOTE
THEY WOULD
HAVE GIVEN US
CANDIDATES

IF THE GODS HAD MEANT US TO VOTE THEY WOULD HAVE GIVEN US CANDIDATES

More Political Subversion from JIM HIGHTOWER, Author of *There's Nothing in the Middle of the Road but Yellow Stripes & Dead Armadillos*

JIM HIGHTOWER

HarperCollins*Publishers*

IF THE GODS HAD MEANT US TO VOTE THEY WOULD HAVE GIVEN US CANDIDATES. Copyright © 2000 by Jim Hightower. All rights reserved. Printed in the United States of America. No part of this book may be used or reproduced in any manner whatsoever without written permission except in the case of brief quotations embodied in critical articles and reviews. For information address HarperCollins Publishers Inc., 10 East 53rd Street, New York, NY 10022.

HarperCollins books may be purchased for educational, business, or sales promotional use. For information please write: Special Markets Department, HarperCollins Publishers Inc., 10 East 53rd Street, New York, NY 10022.

FIRST EDITION

Designed by Lindgren/Fuller Design

This book was manufactured in the U.S. on totally chlorine-free paper made by Lyons Falls Pulp and Paper, and printed with soy-based ink.

ISBN 0-06-019393-X

00 01 02 03 04 ❖/RRD 10 9 8 7 6 5

To Susan DeMarco

No man should ever be president
who doesn't understand hogs.
—HARRY S TRUMAN

CONTENTS

ACKNOWLEDGMENTS

I owe a very special thanks to the research division of my office—our "Department of Betsy," as we call it—which produces so much work that it seems like a whole department of people, but actually consists of a one-woman wonder by the name of Betsy Moon. She is a jewel, capable of unearthing great volumes of information, nimbly sifting through it to find the important nuggets, and producing what's needed when it's needed. She does all of this with great humor, which makes her not only invaluable, but also a delight.

Much of her digging is done in the wealth of materials produced by America's unique and undervalued public-interest groups. Located throughout the country, these small research and advocacy groups are saddle-burrs that have bucked many a pompous corporate executive or government official off of his or her high horse. Since the media have largely abandoned investigative journalism, these underfunded but dedicated truth-seekers are the best source that We the People have for finding out who's doing what to whom and why. In all of my work, including this book, I make use of their information and insights, and I thank them for the enormous public service that they perform.

I owe a great big thank-you, also, to my co-workers Cheri Nightingale and Sylvie Salade, who have done the heavy lifting of production, proofing, and scheduling that has moved this book from my hand scribbles to computer disk (yes, in this exciting electronic era, I remain a proud pad & pen Luddite) and that has moved me around the country for assorted author appearances. Theirs is a difficult assignment, requiring more direct dealings with me than a sane human should have to bear, and I'm grateful not only for the excellent job they do, but also for their great spirit, which allows them to laugh at the impossible, rather than cry.

I'm grateful, too, for the work provided by Chris Johnson, Joe Sexauer and Barbara Strickland, three interns who blessed our office and were assigned to our Salt Mine Division, tracking down sources, checking facts, and doing other essential grub work.

Mentioning such bright young lights as Chris, Joe and Barbara brings to mind how optimistic I feel about young people these days. Despite the media image of teens and twentysomethings being hopelessly self-centered, consumer-obsessed, alienated, and apolitical, my experience has been that most of them are attentive to the big issues of injustice, alert to the possibilities for progressive change, and willing to agitate to get it. I would call them our "most valuable natural resource," but as Utah Philips once said to a group of students, "Have you ever seen what they do to valuable natural resources? Don't ever let them call you a valuable natural resource. They're gonna strip-mine your soul, clearcut your best thoughts for the sake of profit unless you learn to resist. . . . Make a break for it, kids! Flee to the wilderness!" Instead, I'll simply note that I place great hope in this generation, and I thank them for the good spirit, smarts, and sass that they are bringing to the rebellion against the mind-numbing, soul-numbing forces of Corporate World. In addition to the many young people I've been lucky to encounter and work with, I'm especially proud of the ones in my own family, so to put a personal face to this promising generation, I salute my nieces and nephews—Brent, Eric, Jenny, Jerry, Kelly, Kyle, Lisa, and Tommie. Keep agitating.

And I give a big *abrazo* to Adrian Zackheim, my editor and friend ("editor friend" being a concept that would strike most writers as oxymoronic, but it works for me when describing

Adrian). In addition to being a whiz with a red editing pencil, he has also been my savvy guide within the world of conglomerate publishing, moving my hardcore populist work into print and onto the shelves despite its defiantly anti-conglomerate viewpoint. It took some *cojones* for him to do this—and I greatly respect and thank him for it.

PART ONE

ELECTION 2000:
A *Space Odyssey*

OH, GOD!

It's a little-known fact that neck cricks are a common occupational hazard among your politicking class—right up there with wrist sprains, smile cramps, and cologne burn. Politicians suffer neck cricks because, as incongruous as it seems, American politics is damn near eaten up with prayer, so their heads are always bobbing down and up, down and up.

Even Congress begins its daily sessions with a pious bowing of every corrupt head in the chamber—this is not something you'll find normal prostitutes doing. On the campaign trail, too, every public event, whether Democratic or Republican, is kicked off by hauling some minister, rabbi, priest, or whatever to the podium, from whence the cleric beseeches the Almighty to side with the assembled partisans in their righteous cause and smite the infidels of the other party. As one who often speaks at political events—and, I confess, as one who once was a practicing politician myself (you didn't get a virgin here)—I've heard hundreds of these prayerful entreaties. Most are predictable, but every now and then you get a prayer that makes a statement.

My favorite came at a bipartisan meet-the-candidates breakfast in 1990. The head table was stocked with twenty or so buffed-and-grinning aspirants for state legislator, county constable, hide inspector, and whatnot. The collective IQ of the whole bunch wouldn't have outgunned a passel of possums, and none of the candidates had sparked even a flicker of interest, much less enthusiasm, among the yawning public. Nonetheless, about a hundred of their political diehards and kin were in attendance, enjoying the grits and gravy, if not the lackluster campaign.

At 7:30 on the dot, the preacher was called forth. He was a big and imposing man who possessed particularly powerful pipes. He gripped the lectern as the crowd instinctively hushed and bowed. Before uttering a word, the preacher looked deliberately down the line of candidates to his right, then turned and gazed upon those to his left, after which he closed his eyes unusually tight, not so much in prayer, but as though he hoped to block out the sight he'd just taken in. Lifting his face to the heavens, he thrust his arms wide and cried in a booming voice that clearly was seeking deliverance: "Oh, God!" As his plea rumbled across the room, he softly said, "Amen"—and sat down.

As we cast our eyes on today's political process and prospects, most Americans would say to the preacher, "My sentiments exactly." Ask people anywhere in the country what they think about their choices in the forthcoming millennial presidential election and they'll roll their eyes and say, "Oh, God." What about the system itself, with both parties butt deep in the muck and mire of corrupt campaign funds: "Oh, God," they moan, shaking their head. How about your own Congress critter—does he or she represent you? "Oh, God no!" Would you want your kid getting involved in politics? "OH, GOD!!"

What a shame that our nation's politics is so corrupted and worthless these days that our two-party leadership is such an embarrassment, for America really could have used an honest pulse-taking before plunging blindly into the relentlessly ballyhooed "Third Millennium." All hoopla aside, the turning of a century, much less a millennium, is a significant marker, an attention-focusing opportunity to have a thorough public conversation—maybe even a bit of national contemplation—about our people's progress and our national direction. I realize I'm teetering on the brink of squishy idealism here, but golly

Pollyanna, if our political system was not totally fucked, this 2000 election could have been a time when the parties, the candidates, and the media all came out to us plebeians, actually listening to the reality of regular people's situations, debating a plethora of unconventional (i.e., noncorporate) ideas, and generally conducting a kind of two-year, coast-to-coast political Chautauqua—not quite a plebiscite, but at least a "whaddaya think" consultation on charting America's twenty-first century course.

There's plenty to discuss. For starters, enough already with the official pretension that ours is one big fat-and-happy populace whose only real problem in today's "great economy" is deciding whether to stick with the Ford Explorer or move up to the newer and bigger Excursion. Reality check: Sticker price on that Excursion tops $50,000—more than the yearly income of eight out of ten American families. This real-world majority is fortunate if they can afford a used Escort, for the same 80 percent of the people have seen their incomes go flat or go down during the past decade, even as they have been ceaselessly bombarded with assertions that America is wallowing in luxury. For these families, middle-class opportunities are being shut off, and their political voice has been cut off—in both cases by an ascendant corporate/investor elite that now rules supreme, essentially owning the economy, the government, the media . . . and sadly, the 2000 elections.

So, we'll not get the kitchen-table consultation America needs and deserves, nor will the Powers That Be so much as get their feathers ruffled with any bothersome talk by either of the two parties about returning to the gut-level values that working people hold dear: economic fairness, social justice, and equal opportunity for all. Instead, 2000 will be like '98, '96, '94, and '92—another money-soaked, corporate-driven, issue-avoiding, made-for-television snoozer, completely unconnected to real life.

THE CANDIDATES

OK, presidential elections have not been about big ideas, contrasting philosophies, or even about people for several cycles now (going back at least to LBJ v. Goldwater thirty-six years ago), but this one is shaping up to be a particularly surreal space odyssey. If you doubt it for a moment, just peruse the field. In the Democratic primary, you have the unbridled excitement of a Bill Bradley–Al Gore matchup—two policy-wonkish, big-money, corporatists who couldn't fire up grassroots America if we let them use flamethrowers. Listening to them is going to be like having two competing insurance salesmen in your living room at once, both yammering non-stop about the term-life annuity clauses of their respective policies.

But at least Gore and Bradley are slightly sane. Check out the sideshow in the GOP primary. Among the featured acts are Stevie Forbes (a billionaire whose chief idea is to eliminate taxes on billionaires), Gary Bauer (a religious rightist caught up in the conundrum of whether mothers of homosexuals should have aborted), and Orin Hatch (a Utah senator consumed by the ineffable joy of being himself, running on the platform that if everyone else fails, he's ready to be the nominee)—plus Goofy, Pluto, and Dan Quayle. Yes, Danbo! Or at least we had him as a contender for a while, before he dropped out of the race last September, having finished a rather sad eighth in a highly contested Iowa straw poll, running just behind the blue-ribbon heifer at the Iowa State Fair as I recall. Still, it's a measure of how far we've tumbled down Mount Rushmore that Danbo will be recorded in history as having had enough money backers to have been in the running for President of the United States in the Year of Our Lord 2000!

Perhaps some readers are too young to have known The Dan when he was elected Veep with Bush the Elder back in

1988, so as a public service I offer a quick refresher course in Quayle Quotes:

- "It's time for the human race to enter the solar system."
- "What a waste it is to lose one's mind. Or not to have a mind is being very wasteful. How true that is."
- "It isn't pollution that's harming the environment. It's the impurities in our air and water that are doing it."
- "I have made good judgments in the past. I have made good judgments in the future."
- "For NASA, space is still a high priority."
- "I was recently on a tour of Latin America, and the only regret I have is that I didn't study Latin harder in school so I could converse with those people."
- "Welcome to President Bush, Mrs. Bush, and my fellow astronauts."
- "If we don't succeed, we run the risk of failure."
- "Verbosity leads to unclear, inarticulate things."
- "I believe we are on an irreversible trend toward more freedom and democracy—but that could change."
- "Public speaking is very easy."

One notch up on the seriousness level, the Republicans also offer Bush the Younger and others. But peek beneath the surface of all of these "serious" candidates, Democrats as well as Republicans, and you'll find that both parties are offering us the same ol' same ol'—people who have spent their entire careers in service to Wall Street and the Fortunate 500, who are all financed by the same corporate powers, and who are in lockstep support of the corporate agenda. Of those who have a prayer of being either party's nominee, none would do more in the White House than scratch their own ego itch and run errands for their millionaire and billionaire backers.

Cut to the chase: Even before a single primary vote has been cast, the pundits and politicos tell us that the race is

over, that what we'll have as a Democrat-Republican choice
for president on November—is (be still my heart): Gore v.
Bush. Dull and Dullard. Or, perhaps, Bradley v. Bush. Duller
and Dullard.

This is choice? Which one of them is going to stand up for
your family against the whims of the global speculators, the
polluters, the downsizers, the tax loopholers, the corporate welfare bums, the HMOs, the media conglomerates, the finance-
industry finaglers, and all the rest of the establishment, which
is flanked by an elite corps of $500-an-hour Gucci-clad lobby-
ists and armed with enough campaign cash to build an impene-
trable wall around Washington?

Start with Bradley, simply because there's a move to make
him out to be the delightful progressive surprise in the 2000
Cracker Jacks box. He's a maverick with a liberal heart, goes
the spin, and he'll really shake things up if he gets to 1600
Pennsylvania Avenue. Before we hoist him onto our shoulders
as the putative people's champion, however, let's check out
this "maverick."

Quick: name a major progressive cause that Senator Bradley
championed or some courageous crusade that he led in his
eighteen years in Washington. Even on the issues he now says
are at the center of his candidacy (campaign finance reform,
racial healing, concern for poor people), he made no in-your-
face challenge to the power elites, nor is his name attached to
any progressive achievement. Sure he cast some good votes
during his tenure: more money for kids and the environment,
against President Clinton's welfare deform, and for arms control. But voting is merely showing up—it's the least that a senator does and bears little relationship to leadership. Essentially,
he was a plodder in his three senate terms, a neo-liberal without a populist bone in his six-foot, five-inch frame.

This son of a small-town Missouri banker distinguished himself in the senate chiefly as a compliant servant to the Wall
Street crowd. For example, he was the chief Democratic defec-

tor to jump behind Ronald Reagan's 1986 voodoo tax act, which slashed the tax bills for corporations and the wealthy at the same time it jacked up the payroll taxes on working stiffs. Also, in a rare burst of legislative enthusiasm, he was a particularly peppy cheerleader for the passage of NAFTA in 1993, as he was in '96 for the approval of the World Trade Organization—both of which dramatically extended the reach of global corporate power over ordinary folks.

It probably will not surprise you to learn that these same corporate interests were his steady and generous financial backers. The man who now talks loudly of campaign finance reform was tagged in his last senate race as "The King of bundled contributions" by the keen-eyed watchdog group, Center for Responsive Politics. Bundling is a loophole that corporations use to dump otherwise illegal wads of money into a favored candidate's pockets—for example, on June 16, 1989, thirty executives of the Wall Street firm Shearson Lehman Hutton suddenly and individually decided that it would be a good day to write checks of $500 to $1,000 to Bradley's senate campaign. What an amazing coincidence! A week later, thirty-two other Shearson executives were struck by the same spontaneous impulse. In all, Shearson bundled up more than $71,000 for the senator—the largest donation to a senate candidate that year.

Just as he was paid to play for the New York Knicks in Madison Square Garden, Bradley has been a pay-to-play guy for corporations in Washington. For example, in his excellent book, *The Buying of the President*, Charles Lewis of the Center for Public Integrity writes that in Bradley's last senate campaign he took more money from drug companies than any other candidate in the country. These pharmaceutical giants were not giving to Bill because they were old Knicks fans—but because they were avid fans of a loophole in the tax code called Section 936, and Senator Bradley, who sat on the tax-writing finance committee, was their chief defender to keep the loophole in play. Section 936 had been passed years ago as an economic development boost for the commonwealth of Puerto Rico, allowing companies that created jobs there to avoid paying taxes on profits they made from their Puerto Rican operations. Fine, but in the 1980s, legal beagles for the drug makers twisted this good intention into a billion-dollar-a-year boondoggle for themselves.

Here's the trick. Profits from drug making mostly come from the marketing, development, and research stages, with the actual manufacturing of a pill being an almost inconsequential part of the process. The corporations, however, saw Section 936 as a bird's nest on the ground, for it allows them to shift good-paying medicine-manufacturing jobs from workers here in the states to low-wage Puerto Rican workers—not only pocketing a cheap labor windfall, but also claiming that every dime of the profits they make on the drugs are tax free, since they are "Made in Puerto Rico." The bottom line on this Section 936 bookkeeping maneuver is that we taxpayers dole out a tax subsidy of some $70,000 a year to these giants for each and every pill-making job that they move to the island, even though the workers themselves are paid around $12,000 a year. When senate reformers tried in the 1986 tax bill to stop this rip-off, Bradley defended the loophole with more frenetic energy and sprightly moves than he used in guarding John Havlicek in their basketball matchups, and he saved Section 936 for his drug-company contributors.

Asked by the Center for Public Integrity about the connection of such campaign contributions to legislative results, Bradley responded: "The assumption that the only reason anyone donates to a political campaign is to 'buy access to power' is insulting to those who participate in politics." Perhaps he's simply polite to a fault, but the New Jersey senator certainly never came close to "insulting" corporate executives by rejecting their checks, instead showing tail-wagging enthusiasm for them to participate in politics through him. He performed so consistently in their interests that *Investment Dealers' Digest* ranked him among "Wall Street's strongest advocates," and the official voice of corporate power, *The Wall Street Journal*, gushed in 1995 that Bradley was "the most admirable senator of this era."

Now he's running for president because, he says, "I looked in the mirror and said, I'm ready. I'm really, kind of, at the top of my game." But his game is the same—be liberal on social issues, be Republican on economic issues, and stay hitched to the money. No doubt Bradley sincerely feels for the poor and wishes the middle class well, but he hangs out in the power-houses of the rich, which means he'll never offer anything but Band-Aids for the poor and the middle class, because to do more requires challenging the corporate structure and the privileges of the rich.

Probe even a bit beneath his caring demeanor, and you'll find that he's as solid a corporatist as Al Gore, or for that matter, George W. He accepts Wall Street's full agenda of rambo globalization that would enthrone corporations and speculators as sovereigns over workers, farmers, the environment . . . and governments. For the millions of hard hit working stiffs of America who have been downsized and outsourced, seeing their real incomes fall during the "prosperity" of the '90s, he offers the same lame nostrums we hear from Gore and Bush: you need to seek "retraining" and learn to "work smarter." On farm issues, he is clueless, mumbling about more exports and trusting in the "magic of the marketplace"—apparently unaware that magicians don't perform "magic," they perform illusions. On issues of high-tech, biotech, and any other tech he's as gullible as a hick on his first trip to the state fair, gushing about the marvels of technology and nodding approvingly as the gabil-lionaires who run these trendy corporations go down the list of goodies they want from the next president. And don't expect him to stand like Teddy Roosevelt against the mega-mergers that are locking up industry after industry while they also squeeze out competition, raise prices, reduce service, and fabulously enrich the very CEOs and Wall Street bankers who are putting up the bulk of the funds for Bradley's run for the White House.

Even in his proposals to help the poor and middle class he takes care to structure them in a way that will not offend his sponsors. Like Clinton, he would run most of his programs through corporations—an approach that John Kenneth Galbraith once likened to feeding the sparrows by first passing the grain through a horse. An example is Bradley's widely-touted health care proposal. First, give him his due—he deserves high praise for trying to put the issue of *universal* health coverage back on the political table. But the praise stops there, because his idea amounts to a massive, money-sucking subsidy from taxpayers to insurance companies and HMOs. Rather than boldly advocating a single-payer plan that would eliminate the bureaucratic, wasteful, and fraud-ridden insurance middleman, Bradley wants to hook up every American to these very insurance corporations, letting them control our medical decisions and continue their profiteering at our expense.

As always when assessing a politico, to know Bradley, follow the money. "I am raising money from ordinary citizens, not from special interest PACs," he has proclaimed, and indeed he (and Gore) are rejecting PAC funds. But before you swallow that "ordinary citizens" line, note that 82 percent of his presidential funds so far have come not from the $25 crowd, but from the big contributors—a higher percentage of high-dollar checks than even George Bush shows! Also, he has taken more Wall Street money than any other candidate in the race. Technically, corporations can't give money to presidential contenders, but they get around this legal inconvenience by bundling "individual" contributions from their top executives. As of October 1999, the following six bundlers were his biggest sugar daddies:

Goldman Sachs	$239,700
Lehman Brothers	$156,950
Merrill Lynch	$121,940
Citigroup	$74,150
Morgan Stanley Dean Witter	$55,750
J. P. Morgan	$51,600

As a political adviser to institutional investors has observed, "Wall Street likes Bill Bradley. He is a Wall Street kind of Democrat . . . the kind of guy corporate executives feel comfortable around."

And why wouldn't they find him as comfy as an old pair of shoes, since he shares their world view of global economics and, while he has a sweet concern for the underprivileged, he can absolutely be counted on not to rock the corporate boat? Among the CEOs who are Bill's special buddies, actively collecting up bundles of checks for him, are movie and high-tech investor Herbert Allen (who also flies Bill around in his corporate jet), Goldman Sachs president John Thornton, Thomas Labrecque of Chase Manhattan, Disney Inc.'s chief Mouseketeer Michael Eisner, Tommy Hilfiger of fashion fame (and a noted exploiter of sweatshop labor in third-world nations), media mogul Barry Diller, coffee baron Howard Shultz of Starbucks, corporate takover artist Joseph Flan, Citigroup overseer Sanford Weill, John Bryan of Sara Lee (another sweatshop exploiter who is a big backer of extending NAFTA to the Caribbean and Central America, where his company makes clothing), and book-marketing czar Leonard Riggio of Barnes & Noble.

This is the people's champion? Yes Bill Bradley is smart, yes he's serious-minded, yes he's a decent and caring human being, yes he can hit the jump shot from the post—but, no, he won't take on the economic elites who are trampling America's workaday majority.

Then there are Al and George, sons of privilege whose idea of "hardscrabble" is to run out of vowels. They never had to work a drudge shift or worry about making rent, getting good health care, paying bills . . . or getting ahead in life. Neither has a clue what it's like for a family to try to make ends meet on less than $30,000 a year, which is the economic neighborhood for a *majority* of Americans today. George W. Bush is from a wealthier family than Gore, but both have had all the advantages of money since birth, living in an exclusive world of comfort and connections, including entry to the "right" private schools. Gore-the-Democrat, son of a U.S. senator, prepped at Saint Albans in Washington, where his fellow students dubbed him "Prince Al," then off he went to the clubby confines of Harvard Yard. Bush started at Houston's tony Kincaid Academy before moving on to Phillips Academy in Andover; then, despite being a mediocre-to-poor student, he was allowed to follow Daddy and Granddaddy Bush into Yale (the spawn of rich white families being the one American minority that continues to enjoy the benefit of an aggressive affirmative action program, which is why anyone who knows his past guffawed last year when Bush solemnly denounced the practice of "social promotions" in public education).

But an upscale upbringing is not enough to explain Al's and George's fealty to the rich and powerful. After all, this is America, where the handicap of privilege need not bar anyone from becoming a useful citizen. It can be overcome, even by those entering the political realm, if only they have the gumption and internal fortitude to do it (Eleanor and Franklin Roosevelt being a couple of handy role models here). Serving private interests over the public interest is a *choice,* and these two presidential aspirants willingly and eagerly made that choice right from the start of their careers. Rather than using their birth advantages to buck the system on behalf of those who get trampled by it, they joined in solidarity with their brothers and sisters who are similarly advantaged, realizing that they could move up by buddying up with business executives, investment bankers, Washington lobbyists, and other money players who could be valuable to them personally and politically.

BUSH PLAYS BALL

Meet one of George's special buddies: Richard Rainwater. He's little known outside the rarefied world of high finance, but to those denizens he's considered a financial wizard and a skilled corporate deal maker. Having been a bright Wall Streeter at Goldman Sachs, then having made a bundle handling investments for the gabillionaire Bass family of Fort Worth, he subsequently amassed his own portly portfolio, now owning such properties as Pioneer oil company, the huge Columbia/HCA Healthcare corporation, and the sprawling Crescent Real Estate empire, which has billions invested in high-rise office buildings, golf courses, and other developments. He's also into casinos, costume jewelry, health-food restaurants, and a joint venture with the Chinese called Richina (Richard, rich, China . . . get it? Cute). Bottom line is he now ranks among the one hundred richest people in America, with a net worth in the neighborhood of a billion and a half bucks.

Along the way to that posh neighborhood, he got cozy with the President's boy, who had not amounted to much and showed little promise. After a stint in the National Guard (he helped defend Houston during the Vietnam War), Bush spent many years developing his partying skills, gaining the nicknames of "Boosto" and "The Bombastic Bushkin" along the way. With a little help from Daddy and Daddy's friends, George W. went into the oil business, but failed. When Rainwater entered his life, Bush wasn't doing anything but hanging around his daddy's White House, where some of the serious players had bestowed a third nickname on him: "Junior." It was not a term of respect. He was a fortyish overgrown frat boy who, despite a family inheritance, had not made it into the big-money leagues where you're not just a son of wealth, but MR. RICH. To flower, every bush needs to be properly watered, and Rainwater was just what "Junior" needed to grow into real wealth and to gain that "successful businessman" image that later allowed him to run for governor of Texas. Over the past decade, Rainwater has put Bush into oil deals, real estate investments, and other business schemes, with the result that, as R. G. Ratcliffe of the *Houston Chronicle* reports, Richard Rainwater "is largely responsible for Bush's wealth."

The sweetest Bush connection to Rainwater was the purchase and subsequent sale of the Texas Rangers baseball team. In 1989, Rainwater, Dallas financier Edward "Rusty" Rose III, and Cincinnati financier William O. DeWitt Jr. were the heavy hitters in a partnership that bought the Rangers for $86 million. They brought Bush into the deal, too. Even though he put up a relatively insignificant $600,000 (borrowed from United Bank of Midland, where he had served as a director), George was named "Managing Partner," which meant he got to be the team's designated mouth. He served as official spokesman and was the guy with the star-quality family name who was sent by the Rangers to Major League Baseball's formal meetings.

The job was perfect for the affable George, for it involved no heavy lifting—mental or physical—and it paid well: $200,000 a year. So, in his four-plus years as MP, before resigning to run for governor in 1994, Bush was more than able to cover his $600,000 investment in the team, thanks to the generous paycheck his multimillionaire partners stuffed in his pocket each year for acting as the Rangers' general manager. He got something else, too—a high-profile position guaranteed to give him extensive media coverage. He milked this opportunity for all it was worth, and then some, regularly getting his picture made with team stars, signing baseballs in the stands for Rangers fans, and, at the sight of any TV camera, hiking his pants leg to show off his cowboy boots with a red-white-and-blue Texas Rangers logo tooled into the leather. Class will always out.

As managing partner, he also had been given a title that bestowed an aura of business legitimacy, something he'd not been able to get on his own. He clung to it like a drunk grasping his last quart of beer. While giving reporter Ratcliffe a tour of the Rangers' stadium just prior to announcing for governor, Bush waved his arm around and claimed the entire enterprise as his own: "When all those people in Austin say 'He ain't never done anything,' well, this is it."

It's true that the worth of the franchise appreciated richly during George W.'s tenure, but not because of any managerial acumen in the executive suite (and, alas, certainly not because of the team's sad-sack performance on the field during those years). Rather, it was because of a generous dose of corporate welfare from local taxpayers. In 1991, Bush and partners pulled off the old "Build-us-a-new-stadium-you-yokels-or-we'll-move-the-whole-kit-and-kaboodle-to-East-Beelzebub-and-leave-you-with-nothing" heist on local officials. Thus was born the lovely "Ballpark at Arlington," costing taxpayers $150 million or so, paid for by imposing a half-cent hike in the always popular sales tax.

Perhaps I should not be so quick to jump on the partners and compliant local pols for devising such a regressive financing scheme, for it might well have been an act of civic-minded generosity on their part. Since your low-income citizens and average working stiffs can no longer afford to go to the games, due to the jacked up price of admission to the joint, hitting them for half a penny every time they spend a dollar elsewhere in Arlington gives them a way to participate and share in the pride of "owning" the Rangers. Imagine the warm glow they must feel when driving past the majestic stadium alongside I-30, knowing that their every purchase that day—from diapers to beer—will send a few more of their pennies, nickels, and dimes to the Rainwater-Bush partnership.

One other telling tidbit about George W. is wrapped up in his stadium years. As reported by Robert Bryce in the *Texas Observer*, candidate Bush campaigned in '94 on the tried-and-true oratorical chestnut that government power should never be allowed to stomp on people's private property rights. "I understand full well the value of private property," he assured a group of stuffed shirts at a business gathering just before the election, adding, "I will do everything I can to defend the power of private property and property rights when I am governor of this state." He also said, "The best way to allocate resources in our society is through the marketplace. Not through a governing elite."

I'll bet the Curtis Mathes family wishes it could have been there to hear the governor-to-be lecturing on the proper role of government. Until 1991, they owned thirteen acres of land next to the proposed new Ballpark at Arlington—acres the Rangers' brass, including MP Bush, desperately wanted. In April of that year, the team hired lobbyists to push a special bill through the legislature creating a quasi-governmental group that would serve as the legal entity for obtaining their field of dreams. Called the Arlington Sports Facilities Development Authority, it handled land acquisition and other often untidy tasks associated with building a ballpark for the Rangers. This new authority promptly offered the Mathes family $817,000 for their thirteen choice acres, which was only $4 million less than the land was judged to be worth. Naturally, the family refused to sell. The team had prepared for this inconvenience, however, having quietly tucked into the authority's founding legislation a small provision that granted to it the power of condemnation. So—BAM!—the Rangers' owners simply seized the Mathes land by eminent domain, using their specially created authority (the governing elite) to pay way less than market price and allocate the family's private resources to themselves. In the process, Bush and cohorts stomped property rights flatter than a toad on a rainy country road.

The Mathes family sued and were awarded $5 million by a jury. Good luck collecting a dime from the Bush team, however—they claimed that the judgment was not against them (even though they are the ones who engineered the seizure of the land) but against the Arlington Sports Facilities Development Authority: "The sports authority has to pay that," a Rangers spokesman curtly says. For years, the Rangers dillied and dallied, keeping the Mathes family from getting either their land or their money. Finally, after Bush and partners sold the team, the new owners paid the judgment.

Add the confiscated Mathes property to the $150 million that Arlington taxpayers contributed to the team, and suddenly the value of the Rangers franchise had nearly tripled.

When Bush moved into the governor's mansion in 1995 (a move assisted by a $100,000 campaign donation from Rainwater), he made quite a public show of putting his financial holdings into a blind trust. What he didn't publicize, though, was that he left one of his assets out of the trust: the baseball team. This omission let the governor stay informed and involved when Rainwater and the other partners negotiated the sale of the Rangers franchise for $250 million in 1998— the deal that finally elevated George into the class of MR. RICH.

He was paid $2.7 million for his minority share of the sale price—more than a 400 percent return on his investment. But Rainwater *et al.* took better care of their gubernatorial partner than that, awarding him what the Cajuns of southeast Texas refer to as a "lagniappe"—a little something extra. In a Cajun restaurant, the lagniappe might be a small plate of andouille sausage or some extra shrimp for your étouffée, but in Bush's case it was a "bonus payment" of $12.2 million. So, the sitting governor of the great state of Texas, with eyes wide open on an insider crony deal left outside his blind trust, was handed nearly $15 million from the sale—a 2,400 percent profit on the $600,000 he had put up just eight years earlier.

The partners were not merely being generous, they were being grateful. In Bush's first term in office, his former business associates have found state government a most welcoming and profitable place. As documented by reporter Ratcliffe of the *Chronicle,* old Bush buddy Rainwater has been first in line at the government trough, enjoying such favors as:

- Being allowed to buy three office buildings from the state Teacher's Retirement System at bargain-basement rates, including one sold so cheaply to Rainwater's realty firm that the state-administered trust fund for teachers *lost* $44 million on the deal.
- Having the state fund that manages money for Texas universities and public school systems invest nearly $20 million in the stock of his Crescent Real Estate company.
- A Bush veto of a Patient Protection Act that could have affected profits for Rainwater's already troubled Columbia/HCA Healthcare Inc. chain of hospitals and HMOs by requiring more care, instituting a better appeals process for doctors and patients, and prohibiting financial incentives that limit care.
- A Bush-backed tax plan that ultimately failed but would have cut some $2.5 million in annual taxes on commercial properties that Rainwater owns in various Texas cities.
- A $10 million windfall for Crescent Real Estate from a sports-arena financing bill signed into law by Bush in 1997; six months later, Crescent's president put $11,000 into Bush's political fund.

GORE FITS IN

While George W. was born to the manor and summered at the family compound on Walker's Point, which juts jauntily into the Atlantic from Kennebunkport, Maine, Al Gore was born the son of a well-to-do but decidedly maverick U.S. senator from Tennessee. Despite being upscale himself, Al Senior was an advocate of ordinary folks, and he relished getting into the occasional political brawl with the power elites, fighting for the rights and needs of laboring people, small farmers, and minorities. But Al Junior is hardly a chip off that old block of in-your-face populism. Far from it—his own mom, Pauline, has described her second child as "a born conformist." Unfortunately, that fits him like a black suit on an undertaker. As he has confirmed from childhood all the way through his vice presidential years, this is not a fellow who's comfortable coloring outside the lines, much less challenging the corporate order.

You can count on him to stay strictly inside those lines as he methodically moves toward the Democratic presidential nomination, too, despite some Goreheads who want us to think that, deep down, Al might possibly *be* a Democrat. They whisper that he could blossom into some combination of William Jennings Bryan, FDR, and Al Gore *Sr.* now that he's finally in a position to free himself from the Wall Street money shackles that bound the Clinton presidency. Yeah, and Dan Quayle is a closet member of the Mensa Society.

Anyone who thinks Gore is about to leap out in a pair of tights and a red cape to crusade as The People's Champion needs (1) to get professional help if you really fantasize about Al Gore in tights, and (2) to explain why he's been spending such an inordinate amount of time in the company of Rattner, Tisch & Kramer. This is not a firm, but three individuals, although they have been acting as a sort of political brokerage firm, peddling Gore as their sole commodity. Steve Rattner is chief executive of the investment banking house Lazard Frères; John Tisch is scion of the multibillionaire Tisch family, with major holdings in everything from Loews hotels to the New York Giants; and Orin Kramer owns the megabucks money-management firm of Kramer Spellman.

These three gentlemen of the Street have become Al's best pals during the past three years, touting him as hot political stock and working furtively to bring him into the inner sanctums of America's most powerful brokers, bankers, and bond dealers. RT&K's objective has not been merely to introduce him to the conservative (and genetically Republican) world of these high-level money changers but to have them really get to know Al, trust him, teach him, and—dare I say it?—bond with him. According to the *Washington Post*, the trio of Rattner, Tisch, and Kramer has put together dozens of what they refer to as "cultivational" meetings between Gore and a who's who of America's financial heavies, including top executives from Goldman Sachs, Lehman Brothers, J. P. Morgan, Citigroup, AIG Inc., and Bankers Trust. Gore has been courting them like a boar in heat ever since he and Clinton were reelected in '96. He has lunched in Manhattan hotels with them, held tête-à-têtes with them in his Executive Office Building hideaway, had breakfast brainstorming sessions with them in Washington and New York, brought them in for White House coffees (some people just never learn), and even threw three intimate Christmas parties at the Vice President's mansion in 1997 especially to host his new Street buddies and their spouses.

The bonding is complete. Rattner, Tisch, and Kramer have been harvesting bales of campaign dollars from the fertile fields of Wall Street for Gore's presidential run. By midsummer of '99, Kramer was already on record as having baled up more than $100,000 for Gore, and executives from Goldman Sachs, Citigroup, Morgan Stanley, Merrill Lynch, Lehman Brothers, and many more are known to have bought stock in Al.

Check by check, event by event, private meeting by private meeting, Gore has steadily forged and fitted the links of his own Wall Street shackles. What he gets out of this, of course, is a reliable flow of political money from some of the deepest pockets in the country. What do they get? A good boy. One who's well trained, properly grateful, eager to have their continuing approval, and a born conformist. Already, he has demonstrated that he was an attentive student in all those tutorials he got in RT&K's cultivational meetings. For example, the Gore2000 model has toned down considerably the enviro-protecto persona that only a few years ago was his political hallmark. Instead, he now emphasizes a remarkably Republican-like approach that advocates balancing any environmental action with the absolute need to assure that America's "good business climate" (including the stock prices of polluters) is not harmed in any way. I mean, we're all concerned about the climate, right, so why shouldn't the business climate be a natural environmental concern? As Al himself put it, "I believe that anybody who aspires to lead this nation in the twenty-first century needs to be fully conversant with the business environment." Save the Dow, man.

Likewise, Gore2000 has come to the altar of the high church of free-market orthodoxy, becoming almost evangelical in lecturing leaders of developing nations—as he did in Malaysia in 1998—on the imperative of throwing open their borders and their people to the holy whims of Wall Street investors. Never mind that this orthodoxy is crushing the aspirations of those people, even as it drains the life out of the aspirations of America's middle class, Al's focus is on campaign check writers. Jon Corzine, co-CEO of Goldman Sachs, is one of those check writers, as well as one of Gore's tutors, including having had a cup of coffee and an introductory one-on-one session with him in 1998. In a telling understatement about the reelection of Democrat Gore, Corzine told *Washington Post* reporter Ianthe Jeanne Dugan: "The Vice President has tried to understand how the global economy works from the eyes of someone sitting in Wall Street."

Swell. When's the last time Gore tried to understand how the global economy works from the eyes of someone on your street? But, then, unlike Mr. Corzine, you and your Goldman Sachs colleagues haven't written more than $76,750 worth of checks to him, have you?

To keep Gore from getting his streets confused, his pals Rattner, Tisch, and Kramer continue to surround him with the right kind of people. Various Wall Street executives regularly confer with him behind closed doors to explain global financial issues and to counsel him on his economic policies ("Don't touch that Dow!")—and they even vet his speeches. Holy Popalorum! VET HIS SPEECHES? What are the working stiffs, dirt farmers, and other regular folks of America to make of a *Democrat* who meekly submits his thoughts and words for predelivery approval to plutocrats ensconced high in their Towers of Mammon, smugly looking down on the American people?

Not to worry, say some Gore strategists, explaining that Wall Street itself is sort of "populistic" now that so many Internet-browsing, Starbucks-sipping Americans are, like, you know, really into the market in a Third Millennium kind of way, and they see CEOs as celebrity studs, so seeing Big Al rubbing shoulders with them really has its own grassrootsy appeal. Really. None other than Roger Altman, the New York investment banker who first introduced Bill Clinton to Wall Street and later helped shape Clinton's elitist economic policies as deputy treasury secretary, embraces both Gore and his "SmartPolitics" identification with wealth. As Altman told *Post* reporter Dugan: "With a third of American households invested in Wall Street, and mushrooming millionaires made there, Wall Street is more important than ever."

NICE GUYS

Not that Gore means any harm to us nonmushrooming millionaires or to the two-thirds of us who are not immersed in the thrill of the Dow, but—hey—he's taken the money and kissed the devil square on the lips, so what do you expect him to do?

Both Gore and Bush hope that you won't notice, much less take it personally, that their allegiance is to the moneyed elite. Neither has any ill will toward the workaday majority—it's just business. They're certainly not venal in their practice of special-interest politics. Indeed, the public relations people of both parties consider Gore and Bush to be terrific political products for today's market environment precisely because they come across as smooth, family-friendly, safe, comfortable, richly appointed, roomy, with plush leather interiors and superior sound systems—each one a Lexus of status quo politics.

I can't say that I really know Al Gore, though I've talked with him a few times, but I can tell you that he's an awfully nice guy. It's true that he's duller than televised bowling, but he's certainly a sincere fellow and seems to have a fine family. He'll tell you that economic growth is the key to helping everyone, that our fabulous prosperity must be continued (though we simply must do more to help poor people share in it), that he's deeply concerned about America's children, that education is a top priority with him, that we need an aggressive but rational approach to protecting our environment for future generations, that family and quality-of-life issues matter personally to him, and that he believes America will be greater than ever as we cross into the twenty-first century together. "Practical Idealism," he calls it.

I don't know George W. Bush personally, but by all accounts he's an awfully nice guy. It's true that he's not the brightest puppy in the litter, but he's certainly a sincere fellow and seems to have a real nice family. He'll tell you that economic growth is the key to helping everyone, that our fabulous prosperity must be continued (though we simply must do more to help poor people share in it), that he's deeply concerned about America's children, that education is a top priority with him, that we need an aggressive but rational approach to protecting our environment for future generations, that family and quality-of-life issues matter personally to him, and that he believes America will be greater than ever as we cross into the twenty-first century together. "Compassionate Conservatism," he calls it.

Old Mr. Powerbroker watches George W. Bush swing with his slow roundhouse right of Compassionate Conservatism, then watches Al Gore counterpunch with his feeble left jab of Practical Idealism, and he just laughs and laughs, not caring one whit whether Compassionate Practicality, Conservative Idealism, or any combination thereof wins in November— because he owns both of these pugs. Among the corporations already represented on the money lists of *both* the Bush and Gore campaigns are:

Aetna	Intel
AT&T	Lazard Frères
BellSouth	Lehman Brothers
Boeing	Merrill Lynch
Citigroup	Microsoft
Du Pont	Monsanto
Enron	Morgan Stanley
Ernst & Young	Raytheon
Goldman Sachs	Roche
IBM	Time Warner

CLINTON'S LAST ERECTION

As the great Mexican revolutionist Pancho Villa lay dying, he suddenly realized his followers would expect some memorable last words from him. But his final breath was quickly upon him, and he hadn't prepared for the moment, so Villa passed into history with this desperate utterance: "Don't let it end like this! Tell them I said something."

Alas, poor Bill Clinton's eight-year presidency is gasping to a close, and you can hear him pleading: "Tell them I *did* something." For most of his two terms, Clinton has fretted over his "legacy" rather than doing what it takes to create one. For example, this was the guy who boldly decided in 1997 to join Abraham Lincoln and Lyndon Johnson in addressing the great hurt of racism in our society. His race initiative, crowed the president's team of cock-a-doodle-dooers, would be "The Legacy." Indeed, it was an opportunity for greatness, a matter worthy of Herculean presidential effort. And Clinton, having grown up in the mire of Arkansas's racial divide and been governor there for years, already knew the problems. As a modern son of the South he was perfectly positioned to go beyond a rehashing of problems and delve into solutions, quite possibly achieving some genuine measure of progress. What a way to step into the new millennium!

It was no small task—legacy building never is. It requires whacking the bastards right in the face, spending enormous amounts of presidential capital, taking hard political risks, and confronting the power structure of America—all things that Lincoln and LBJ did. Clinton, too, started strong, launching his initiative with a gusher of eloquence about what he termed America's "constant curse." But rhetoric was all we got—turn on Clinton's spigot, and he's all foam, no beer. His boldest "action" was to appoint a study commission. He did attend a couple of hoked-up, town-hall-style meetings on the subject, including one ill-conceived evening with sports figures that was broadcast on ESPN, but he didn't spend a nickel of political capital.

After meandering around the country talking about the issue for a couple of years, the commission finally sputtered to an end, and in 1999 Clinton announced the conclusion of the whole pathetic exercise—he created a new and shiny bit of bureaucracy called (cue the trumpets): "White House Office on the President's Initiative for One America."

All you need to know about the importance of this office in Washington's hierarchy of power is that it does not have cabinet-level status, it is not a separate agency, and it does not report to the President, vice president, attorney general, chief of staff, or even Buddy, the presidential pooch. Instead, it is headed by the deputy director of the office of public liaison. The *deputy* director! Presumably he reports to the actual, full-fledged director of the office of public liaison, who I understand *does* report to Buddy.

So our pantheon of presidential race healers proudly boasts Lincoln with his Emancipation Proclamation, Johnson with his Voting Rights Act . . . and now Clinton with his WHOOPIFOA. Legacy-wise, he would have been better off if he'd just led America in a one-time, nationally broadcast sing-along of all ninety-seven verses of "Kumbaya."

But every president is remembered for *something*. In college, the textbook for my American history class had photographs or drawings of the various presidents scattered through it, complete with a three- or four-sentence caption describing their major accomplishments in office. I recall that the captions were quite spare for the line of decidedly undistinguished presidents during the Robber Baron days, extending roughly between Lincoln and the trust-busting T. R. at the turn of the century. Under the photo of one of these mediocre to miserable presidents (it might have been Rutherford B. Hayes or Chester A. Arthur) was a one-line caption noting that "the White House was wired for electricity" during his administration.

I thought of that president's lame claim to fame one day late in Clinton's first term. By then, he had already scuttled practically all of his major campaign pledges, including promises that he would produce good jobs at good wages, raise the minimum wage so no one who works full-time lives in poverty, provide health coverage for all, and stop any international trade deal that failed to protect workers or the environment. Clinton, who says he often dreams of being remembered as another FDR, was facing a fate of not being remembered at all, much like Hayes and Arthur. Then, in 1995, came a proud announcement from Clinton's office that "the White House has been wired for the Internet."

He would have been stuck with this as his epitaph, except that soon afterward he was overcome by his renowned lust, which ultimately led him to make the indelible and infamous mark for which he'll always be remembered—and I don't mean the mess on the dress. Clinton's most ardent and damaging presidential passion was not for Monica but for money.

From mid-1995 forward, he amassed a monument of corrupt, corporate campaign moneys—hundreds of millions of dollars that, if stacked together, would thrust higher into the capital sky than the Washington Monument itself—Clinton's final erection.

Particularly harmful was his innovative and tireless pursuit of "soft money," a category that is just as pornographic (politically speaking) as it sounds. This is unregulated money, in terms of where it comes from and how much of it can be given by one source. You see, corporations themselves are forbidden to contribute to candidates or political action committees—and the executives, lobbyists, and PACs of corporations are limited to giving no more than $1,000 each to candidates or $5,000 to their committees. Running around collecting these "small" checks was not building a big enough political war chest fast enough to satisfy the cash-hungry Clinton campaign operatives in the spring of '95. If only they could uncap the deep well of corporate funds, from which they could draw $100,000, $500,000, even a million dollars at a time. Then late one night, from a cubicle somewhere in a Washington basement, someone shouted, "Eureka! Voilà! Bonanza! Bingo! Come to Papa!"—and the soft-money loophole was found.

CLINTON CHANGES THE MONEY RULES

It's not that the Clintonites were the first or only ones to use soft money for their own political purposes—that honor must fall to the GOP, which seems genetically programmed to sniff-out a dollar bill, no matter where it's tucked (Sen. George Voinovich, Republican of Ohio, could be the poster boy for this genetic proclivity—his press secretary confirms that Voinovich once stepped up to a urinal, looked down, spotted a penny in it, reached into the urinal to snare the coin, rinsed it off, and put it in his pocket). Republican leaders have been hauling bags of soft money into their coffers since at least 1991. But they lacked the vision of what could be done with this money . . . and the audacity that Clinton and his campaign showed in going after it.

Ironically, soft money was designed to help political parties return some small measure of importance to "people-politics." Instead of financing campaigns, this money is supposed to develop grassroots networks and to talk *issues* with voters.

Corporations can give directly to these efforts (though relatively few did before 1995), and there is no limit on how much can be donated. The only proviso is that the money cannot go to a candidate, nor can it be spent in coordination with, much less under the direction of, a candidate's campaign. Pure in concept, this little flower was about to be violated on a massive scale by Bill Clinton.

Dick Morris, the well-known low-life political hack and sucker of prostitutes' toes, was Clinton's guru back then, and he says it was the prim Erskine Bowles, a corporate chieftain who later became Clinton's chief of staff, who first told him about "something called issue advocacy advertising." The deal was that they could raise truckloads of corporate soft money through the Democratic National Committee, then have the DNC spend it on an early blitz of image advertising to promote the president's reelection. Clinton himself was wildly enthusiastic about this shell game, grinning like a pig that had finally found a way into the corn bin. You can even see him grinning and talking about the plan on tape, thanks to Sherry Jones, producer of a Bill Moyers television documentary called "Washington's Other Scandal." She got her hands on a grainy videotape made with a camcorder by someone at a Clinton fund-raiser in Washington's swank Hay-Adams Hotel. There was Bill, sipping fine wine and schmoozing with a roomful of suits who had given a ton of soft money to the DNC, candidly telling them about the scam they were running:

CLINTON: It means that we can finance this campaign in 1995, so I don't have to worry about it in 1996. So this is a brilliant thing that they have done, this plan that you have participated in.

He tells them that soft-money contributions like theirs have already bought ads in key markets—ads paid for by the Democratic Party, but touting him:

TV COMMERCIAL: As Americans, there are some things we do simply and solely because they are moral, right, and good. . . . The Republicans are wrong to want to cut Medicare benefits. And President Clinton is right to protect Medicare. . . ."

The president confides to them that the DNC soft-money commercials have been a big boost to his reelection chances:

CLINTON: The lead that I enjoy today in the public opinion polls is about one-third due to that advertising and the fact that we have been able to shape the debates in that way. And it makes a huge difference.

By raising the money through the DNC, he tells his Hay-Adams co-conspirators, he is also able to skirt the legal limit on the total amount his campaign can spend:

CLINTON: We realized that we could run these ads through the Democratic Party, which means that we can raise money in twenty- and fifty- and hundred-thousand-dollar lots, so we didn't have to do it all in thousand dollars and run down my . . . you know, what I can spend, which is limited by law. So that's what we've done.

This discovery by Clinton and his clever boys produced a watershed change in the way presidential elections are financed, and it turned him into the most indefatigable, prodigious, and shameless money hustler in American history—and I'm counting Nixon. They did not merely find a loophole in our nation's campaign funding laws, they took an earth auger and bored a hole through the whole damned book, then they shredded the pages, burned the shreds, and buried the ashes in the Rose Garden during a lunar eclipse, howling deliriously as they sacked up unprecedented sums of money piled in front of them by corporate executives, Wall Street speculators, con artists, international schemers, hapless and naive tribal leaders, manipulative Chinese generals, and even a few clueless Buddhist nuns—all of whom were shelling out big bucks because the word was on the street: The White House is in play again. Clinton's personal hustle would make Willy Loman wince—partly in envy of his energy, partly in disgust at his tactics. The President of the United States turned the Lincoln Bedroom into a one-nighter flophouse, created "A Day at the White House" theme park for big donors, converted the historic Map Room into the Koffee-Klatch-for-Kash Kafe (532 people slurped a cup-a-joe there in '95 and '96, leaving an average tip of $50,000 each), put John Huang in both the Commerce Department and the DNC to handle the China franchise, personally dialed for dollars from the Oval Office (did he use his cigar, one wonders, to punch out the numbers?), and generally engaged in political obscenities with wild and reckless abandon, making the Monica dalliance seem like an almost sweet flirtation. Since 1995, Clinton has raised more than $145 million in soft money.

The money, of course, has not been given altruistically. You might give $100 or even $1,000 because you believe in what so-and-so is trying to do—but you give $100,000 because of what so-and-so can do for *you*. These are, after all, mostly bottom-line-minded corporate executives who are putting up the money, so from the start of Clinton's carny-barker come-on, contributors had expectations, and they were not often disappointed. From launching a banana war with Europe on behalf of $500,000 donor Carl Lindner of Chiquita Inc. to arranging a billion-dollar technology deal with the Chinese for $455,000 donor Bernard Schwartz of Loral Corporation, cash to Clinton became a good business investment. There have been no shortage of eager givers, all of whom are thrilled to have this side door into the White House opened exclusively for cash customers.

Clinton's people saw nothing wrong with this. Truman Arnold, an oilman and longtime Clinton financier from Texarkana, was moved into the DNC in 1995, handpicked by the President himself to set up the soft-money scheme. Arnold told Jane Mayer of *The New Yorker:* "I've been in sales all my life. It's a bit like romance. You go to dinner, and if everything feels right, you proceed to the goodnight kiss—or the Lincoln Bedroom."

Clinton money operative Harold Ickes was asked by Bill Moyers a direct question about the President's personal awareness and concern about the slippery ethical slope he was on.

MOYERS: Did he raise a moral question?
ICKES: He did not. He wanted to know whether it was legal. His order to me was, "It's got to be legal." And it was legal.

Nonsense. The White House's soft-money scheme was not the slightest bit legal, much less ethical. Aside from raising what amounts to bribery funds, Clinton and team flagrantly violated the absolute proviso that any expenditure of soft money must be kept at arm's length from the candidates. God doesn't make arms this short:

1. The Clintonites raise millions in soft money from July of '95 to July of '96, properly storing the funds at the DNC.
2. During this same period, the DNC distributes $18 million of this money to the Democratic Party organization in each of twelve large states, so those organizations can run "issue ads" to educate the public; so far, so good, but then it starts to get funky.
3. All twelve state parties send the money they received from the DNC right back to Washington—all of it posted to two national media firms that just happen to be handling the Clinton-Gore reelection campaign; for example, on August

22, 1995, the DNC sends $30,376 to the Florida Democratic Party and THAT SAME DAY the Florida party ships $30,376 to the Clinton-Gore advertising firms in Washington.

4. These two firms design and produce the exact same "issue ads" for each of the twelve states; the firms also decide which stations will run the ads and at what times in the various states; then, Clinton's two media firms pay for the chosen air times in each state (even Mussolini didn't pay this much attention to the details of making the trains run on time).

5. The ads that run are not generic party ads or issue ads—they are "Bill-Clinton-is-the-best-thing-since-twist-off-caps" ads, and "Bob-Dole-is-the-cause-of-halitosis-and-genital-warts" ads; whether you agree with either of these views or not (I personally doubt the genital wart claim, but . . .), they clearly were not meant to be broadcast under the sponsorship of soft money; but there they were.

Yet, Ickes called this "legal," not only when asked by Moyers but also when pressed by prosecutors. So did Bill Clinton, Al Gore, Don Fowler (then the chairman of the DNC), and all the President's men. Riddle: How many legs does a dog have if you count its tail as a leg? Answer: Four. Calling a tail a leg doesn't make it one.

Common Cause, the watchdog of political corruption, traced practically every dime of this soft money's amazing ride along the financial loop-the-loop from the local TV stations to the Washington ad agencies to the state parties and back to the DNC. The organization's muckrakers determined that the entire effort was directed from the White House (Clinton himself was involved in designing the content of the ads). The DNC and state parties played zero role—except to launder the money. As Common Cause put it, "These are not technical violations of the campaign finance laws. This is not pushing the envelope to take advantage of loopholes in the law. What is at issue here are massive illegal schemes [in which the Clinton campaign] knowingly and willfully violated federal election laws."

So, why are none of these characters in the federal pokey? Because Bob Dole did it too. He got a later start, but once he saw what Bill and the boys were up to, he decided Republicans could violate the law just as flagrantly as Democrats, so in 1996 he did the exact same thing. He raised $8.8 million in soft money to pay for his "issue ads," ran the money through the Republican National Committee, which disbursed the money to state Republican parties, which funneled the funds directly back to the two ad agencies handling the Dole campaign, which then designed, produced, targeted, and paid for the ads.

In a pathetic effort to claim that these were not "candidate ads" per se, both campaigns have pointed to the legal nicety that they were careful not to include the punch line of "Vote for Me for President." But in a candid moment, Dole himself winkingly conceded the patent absurdity of this legal distinction: "It never says that I am running for president, though I hope that is fairly obvious since I'm the only one in the picture."

Neither party wants to stop the soft-money merry-go-round for obvious reasons, so even though they both periodically express high indignation that the soft-money law is being grossly violated and should be eliminated, it's still there. In the Congress of 1997 and '98, the Republicans had five different committees chasing Clinton's soft-money outrages, but for all their huffing and puffing they were not about to blow down the house built of corrupt political money, because they were inside it, too. Even His Oily Eminence, Rep. Henry Hyde, threatened loudly for a while that he would add soft money to his Clinton impeachment charges, but his threat was as hollow as the charge itself was meritorious. Chairman Hyde's feigned indignation at fund-raising excesses was rendered hilariously hypocritical when, at one point in the hearings, it was noticed that he kept switching out gavels, giving a single rap with one, handing it to an aide who then handed him another to make the second rap, and so on. Apparently, Republican fund-raising officials had hit on the bright idea that these "100 Percent Authentic Impeachment Gavels Actually Used by Chairman Hyde in the Historic Proceedings Against William Jefferson Clinton" would make nifty premiums to attract major campaign donors.

Every Republican investigation into Clinton's money mess fizzled because, first, the public hooted at the chutzpah of money-drenched Republicans getting all pious about campaign-finance corruption—this is the party of Nixon after all, and the party that has clubbed to death every reform measure that has raised its tiny head inside Congress. Second, GOP fund-raising operatives and nervous Republican presidential aspirants wanted the investigators to just "shut the hell up" and stop shooting at Clinton on this issue because they knew that they could get caught in the crossfire and, worst of all, the Golden Goose could be killed.

CLINTON *TALKS* REFORM

When first running for president in 1992, Clinton's campaign manifesto offered this poignant piece of political rhetoric [WARNING! Certain readers might feel a sudden need for Pepto-Bismol after reading the following; it is only one sentence, but be prepared]: "On the streets where statesmen once strolled, a never-ending stream of money now changes hands—tying the hands of those elected to lead." Once elected, the rhetoric continued to roll—in his first Inaugural Address the President pledged to "reform our politics so that power and privilege no longer shout down the voice of the people." Great stuff. So great that he made it a regular refrain in his annual State of the Union addresses. Every January, like a drunk making yet another New Year's resolution to swear off the booze, Clinton has stood before Congress with his pockets full of corrupt money, but with his heart filled with the gospel of reform:

> **1993—"I am asking the United States Congress to pass a real campaign reform bill this year." (Cheers)**

> **1994—"I also must now call on you to [pass] tough and meaningful campaign finance reform and lobby reform legislation this year." (Cheers)**

> **1995—"We should also curb the role of big money in elections. . . . This year, let's give the folks at home something to cheer about." (Cheers)**

> **1996—"Now I challenge Congress to go further—to curb special interest influence in politics by passing the first truly bipartisan campaign reform bill in a generation." (Cheers)**

> **1997—"Let's work together to write bipartisan campaign finance reform into law . . . by the day we celebrate the birth of our democracy—July the Fourth." (Cheers)**

> **1998—"I ask you to strengthen our democracy and pass campaign finance reform this year." (Cheers)**

> **1999—"Now, we must work to renew our national community as well for the twenty-first century . . . [by passing] the bipartisan campaign finance reform legislation." (Cheers)**

Problem is, like that drunk on New Year's Day, he never really wanted reform and never pushed it. Even in his first two years when Democrats controlled the Congress, he made no effort to pass a bill, and thereafter he grew ever more addicted to high-dollar fund-raising.

Besides, the last glimmer of hope that the two parties might ever do something about their corruption had already been snuffed out. The chance for them to act came on June 11, 1995, in Claremont, New Hampshire. In a rare happenstance, Clinton and then-speaker Newt Gingrich appeared together at a town-hall confab, answering questions from the audience. Local citizen Frank MacConnell made national news that day by rising and asking the two of them to clean up Washington by stopping big-money political contributions. Right then and there, Clinton and The Newt impulsively pledged to go to work on it and shook hands on the deal—a handshake that ran on every TV news broadcast on every front page in America. It seemed to be such a genuine moment, so filled with promise, that the audience burst into heartfelt huzzahs. Mr. MacConnell later said that he and others dared to hope that "the handshake seen 'round the world'" symbolized the start of a new age in which "a politician's word could still mean something." But Clinton and Gingrich never met again to discuss the topic, and within a month, Clinton was squirreled away in the White House with Dick Morris, plotting their soft-money subterfuge of our election laws. A year and a half later, just before Clinton defeated Dole in a campaign distinguished only by the fact that it burst through the bottom hatches of political hell to wallow in a squalid and horrendous new level of money corruption, Frank MacConnell passed away.

NO LIMITS, NO FEAR

Raw political cynicism is Clinton's lasting legacy. By his careless use of soft money, he has authorized all future presidential and congressional candidates to disregard the law and treat public office as a commodity to be retailed for unlimited sums of campaign money. It turns the political clock back to the utterly corrupt days of Nixon, who literally kept wads of corporate cash stashed around the White House. One of those stashes included $25,000 from Archer Daniels Midland CEO Dwayne Andreas— money used to pay the Watergate burglars. A quarter of a century later, there was Bill Clinton with his 1996 unregulated stash of political money, including $295,000 from Andreas.

Oh, the soft-money prohibitions still are on the books, but they're now like one of those quirky old laws that occasionally pops up in news features: "A 1913 Iowa statute makes it illegal, even today, for a farmer to be naked in the cow barn at milking time."

There was a chance to clamp the lid (if not the cuffs) on those who so openly broke the law in 1996, both in the Clinton and Dole campaigns. To their credit, the gutsy staff auditors of the Federal Elections Committee tried to do just that, concluding that Clinton's campaign spent $46 million more than was legal and that the Dole campaign was $17 million outside the law—nearly all of which had been spent on their bogus "issue advocacy advertising." The auditors were gutsy because their bosses, the six FEC commissioners, are political appointees (three appointed by the Democrats, three by the Republicans). The commissioners are appointed to prevent trouble for the parties, not cause it, and they've shown that they'd sooner try sandpapering a bobcat's butt than to stand in the way of the free flow of this illegal money into the coffers of their parties.

Unhappy to see this ugliness suddenly surface and be dumped in their laps, the commissioners were angrier at their auditors than at the outlaws. When the report hit the media, David Mason, who had been an aide to Republican leader Trent Lott before being named to the FEC, snapped: "It's a virtual certainty that these things won't be adopted." He was right. A week later, the commissioners voted 6–0 against any punishment for the Clinton and Dole campaigns.

This left Janet Reno as the last sheriff in Dodge. The attorney general's office had subpoenaed an early draft of the FEC auditors' report and was considering whether its charges warranted the appointment of an independent counsel to investigate Clinton's unlawful spending. Since she had proven to be a mighty slow draw on other Clinton-Gore fund-raising violations, there were very low expectations that General Reno would do anything this time, and she actually underperformed on the expectations. Just before Christmas of '98, Reno delivered a nice stocking stuffer for Clinton, ruling that there should be no further legal inquiries into his soft-money sleight of hand because there was "clear and convincing evidence that the President . . . lacked the criminal intent to violate the law."

Huh?

Clinton was known to have been intimately involved in the whole scam—raising the money for it, developing the ad strategy, critiquing and changing the content of the ads themselves. The law plainly says that a candidate can't do this. What part of "can't" had the lawyer-president not understood? Maybe Reno discovered that Clinton had said "KingsX" or had his fingers crossed behind his back while plotting with Morris, or that he hadn't inhaled the whole time. But, no, it was nothing so logical as that. Her ruling was that (follow the bouncing ball here) (1) while the President might have violated the law, (2) he didn't *intend* any violation, as proven by the fact that (3) his lawyers told him his actions were legal, so (4) he "lacked the criminal intent," and (5) *ergo, ipso facto, habeas corpus delecti and dipsy doodle,* Bill Clinton can walk.

The new legal standard on soft money, then, is that candidates may violate the law with impunity as long as their lawyers tell them it's OK. And every lawyer will say it's OK, because the Clinton precedent now exists, having been sanctioned by the FEC and the Justice Department.

DRAGGING A SACK

I never had to make a living picking cotton, but as a tyke growing up in northeast Texas, I did spend time in the fields as a "toesack cotton picker" during the summers that my brother Jerry and I spent on my Uncle Ernest's small farm at Duckworth Flats, near the town of Bonham.

This was when I was about six or seven and was way too small to pull a real cotton sack down the rows—sacks that could hold a hundred pounds of cotton and would strain the backs of even the strongest workers who filled them again and again during the day, getting three cents a pound to bring in the crop under a brutal Texas sun. But my brother and I were out there among them, doing our little part for the family by "dragging a sack," as cotton pickers called their work—even if ours were "starter" sacks that my aunt Eula fashioned for us out of burlap feed bags with rope straps attached to them.

Years later, I found myself dragging a sack again—not in the cotton fields but in the money fields of Texas politics. This is the term we statewide politicos applied to the drudgery of fundraising, and I dragged my bedraggled sack through these hardscrabble fields during the 1980s, when I was elected to two terms as state agriculture commissioner. Yessiree, there's nothing like crawling out of bed in the early A.M., knowing that you've got a long, hard row of fund-raising calls to make that day, 80 percent to people you don't know personally, 90 percent of whom will not take your call, and of the 10 percent who do, at least half will say something ego-boosting like, "You're running for what?" or "How did you get my number?"

It did not take me long to figure out that this way of fundraising was not for me. I didn't have the stomach for the suckup. Plus, I wasn't called "Whole Hog" Hightower for nothing. My undiluted populism—fighting for family farmers, farmworkers, and consumers against the greed of the commodity traders, speculators, bankers, pesticide companies, and giant processors—was not exactly tailored for successful, high-dollar fund-raising. So I counted on a lot of low-dollar events and direct mail to fill my sack.

But if you're out to raise $20–25 million as Bill Bradley, John McCain, and Elizabeth Dole have been, or out to raise in the $50 million range as Al Gore and George Bush have been—then you're not going to be a populist. Hell, you won't even be a Democrat.

Raising $25 million in a year's time, as some of these candidates have done, meant hauling in $68,495 a day *every day* of the year, counting Saturdays, Sundays, and the Fourth of July. This leaves you no time to be with the folks, raising issues, raising hope, and raising hell—which is what the 2000 race should be about. Instead, it means spending your time and focusing your message on a carefully culled constituency of about sixty-five thousand very atypical Americans. This is about how many people there are (out of 270 million of us) who can and do give the big bucks to candidates.

The thought of having to telephone this particular breed day in and day out; of having to trudge door to door on Wall Street to woo them; of spending long weekends hanging out in Palm Springs or Palm Beach trying to collar them for a quick pitch over drinks or at poolside; of standing in their Martha Stewart–designed living rooms night after night to charm yet another small gathering of their divine friends; of taking the private elevator to corporate suite after corporate suite to sell another piece of yourself; and of generally having to drag a silk sack for months among these elites has shoved lots of prospects out of the field. Senator John Kerry considered challenging Al Gore in the 2000 presidential primaries, but declined in February of '99, saying, "My heart wants to talk about the issues I care about, but my head was telling me the ten months I have to raise a huge amount of money is difficult." When New Jersey senator Frank Lautenberg announced that he would not run for reelection, he said, "It dawned on me I'd have to spend half of every day for the next eighteen to nineteen months fund-raising." Likewise, when John Glenn announced his retirement from the senate, he said, "There are a lot of things I won't miss, like fund-raising, which is a stinking, miserable way to lead your life."

Of course it is. It's a stinking, miserable way to choose a government, too! And it sure makes you wonder about the mind-set of those who do it. Check the flock of odd duckies running for president. Let's be honest—these are not sane people. The cash chase demands and attracts candidates who are comfortable with, good at, and seem to enjoy prostituting themselves to the privileged and powerful.

And, like Bill Clinton, they can be highly creative when it comes to designing new sacks to drag and finding innovative ways to fill them. When George W. Bush, for example, began in November 1998 to concentrate on his presidential run, he was in a PR bind because he had just been reelected governor and had promised Texans that he would put his national ambitions on hold so he could be their full-time governor until the legislative session ended the next May. Yet, while he sat in Austin, the other GOP wanna-bes were scampering across America like ground squirrels, lining up money support. Shrub worried, a frown creasing his tanned and sloping brow. He needed to be in touch with these contributors, too. What to do, what to do? "I know," piped up one of his bushy-tailed aides. "You can make a nifty video that talks about your virtues and family and stuff, really puffing you up, you know, and send it to the big donors." "Bully idea," exulted everyone around Prince George!

Yes, but how to pay for the video? He couldn't establish a federal campaign fund yet, because that would break his eyes-for-Texas-only pledge. "No sweat," growled a knowing adviser with a slanted, Clinton kind of smile. "You've had a ton of cash put in your state campaign fund by lobbyists who need your help in the legislature. Use that money for the videos." It was true. From Aetna to Wal-Mart, corporate money had flooded into Bush's fund—there was $50,000 from AT&T, $20,000 from Dow Chemical, $27,000 from GTE, $20,000 from Bank One, $103,000 from the Hunt brothers, $25,000 from Bell Helicopter, $55,000 from NationsBank, and dozens of other similar-sized checks. These companies could not legally give this much money to Bush for President—in fact, corporate funds could not be given at all. But, said the sly adviser to young George, "There's a little loophole." Indeed there was—a legality that allows state campaign funds to be used to promote issues nationally. "That's all you're doing, isn't it, George?" asked the adviser. "You're just sending out videos that promote issues, aren't you? It's 'legal,' George. As long as the thing doesn't say 'Vote for George W. Bush for President,' you're in the clear."

Shrub just beamed, his sloping brow unfurrowed now, very satisfied with himself that such clever people had come to help him be president. And out went the videos.

Sadly, there is no traffic jam on the high road of politics this year. All the White House contestants are too busy working the low road, finding ever more cunning ways for their big givers to get past that irritating law that says a person can give "only" $1,000 to a presidential candidate. Fund-raising consultants derisively refer to this level of giving as trying to fill a bathtub with a teaspoon.

The easiest two-step around the limit is for the donor's spouse to put in a $1,000 check, too, doubling the donor's purchasing power. But ambitious contributors don't stop there.

Let me introduce you to Skye Stolnitz, a thousand-dollar contributor to Lamar Alexander; Asher Simon, who gave $3,000 to Sen. Dianne Feinstein and two other Democrats; and Lindsey Tabak, a $20,000 soft-money contributor to the Democratic Party. What's unique about these generous givers is that when they became political money players, they were too young to vote, drive, or buy a beer. Skye was ten; Asher, nine; and Lindsey, fifteen. The *LA Times* reports that they are part of a national Korps of Kiddie Kontributors who now put millions into the political money process under the guiding hand of their politically enthusiastic parents.

Skye's dad, Scott, and her mom each put their $1,000 down on Alexander's ill-fated presidential climb. On the same day, Skye also chipped in $1,000. "It was my decision based on what I thought was in her best interest," Scott told the *Times*. He said the money came from her very own checking account, and that he had talked it over with the ten-year-old. "I told her what I was doing and why. She did not object." He said he was unaware of federal laws that require donors to make contribution decisions on their own.

John Price is another big giver who believes in the family plan. A multimillionaire from Salt Lake City, Price has raised hundreds of thousands of dollars for his man, George W. On March 24, 1999, he wrote his own $1,000 check to the campaign. His wife wrote a $1,000 check to Bush that day, too, as did his two children, both of their spouses, and five of Price's grandchildren—a surprisingly spontaneous outburst of check-writing enthusiasm by the Price family. Especially surprising were the $1,000 donations from twin granddaughters Alexandra and Hannah, who are three years old. In the Bush campaign contribution report to the Federal Election Commission, Alexandra's and Hannah's occupations are listed as "student." So far, Bush has taken $164,000 from donors listed as students.

But even Price's three-year-old granddaughters are not the youngest givers on record—Bradford Bainum has that distinction. He was eighteen months old when he made his first contribution—and he'd donated $4,000 by the time he was two.

Still, this is peanuts in the big money game, so let's take a step up to the "leadership PAC." This is a money funnel engineered by congressional Republicans through which corporations could legally pour $5,000 at a time into the coffers of key lawmakers. Newt Gingrich had his GOPAC, Trent Lott has his New Republican Majority Fund, Speaker Dennis Hastert has the Keep Our Majority PAC, Republican whip Tom DeLay has ROMP-PAC (Retain Our Majority Program), and even the thirteen GOP managers of the impeachment case against Clinton have their own house manager's PAC.

It didn't take long for presidential possibles to sniff out this new sack, realizing not only that a leadership PAC would allow them to rake in merely $1,000 each from contributors to their campaign fund, but the same people could also give $5,000 each to their PAC, which can be used to pay expenses for their presidential ramblings. A good loophole gets around, and all the 2000 wannabes quickly established leadership PACs to inject more dollar-fuel into their campaigns from big money interests: Dan Quayle sacked up more than $6 million in his Campaign America PAC before he dropped out, Bill Bradley's Time Future PAC has about $2 million in it, and Lamar Alexander loaded more than $5 million into his Campaign for a New American Century PAC, before he packed in his candidacy.

Al Gore has a PAC, too, named Friends of Al Gore Jr. Inc. Deciding early on that this was a bit stiff and corporate, even for Al, the PAC was renamed Leadership 98, apparently oblivious to the fact that the name had a built-in Y2K problem. What the hell, said one of Gore's political operatives to the *New York Times,* "We're more concerned with the purpose than the name." Fair enough. The purpose is to bag as much special-interest cash as quickly as possible, and Leadership 98 has bagged $4 million, including $5,000 each from the top executives of Netscape, 3Com, Bell Atlantic, Lucent Technologies, Lazard Frères, SunAmerica, AT&T, Disney, Goldman Sachs, AIG, Dow Jones, Travelers, Cablevision, Prudential, Dreamworks, Rite Aid, Playboy, Merrill Lynch, Northwest Airlines, Bear Stearns, Qualcomm, America Online, the Chicago Mercantile Exchange, Genentech, Bankers Trust (now Deutsche Bank), Fleet Bank, Morgan Stanley, LongTerm Capital Management, BankAmerica, Solomon Smith Barney, SmithKline Beecham, Enron, Pfizer, Lockheed Martin, Miramax, Lehman Brothers, and BellSouth. In many cases, the spouses of these executives also chipped in $5,000. Other family members did, too. So did business partners and fellow executives. It's hard to know how many babies, nannies, and pets are on the list (there's a "Candy," a "Tandy," a "Bud," a "Dixie," and a couple of "Bobs" that look suspicious to me—people . . . or parakeets?).

Still, even sacking up money in $5,000 batches can be slower and more tiresome than some of today's go-go candidates want to mess with in their search for $20–55 million, so they sicced their green-eyeshade boys on the election laws once again to see if they could find still more ways around the rules and grab some really big money. Leave it to Lamar! Lamar Alexander—the former Tennessee governor, GOP cabinet member, and second-time presidential runner—has a history of political slickness that makes Bill Clinton look like a straight shooter. When he announced his first run for the Rose Garden in 1996, he wore a plaid flannel shirt to show that he was one of the regular folks, not one of those Beltway Boys in suits. Unfortunately, his crack campaign staff didn't know enough to launder Lamar's costume first, so there stood Mr. Regular Guy up on the podium with his right-off-the-shelf flannel shirt all stiff and showing telltale crease marks, having just been unfolded for the media event. (No word as to whether the little cardboard piece was still in the collar.)

After falling early and hard in the '96 race, Alexander whined loudly that the $1,000 limit on contributions to candidates and the $5,000 limit on donations to a candidate's PAC had killed him. He had many fat cats in his political house, he said, and it was unfair that they couldn't buy in at a higher level. Take off the limits, he cried to Congress! Congress didn't. So, for this year's run, Lamar simply created his own loophole: "the nonfederal account." The *Boston Globe* reports that he set up a state PAC back home in Tennessee, where the law allows any person to give an unlimited amount to a candidate's PAC. Then, thanks to a slippery loophole that his legal beagles found, he slid the money from his state sack directly into his federal sack, using the funds to cover travel, staff salaries, rent, and other "overhead" costs associated with informing the public about issues. As the *Globe* put it, Alexander has pioneered "a state-based 'soft money' machine," and in just the first six months of 1998 he filled it with nearly $2 million donated by only sixty-one people—an average of roughly $30,000 a pop.

One of those was Donald Lamberti, an Alexander supporter and CEO of a chain of 1,100 convenience stores based in Iowa. The *Globe* reports that Alexander took Lamberti to breakfast and told him to forget the federal limits and dump as big a wad as he could into the Tennessee PAC. "I wanted it to be legal," Lamberti later told the *Globe*. "I said, 'Can I give that?'" With a big smile and a wink, Lamar said "yes"—and Lamberti agreed on the spot to put $95,000 in Alexander's state PAC. The candidate was so enthused by this "innovation" that he ultimately set up these shells in more than a dozen states.

It was all to no avail for Alexander, however—his campaign crashed and burned in mid-September '99, with the Tennessean withdrawing from the race after unleashing a comically hypocritical tirade against the power of political money to overwhelm political ideas. Lamar was gone, but not his legacy of the state PAC fund-raising gimmick. When Dan Quayle's political director was told about Loophole Lamar's shell game, he exclaimed, "That's incredible. I didn't know you could do that. I'm flabbergasted." But he wasn't repelled. In short order, Quayle had a state PAC of his own and was siphoning the money out of it into his federal PAC. Dan even added a little twist to the idea—since he lives in Arizona, which doesn't allow unlimited money to go into a PAC, Quayle set up his state PAC in Virginia, which does allow unlimited money.

If you thought surely there are no more money tricks to be discovered, you forgot about Newt Gingrich. Like his nemesis Clinton, the Newtster was always looking for an edge, some new way to let corporate interests bring even more checks to his table. His evil genius was that he not only worked the campaign laws to the max and beyond, just as Clinton did with soft money, but he also pulled off the political equivalent of turning water into wine—he found a way to bring *tax-exempt* contributions into politics.

While others were going word by word through the *campaign* laws to find ways over, around, and under them, Gingrich went boldly where only fools had dared to tread: into the tax laws. It's a measure of how insane the quest for money has become that a politician would risk using tax-deductible funds for partisan purposes. Until now, such an effort would have been considered slack-jawed, mouth-breathing, bone-deep stupid—akin to opening the gas cap on your lawn mower in the dark and striking a match to see how much gasoline you have. The IRS has been especially humorless on this matter of mixing politics with tax-exempt money. As one who has received tax-exempt funds for research work in the past, I can tell you that you have to sign a document certifying that your efforts are for "charitable and educational" purposes only, and that you will not spend a dime of the money for partisan political activity. I know people who will testify that even the slightest, most unintentional violation can produce a long and unhappy experience with IRS agents who have been specially selected for this duty because they have a genetic deficiency, being entirely without the human smile gene.

Newt, on the other hand, was born with a complete absence of the humility gene. His ego is so big it's got its own area code. This is the guy who once proclaimed himself to be the "defender of civilization, teacher of the rules of civilization, arouser of those who form civilizations . . . and leader 'possibly' of the civilizing forces." He was also the very powerful speaker of the House of Representatives, so his volatile mix of raw ego and institutional power made him a likely candidate to strike the match and look into the gas can.

Gingrich was the moving force behind the Progress and Freedom Foundation, organized for charitable and educational purposes under section 501(c)3 of the tax code and funded by such "charitable and educational" concerns as AT&T, FedEx, GE, Golden Rule Insurance Company, IBM, Lockheed, Seagram, BellSouth, Coca-Cola, Ford, and Johnson & Johnson. Making donations to Newt's foundation was a painless way for corporations to curry favor with him for their legislative agendas, since every dime could be deducted from their income tax. What a deal! If you're a corporate executive, getting a tax deduction for buying a politician is about as much fun as you can have with your clothes on.

The foundation itself was a long way from being a philanthropic cause, unless you count Newt as a charity case. PFF was referred to by Democrats as "Puff," for it clearly was a front group for Newt's highly partisan agenda. Not only did the foundation do work directly tied to Republican campaigns and legislation, but it also made little pretense of being anything more than an arm of GOPAC, Newt's political action committee. The PAC and the PFF shared staff, offices, agendas, funders . . . and, of course, Newt.

As a result of a House ethics committee investigation into a few of Gingrich's corrupt connections to money (an investigation that led to the sitting speaker being censured and fined by the very Congress he controlled), the IRS went eyeball to eyeball with Newt over his foundation's tax-exempt status. Amazingly, the IRS blinked!

There has been a lot of harrumphing and finger-pointing as to why it did so, but the bottom line is that the IRS validated Newt's political use of tax-exempt funds. The seventy-four-page decision in February of '99 overturns decades of IRS rulings, drastically changing the way charitable organizations can relate to campaigns and putting a big new fund-raising sack into a political process already saturated with special-interest money. Tax law professor Fran Hill, an expert on the separation of charitable funds from politics, says there is no separation now. After the ruling, she told *Roll Call,* "Every candidate for public office ought to immediately incorporate a 501(c)3 charitable organization into his or her campaign finance structure. And they should do that sooner rather than later. And they should run all of their research activities and all of their dissemination of ideas through the (c)3." Rep. Nancy Pelosi, astounded by the IRS's flip-flop, told *Roll Call* that "the ruling means that my colleagues and I can set up a (c)3 charitable organization, the easiest way out there to raise money. That's why the Republicans were setting them up. It's an easy way to raise money. Now you would be a fool not to do it."

So the top leaders of our country are equipped in 2000 with an array of sacks, presenting multiple opportunities for the wealthy few to deposit their bribery funds—sacks for soft money, hard money, PAC money, money from toddlers, non-federal money, taxpayer-subsidized money, and other forms we've yet to learn about. Change will have to come from outside, for those in the system are both addicted to the money and completely in denial about its totally corrupting impact on them, the political process, and the government.

At The Breakers, an Italianate resort in Palm Beach, Florida, that pretty well defines opulence, senate majority leader Trent Lott and several Republican committee chairmen were wallowing with members of "Team 100" during a three-day winter retreat and hog-mating ritual. The name of this GOP money club does not mean that it allows only a hundred members but that membership starts at a hundred. (In the social swirl of political fund-raising, it's considered tasteful when discussing money to avoid any reference to dollars and to drop the last three zeroes—so when someone says "a hundred," everyone knows that's $100,000; similarly, reference to "a half" means half a million dollars.) Among Team 100 members are top executives of Amway, Philip Morris, RJR Nabisco, ARCO, TCI, Union Pacific, Pfizer, Eli Lilly, Enron, Seagram's, ADM, AT&T, Burlington Northern Santa Fe, GM, Bristol-Myers Squibb, Merrill Lynch, Travelers, Chevron, PepsiCo, Coca-Cola, MCI, Mirage Resorts, Dow Chemical, Circuit City Stores, and Trump's Castle Casino Resort—and these are just some of the corporations that gave more than $250,000 each. (In an escalation for 2000, the good old GOP has created a new platinum-level club for corporate interests that give at least $250,000 for each of the four years leading up to the presidential election—"Team $1 Million" they're blatantly calling it, and they expect to enlist 100 members, each of which will be treated to a smorgasbord of private sessions with our lawmakers.)

The Breakers gathering gave the big givers three days of closed-door meetings, long dinner conversations, leisurely golf chats, and plenty more chances to bond with the top congressional leaders. The business and social sessions were closed to the media, but reporters were able to grab a brief, walking interview with Senator Lott. Why was he blocking legislation to stop this kind of gross selling of legislative power, he was asked. "Look, I support people being involved in the political process," he replied. Oh, a reporter asked, so should corporate executives like those of Team 100 be allowed to spend an unlimited amount of money to buy such exclusive access to policy makers? Lott declared: "I think for them to have the opportunity to do that is the American way."

BEELZEBUB'S BUZZWORDS

Being a glossary of political corruption, consisting of words and phrases, from *A* to *Z*, actually used by the buyers and sellers of political influence in these modern times . . .

ACCESS, n. The Yellow Brick Road. It leads straight into the back rooms of Washington. Access is what the buyers of political favors profess to be purchasing from the sellers, as in: *Our contribution to the senator merely reflects our desire to have access to the legislative process*. Buying access is distinguished from bribery chiefly by the fact that the latter has been officially declared illegal, while the former is still at large. Despite protestations by political pettifoggers, experience teaches that there is no practical difference between buying an official's action and buying exclusive access to the official. *Slang*: Greasing the skids. "There is no question—if you give a lot of money, you will get a lot of access," a satisfied executive told the *New York Times* after his corporation had given $500,000 to the GOP. "All you have to do is send in the check." Many citizens are unaware that access is for sale, so out of ignorance they don't bid.

ASK, THE, n. The key moment. After all the wine has been drunk and the dancing done, finally comes The Ask, the naming of a specific price; e.g., *The chairman has the material you wanted him to see on that tax problem, Bob, and he hopes you'll* *consider donating 50 and raising another 50. Also called The Pucker.*

BAIT, n. Officeholders and candidates. To hook a major donor, the bait is offered in many forms: *We can arrange a private meeting for you with the Speaker;* or, *The President will be golfing at Windswept on the 25th and there's an opening in his foursome;* or, *The Senator hopes you might sit at his table at the fund-raiser.* All bait opportunities are based on market price and availability. Overnights in the Lincoln Bedroom and appearances in Buddhist Temples have been discontinued for the 2000 season.

BREAKFAST CLUB, n. A well-appointed den of self-appointed thieves. On Capitol Hill, a breakfast club is organized around a powerful lawmaker who meets periodically in a private and swank setting with a group of lobbyists and other big contributors for a convivial discussion of their legislative needs. (The discussion is discreetly referred to as "platter chatter," as in: *Oh, nothing happened—we just had breakfast and some platter chatter.*) When the chatter is done and the last bit of sausage swallowed, an envelope is slipped into the hands of the lawmaker, who later discovers to his or her delighted surprise that it is filled with checks; e.g., when Rep. Dennis Hastert ascended to the speaker's chair in 1999, he immediately instituted a regimen of breakfasting every couple of weeks with a different lobbying firm and their clients; they would devour eggs, talk legislation, and fatten the speaker by $20,000 to $100,000 each time; as a Hastert aide put it, "Dennis likes to do breakfast."

BUNDLING, v. To get close, but not go all the way. Corporations cannot give money directly to a presidential or congressional candidate, which frustrates many CEOs who miss the old days. Hence, the artful dodge of bundling. Since corporate executives (plus their wives and children) can each write

$1,000 checks to candidates, the CEO simply collects, say, a hundred of these individual checks from those in the executive suite of Great Big Global Corporation Inc., bundles them together with a tasteful gold ribbon, and personally hands them to the candidate in the name of the company: *George, here's a hundred grand we've bundled for you at GBGC—don't forget us now, you hear?* Technically, the law is not violated, and the corporation and candidate both get what they want.

CLEAN ROOM, n. (sometimes preceded by *ethically*). A legally sanitized place for raising bribery funds by telephone. The law is prudish about money calls being made from such hallowed sanctuaries as the Capitol, congressional offices, and the White House. (Oops, a couple of slipups there by Clinton and Gore, but see what a fuss it caused, and besides, there was *no controlling legal authority,* according to the vice president, and Janet Reno gave him an official kiss on his boo-boo, so it's all better now.) To avoid calling donors from their congressional offices, lawmakers can dart one block away to either the Republican Club or the Democratic Club, where dozens of fully equipped small offices, cynically referred to as Clean Rooms, are available for members to do their daily telephone solicitations of special-interest money givers. Both clubs provide showers for the more fastidious members.

CLOSER, n. The one who does *the ask* (see above). Usually, the closer is not the candidate but a campaign official who is brought in to do the dirty work of asking a potential contributor for a certain amount of cash; some candidates, like Al Gore, are exceptions: "He's an excellent closer," a Gore confident says. *Colloquial:* One who seals the deal.

CONCIERGE, n. (also, the *arranger,* the *fixer,* the *handler,* the *contact*). Each major donor to either the Democratic or Republican parties is assigned a staffer in that party's Washington office who serves as their personal, governmental-affairs concierge. Is your legislation hung up in subcommittee, do you want to get on a trade mission to China, is a regulator bothering you? Call your concierge.

CONSULTANT, n. (usually preceded by an adjective, such as *fund-raising, media, polling, issue, speech*). The lowest life form in politics. Also, the highest paid. "Consultants" is the correct answer to one of today's oft-asked questions: *Why do campaigns suck?*

CONDUITING, v. Playing traffic cop on the Yellow Brick Road. Many industry associations give very little money directly to candidates, but they steer truckloads of it to politicians they favor by calling on member companies to send in checks made out to the chosen ones. The checks are then packaged (see *Bundling*) and conduited to the candidates by the association. There is no limit on how much can be conduited to a candidate, and conduiters claim to provide a service for donors who need guidance; a sort of *Political Bribery for Dummies* approach.

DAISY CHAIN, n. A cooperative effort to weave flowers into links, like innocent girls do in the early summer, gaily linking daisies into beautiful chains. The difference here is that the "daisies" are dollars, the "girls" are lobbyists, and "innocence" was deflowered long ago. To raise a lot of money in a hurry for a candidate, a group of lobbyists will set a goal of, say, $2 million in one month. Then they rush into the money fields, quickly plucking checks from their clients and other interested parties. They link these checks, one by one, into what is called a daisy chain for the candidate.

DONOR, n. One who gives to get; a political investor; the most valued citizen in today's political system.

DOUBLE DONOR, n. Companies that give without the burden of ideology or political passion, concerned purely with making certain that no matter who wins, they win; a nirvana achieved by the fact that they contribute generously to both candidates in a race and/or to both parties; e.g., American Airlines, American International Group, Anheuser-Busch, ARCO, Archer Daniels Midland, Bell Atlantic, BellSouth, Blue Cross & Blue Shield, Bristol-Myers Squibb, Citigroup, Coca-Cola, Eli Lilly, Enron, Federal Express, Flo-Sun Sugar, Intel, Lockheed Martin, Microsoft, New York Life, Pacific Gas & Electric, SBC Communications, Schering-Plough, Sprint, TCI Communications, Time Warner, Union Pacific, and United Airlines are among those that have given at least $50,000 to both the DNC and the RNC in 1999. *Informal:* In some circles, the Double Donor is referred to as *Double Crosser* or, more colloquially, as *chickenshit*.

FACE TIME, n. A rare and prized commodity, now mostly for sale. The chance to sit face-to-face—constituent to Congress member—for maybe a half hour or more to talk about a particular issue of concern is about as unlikely for regular citizens (i.e., *noncontributors*) as coming face-to-face with a talking pig. It is, however, an opportunity that grows more likely in direct proportion to the amount of money brought to the trough; as a notoriously whorish Texas state senator used to say, "Write your problem on the back of a check for me, then we'll talk."

FLOPHOUSE, n. see *Lincoln Bedroom*.

FUND-RAISER, n. The organizer of the bribery.

GOOD GOVERNMENT, n. The altruistic objective of big givers, so long as good government is defined as government good for them; e.g., the chief lobbyist for the giant energy firm Enron, explaining her corporation's $50,000 donation to George W.

Bush's 1999 gubernatorial inaugural bash, said: "We clearly never expect to receive anything other than good government as a result of any kind of contribution we make." Subsequently, one of Governor Bush's good government priorities in the '99 legislative session was to pass an electricity deregulation bill pushed by Enron.

HOUND-DOG, v. *Slang,* to sniff out and pursue new or reluctant contributors, like a hound dog after game; to have an instinct for the hunt, as in: *He hound-dogged that rabbit right out of the bushes when no one else even knew it was there.*

IN COMPLIANCE, v. The first resort of scoundrels. The blissful state of being legally covered when accepting obvious bribes; e.g., when the Republican congressional leadership killed anti-smoking legislation the day after the Republican Party took $220,000 from tobacco companies in 1998, reporters were assured that the transaction was *in compliance with all the ethics rules.* Alert citizens will note that those who proclaim the loudest to be in compliance with the rules are those who write the rules.

INTERESTED MONEY, n. The golden goose of the political system. Potential donors who need particular political favors are the biggest, fastest growing, and most reliable category of big-money donations: "Both parties go through donor lists to find people with particular concerns at stake in the legislative process or the executive branch, and they go out and hit them up," a GOP fund-raiser confessed to *USA Today.* Synonym: *bribery funds.*

KISS, v. To score: *We kissed Exxon today.*

LEADERSHIP PAC, n. The legalized slush fund of a powerful politician.

LEVERAGE YOUR VOICE, v. Euphemism for *money talks, bullshit walks:* Rep. Ellen Tauscher, telling *Roll Call* about the sudden flood of political money now surging out of Silicon Valley high-tech corporations, explained: "I think clearly it is important to be able to establish yourself as to how the political process works. I think that they understand that this is part of the process and that they want to leverage their voices." Synonym: *pay to play.*

LINCOLN BEDROOM, n. See *Flophouse*.

MAINTENANCE, v. Taking care of big donors. Both national parties keep skilled mechanics available twenty-four hours a day, seven days a week, including road service. *Preventive maintenance* includes keeping donors well oiled with high-level phone calls, greasing any governmental problem they have, and periodically bringing them in to Washington to check their engine pressure and give them special briefings; e.g., former senator Lloyd Bentsen used to hold a monthly breakfast open only to those who gave $10,000 or more, and former senator Rudy Boschwitz issued special blue stamps to his contributors so his staff would expedite their mail. *High maintenance:* donors who demand lots of attention; *slang:* Whiners.

MATING DANCE, n. The cooing, wooing, flourishing of feathers, prancing, and dancing performed by political candidates in front of possible contributors; often done in flocks, where several contributors are assembled for, say, a cocktail reception, then several candidates join them and proceed to strut their stuff, hoping for one or more matches.

MEMBER, n. A first-class citizen. Membership in the high-donor clubs of either party puts you in the skybox of American politics. Democrats have their "Majority Council" ($50,000-plus) and two clubs, "Team 2000" and the "Trustees," for givers of $100,000 and up, while Republicans have their gold-card "Eagles" ($15,000-plus) and their platinum-card "Team 100" ($100,000 and up). Membership definitely has its privileges—e.g., a GOP fund-raiser explained to an undercover MSNBC reporter that while they can't guarantee private meetings with key lawmakers, the party will always try to set one up whenever a major donor needs it, adding: "I've never heard of a Team 100 member being denied a meeting."

MENU, n. The price list for access. The parties have become so flagrant in their disdain for even the appearance of ethical pro-priety that they have published brochures that offer specific access for specific levels of giving—from $5,000 photo ops with the vice president and $25,000 skeet shoots with GOP committee chairmen to $10,000 private work sessions with committee staff and $100,000 Florida retreats with senior White House staffers; "We had a brochure from the GOP, and we virtually copied the format," said the DNC's 1996 soft-money coordinator to *The New Yorker.* "I wanted some sort of consistency to [the pricing of access]. I didn't want the people in L.A. to get better access than the oil jobbers in Texas."

NO QUID PRO QUO, n. As low as it gets. The final defense politi-cians offer for accepting corruption funds from corporations is that there was no explicit promise to deliver a goodie for a gift: *"The lobbyist asked for no quid pro quo,"* said the chairman, *"and I promised none."* This lowers the ethical bar to ground zero. *Anec-dote*: The Texas legislature consistently shortchanges poor peo-ple so badly that the Lone Star State regularly ranks number forty-nine in various measurements of basic human decency, usually positioning us barely ahead of Mississippi; beleaguered progressives in our state are, therefore, reduced to being proud we're not dead last, cheering heartily, *Thank God for Mississippi!* This is now the sad standard of national political ethics—*thank God he never came right out and promised a quid pro quo!*

REPUBLICAN/DEMOCRAT, n. The two-faced mask of evil intentions worn by most lobbyists, all corporations, and too many politicians: *I am neither Republican nor Democrat, but both.* Like Beelzebub himself, this is a creature that can take many forms but serves only one interest: his own. *Slang:* Republicrat.

ROLODEXES, n. Money people with networks of money people and a willingness to work them. The Rolodexes are the prize catches of all major campaigns, for they are peers of the big givers, they speak the native tongue and know the secret handshakes, and they can harvest checks faster than a John Deere haybaler: "You could care less about a guy who can give $100,000," said the former finance coordinator for Bill Clinton—it's the individuals who can work their Rolodexes to tap dozens of others for twenty-five, fifty, or a hundred thousand dollars each who truly matter. Shopping center mogul Mel Sembler for George W. Bush, superlobbyist Peter Knight for Al Gore, real estate baron Ted Welch for Lamar Alexander, Gateway lobbyist John Heubusch for Elizabeth Dole, AIG honcho Hank Greenberg for John McCain—these are a few of the big-league Rolodexes in the 2000 presidential campaigns. Another Bush Rolodex, Christopher Burnham, who heads a Wall Street investment firm, says, "I am absolutely enthused about this. I have called my Christmas card list, my professional list, my own political lists from fund-raising over five campaigns. When I get through with that I'll turn to the phone book."

SEASON TICKET HOLDER, n. The Brahmans of the political caste. Both parties now have an ultimate pedestal for super-givers who put more than $250,000 a year into their respective cups, though it is the Republicans who designated theirs the Season Ticket Holders. *Origin:* It seems that the GOP's weekend getaways for donors and politicians at Aspen, Palm Beach, and elsewhere were becoming so overrun with the riffraff who contribute only $100,000 each that your true elites were finding these events "crowded" and difficult to get quality face time with the politicians; thus was born, in 1996, the Season Ticket Holder class, with members awarded carte-blanche access to the party's top officeholders and granted entree to the most intimate gatherings with GOP politicians. Those with their tickets punched are also said to hold *season passes,* as in: *Make time this morning for me to see the gentleman from Philip Morris, for he's got a season pass.*

STROKING DOLLARS, v. The political art of wooing major donors, stroking their egos, and eventually stroking dollars from them for a campaign. Commonly practiced by candidates at gatherings of the GOP's "Team 100" or the Democrat's "Team 2000," where numerous stroking opportunities present themselves. *Archaic*: wining and dining. *Regional*: In parts of the South, candidates refer to themselves as pickpockets, as in: *I've got to go to that black-tie dinner in Houston and pick a few pockets.*

UNILATERAL DISARMAMENT, n. The ultimate dodge, used most often by Democrats, to avoid any slowdown in the fund-raising arms race, as in: *I strongly support campaign finance reform, but the other side is raising millions, and you can't expect us to unilaterally disarm, so we're going to keep raising the big money, too.* It is a version of "The devil made me do it." The disarmament dodge ignores other choices, from emphasizing low-dollar fund-raising to pushing for public financing; e.g., Sen. Russ Feingold of Wisconsin, a reformer running for reelection in 1998, did not disarm, but did have the integrity to de-escalate, refusing to use soft money and imposing a spending limit on his campaign; his Republican opponent was forced by this stand to de-escalate, too, though he didn't go nearly as far; the result was that Feingold was significantly outspent, yet he won anyway, in big part because of voter appreciation for his effort to restrain the whoring for dollars. Back in Washington,

Feingold's reward was to be reviled by his own Democratic colleagues for showing them up.

VACUUMING, v. Going far beyond a candidate's or party's usual base of donors to try gathering contributions from interests they really don't know. Vacuuming can find some real treasures, but it can also find some real problems, as in: *The Casino boys ought to like my tax-incentive plan, so let's run our vacuum through Las Vegas and see what we pick up.*

WHORE, n. A term of endearment among insiders; a politician who engages in promiscuous legislative intercourse with a donor for money. While politicians never want to be called a whore in public, they often refer to each other as such in private as praise for being a successful fund-raiser, as in: *Why you old whore, I heard you scored a big one with Globex International!*

ZIPS, THE, n. The most bountiful hunting grounds for bagging campaign contributions by presidential and high-profile congressional candidates. In order, the top-ten most lucrative zip codes, based on total amount of money given, are: 10021 and 10022 (Manhattan, NY), 90210 (Beverly Hills, CA), 10017 (Manhattan, NY), 20008 and 20007 (Washington, D.C.), 10128 (Manhattan, NY), 33480 (Palm Beach, FL), 10028 (Manhattan, NY), and 90067 (Century City, CA). The five Manhattan zip codes run contiguously up the posh east side of the city, from Forty-sixth Street to Ninety-sixth, stretching from Fifth Avenue to the East River—these are the penthouses of the clans that run Wall Street; the two Washington zip codes are the Georgetown and Rock Creek Park neighborhoods, where the top lobbyists dwell; fund-raising consultants refer to these prestigious addresses simply as The Zips, as in: *My candidate is having good luck in The Zips.*

PLUTOCRACY IS NOT GOVERNMENT BY A FAR-OFF PLANET

Ask someone to name a bizarre Texas billionaire and chances are Ross Perot's name will pop out.

Ah, how short our national memory is. On the scale of billionaire bonkerdom, Perot is barely a 1 when compared to the perfect 10 of Mr. H. L. Hunt, a Dallas oilman, who was ridiculously rich, severely right-wing, and nuttier than a hundred-pound sack of goobers. He was a billionaire back when that was unusual, in the 1950s and 1960s, and he was given to such egomaniacal tendencies as living in a mansion that was a replica of Mount Vernon only, to put the father of our country in his place, H. L.'s was built a wee bit bigger.

How right-wing was he? Start with the John Birch Society and keep moving out there, *way out there*, to the point where you could call Dwight D. Eisenhower a tool of the communist conspiracy. Hunt went that far, and farther, using his *Life Line* radio program to make his daily dump into the intellectual discourse of the time. (I used to hear his program as a teenager growing up in Denison, north of Dallas and a lot closer to Earth than whatever planet Hunt was beaming from.) But the apogee of H. L.'s strange political odyssey came with the 1960 publication of *Alpaca*, a novel that he personally penned to set forth his utopian vision for the governance and safekeeping of America. The essence of his utopia was that the richer you are, the more votes you would get. Seemed only fair to him. In this transparently self-serving vision, Hunt himself would have outvoted all of the people of the Corn Belt, South Side Chicago, both Dakotas, and Duval County, Texas.

Alas, poor H. L. couldn't get anyone to take him seriously at the time. Yet, the spawn of his genius is with us today in the form of a political system that does indeed allow a few corporations, lobbyists, and superwealthy individuals a much larger vote than all other Americans combined. In today's *Alpacian* system, money is the ballot that counts and the people who vote with money are the citizens who matter. STAND BACK, BAR CHART COMING THROUGH! These things are usually so tooth-grindingly wonkish that they can cause your fillings to pop out, but the disparity between those who are treated as serious political players and the rest of us is so extreme that it cries out for a graphic, so here it is, ready or not:

PERCENTAGE OF THE AMERICAN PEOPLE WHO DONATE MONEY TO NATIONAL POLITICAL CANDIDATES

Donate $0	▇▇▇▇▇▇▇▇▇▇▇▇▇▇ 96%
Donate up to $200	▇▇▇ 4%
Donate $200 to $1,000	▮ .09%
Donate $1,000 to $10,000	∣ .05%
Donate $10,000 to $100,000	← (Need magnifying glass) .002%
Donate $100,000 or more	← (Need Hubble telescope) .0001%

Source: Center for Responsive Politics (www.opensecrets.org)

Since it takes at least a three-zero donation for your name to get noticed by presidential candidates or top congressional officials (and four zeroes to get any attention paid to your political concerns), the arithmetic of today's politics is pretty straightforward: 99.9 percent of us are invisible and irrelevant to those who run the game, and the real "majority" is the one-twentieth of 1 percent who put $1,000 and up into it. We're talking about only 136,000 people in a nation of 270 million.

Richard and Helen DeVos of Grand Rapids, Michigan, are among this moneyed "majority," ranking in the very top echelon. These two are the founders of Amway, the direct-sales powerhouse that peddles everything from Nestlé to Wonderbras through a network of in-home sales reps. *Mother Jones* magazine reports that in April of 1997, Richard and Helen each wrote $500,000 checks to the Republican National Committee, instantly crowning them as the party's largest individual soft-money donors and, of course, making them much beloved, celebrated, consulted, and pampered by Newt Gingrich, Trent Lott, and other cooing party officials. But the DeVoses were not parting with a million cool ones simply to express their love for the GOP or the free-enterprise system. No, no, Nanette—three months after their checks were written, Newt and Trent teamed up in a closed door, eleventh-hour tax-writing session to slip a little ol' amendment into the massive 1997 tax bill. Provision C, section XI, reads: "Modification of passive foreign investment company provisions to eliminate overlap with subpart F and to allow market-to-market election, and to modify asset measurement rule." Abracadabra and Hocus Pocus! This arcane provision gave Amway a special annual tax break worth at least $19 million. The Amway amendment can also be used by a couple of other corporations, but Amway lobbyists admit that they engineered the loophole. There had been no consideration of this giveaway in either the House or Senate—no debate, no votes, not even a bill. Newt and Trent simply arranged to sneak it into the bill in the dark of night—a little "thank-you" for Richard and Helen, courtesy of us taxpayers.

Mother Jones also found that "Kissing Bob" Packwood, the sexual harasser and former senator who fell so far from grace that he became a lobbyist, had been hired by Amway shortly after the million-dollar DeVos donation to the GOP. His job was to grease the skids for the tax break with his former colleagues. Conveniently, one of Packwood's former staffers had moved over to become Lott's staff counsel for tax issues, so the deal was quickly sealed. To prevent a flare-up from the Clinton administration, Amway lobbyist Roger Mentz, a former Treasury official, was dispatched to work his magic on his former colleagues, which he did, getting them to put Treasury on record as "not opposed" to the break. Since it was known inside the White House that this was one that both Gingrich and Lott wanted, Clinton didn't fight them, signing the tax bill without excising the Amway giveaway, which he could have done by exercising the line-item veto that was available to him at the time.

The DeVos family continues to be big-time benefactors of the GOP, keeping up payments on their private parcel of "democracy." As daughter-in-law Betsy DeVos put it in an op-ed that ran in *Roll Call,* "I know a little something about soft money, as my family is the largest single contributor of soft money to the national Republican Party. I have decided, however, to stop taking offense at the suggestion that we are buying influence. Now I simply concede the point. They are right. We do expect some things in return." What things? Specifically, she wrote, "We expect a return on our investment." Score one for candor. Betsy also said, "We expect a good and honest government." Well, the DeVoses seem to have bought one "honest" enough to give them a nineteen-to-one return on their million-dollar investment. She calls that "good" government—you might call it "corrupt."

The DeVoses, joined by a few hundred other individual money givers (and getters) and by a who's who of brand-name corporations that give (and get) even more, have risen to become America's ruling class as we turn the calendar to a new millennium. Individuals like Bernard Schwartz (Loral Space & Communications Inc.), who personally gave $555,000 in 1998; Carl Lindner (Chiquita Brands Inc.), who gave $536,000; and Jon

Corzine (Goldman Sachs), who gave $257,800, are among the reigning nobles, as are such corporate barons as Union Pacific ($1 million in '98), RJR Nabisco ($1.1 million), FedEx ($1.2 million), Lockheed Martin ($1.3 million), Bell Atlantic ($1.4 million), UPS ($1.5 million), Travelers Group ($1.6 million), AT&T ($1.7 million), and Philip Morris ($2.5 million).

"Money has come to be the moving power in American politics," said Sen. William E. Borah back in 1926. A progressive Republican [*dinosaurus republicus progressus*—extinct circa 1980], Senator Borah of Idaho continued: "Some years ago, politicians got into the habit of seeking contributions from men of great wealth. . . . It was inevitable, if the large sums were to be given, that large sums would have to be returned in some way. Hence, money and politicians joined forces, and money has its say in shaping legislation and in administering the laws of the country. . . . It is a fearful national evil and will in the end, if not controlled, destroy the government of the people and substitute, therefore, a government of the few — the few who have sufficient money with which to buy the government."

In Borah's time, it was the likes of Andrew Mellon, the imperious multimillionaire banker, who reigned. Not only did money men like him buy the government of the day, but Mellon himself was ensconced as secretary of the treasury for *three* consecutive Republican administrations—those of Harding, Coolidge, and Hoover. He was there (as Robert Rubin of Goldman Sachs has been in the Clinton years) to ensure that the nation's governmental policies enrich the elites, even when such policies wreak havoc on workers, farmers, and everyday Americans. In Mellon's case, the myopic policy of upper-class enrichment led to the farm depression beginning in the 1920s and ultimately to the Great Depression that engulfed the entire country.

Three-quarters of a century later, we are living again under the "fearful national evil" that Borah spoke of, with modern-day Mellons controlling both our politics and our government, merrily enriching themselves at the expense of the many while blithely declaring that these are the best of times and that our democracy is sound. Bullfeathers. America's democracy has been buried in a stinking heap of bribery money, and people know it. Polls consistently find that the vast majority of Americans—75 to 90 percent, depending on the question—believe that their voice doesn't matter, that politicians do what their big contributors want rather than what ordinary voters want, and that neither party is interested in them. They believe this for the best of reasons: It's true! Look at our corporatized health-care system, at our butt-kissing corporate-driven policy toward China, at job-sucking trade deals like NAFTA, at the rubber-stamping of megamergers leading to price-gouging cartels in everything from banking to drugs, at the promotion of factory farms over farm families, at the selling of America's sovereignty to the World Trade Organization, at our tax laws that reward speculators and punish workers, at Wall Street's grab for the people's Social Security funds, at the push to allow corporate manipulation of the very genetics of our food supply, at the accelerated poisoning of our air and water, at the gorging of weapons manufacturers with ever larger piles of our tax dollars, at . . . well, at practically the entire agenda of both the White House and the Congress.

Washington and their Wall Street cohorts might think they're fooling the people, but they're fooling themselves if they think the people don't see what's going on. Humor columnist Phil Proctor tells of a first-grade teacher who gave her class the first part of some well-known proverbs, then asked them to fill in the rest. To the biblical adage "As you shall make your bed, so shall you . . ." a student responded, "mess it up." Out of the mouths of babes, huh? Indeed, the economic and political elites have made their corrupt bed and messed it up for the great majority of people. In this momentous year of 2000, the United States is no longer a democracy but a *plutocracy*. As former speaker of the house Jim Wright puts it, plutocracy is not government by a far-off planet. It is government of, by, and for the wealthy. Today, a million dollars easily outpolls a million voters—and wouldn't that cause H. L. Hunt to bust out in a great big grin?

Some would say that "plutocracy" is not quite expressive enough to describe what we have. So here's a selection that you might find more apt:

Diabolracy—government by devils.

Pornacracy—government by prostitutes (also, Strumpetocracy).

Foolocracy—government by . . . well, it's obvious.

Kakistocracy (my favorite)—government by the worst people in society.

Now we surge into this year's presidential and congressional elections, with dozens of state primaries ahead, the nominating conventions coming in July and August, the solemnity of presidential debates in the fall, a cacophony of TV ads to be run, and finally the national drama of election night, November 7. But guess what? *IT'S ALREADY OVER!*

Even before the voting starts, the election is over. OK, still up for grabs is which personality will get to sit in the big chair with the Presidential Seal on it and which party will have a congressional majority. But already decided is the basic issue of who government will serve, with the status quo assured on middle-class job loss, trade scams, environmental gradualism, mergers, corporate welfare, biotech insanity, campaign-finance corruption, and the other policies that most affect Americans at the kitchen-table level.

This year's election is about personalities rather than policies because the policy election—the *real* election—was held last year in the corporate suites and the living rooms of the rich. Any and all presidential candidates who have banked the money it takes to have a real shot at winning this year were vetted last year by these privileged few, meaning the candidates' views on all the kitchen-table issues have been pretailored to get the money—a tailoring that lacks much subtlety, essentially coming down to this obsequious pledge: "I [name of candidate], will put your financial interests above all others, and I will do nothing without clearing it with you first." It's a pledge that's also expressed more colloquially as "You da Man!"

Sure, we still get to vote, but the moneyed interests are the ones who have *chosen our choices*. For example, Goldman Sachs and its executives have put thousands and thousands of dollars into Al Gore's campaign. And into George Bush's. And into John McCain's. And into Bill Bradley's. No matter who wins, Goldman Sachs has a friend in the White House—and probably will get at least one of its own executives appointed to a key administrative position, from which to keep an eye on the company's political investment.

But Goldman Sachs and the other plutocrats also win because their donations assure that Gore, Bush, Bradley, and the rest won't be making trouble in the campaign by taking any nonconformist, nonauthorized positions that could spark a bothersome debate about the plutocracy itself, inflaming the peasantry's simmering economic and political resentments. By purchasing candidates wholesale, they guarantee a campaign that is much ado about nothing, with the debate restricted to *social issues* like abortion, *hokey issues* like who can downsize government the most (while hypocritically lavishing ever more wasteful spending on the Pentagon, the antidrug war, and corporate welfare—hypocrisy being a valued trait in recent U.S. presidents), *local issues* like zoning and traffic jams, and *nonissues* like which candidates can be the most pious about never ever even thinking about doing cigar tricks with White House interns.

And they wonder why people aren't voting? The noted political theorist Dan Quayle has observed that "A low voter turnout is an indication of fewer people going to the polls." (It must be true, as I've been told, that if you stand close enough to Dan, you can hear the ocean.) You could dismiss his tomfoolery, except that he's not that much more ludicrous than the others. This is why, given a choice between the likes of Al Gore and Shrub Bush on November 7, most folks are going to say: "Oh, hell, I need to work on my car."

YOU DON'T MATTER

POLITICAL PASSIONS FLARE

Monroe County, KS.—The campaign culminated in a bloody tragedy at Clarendon Saturday afternoon. The candidates were to speak and a great crowd had gathered. The debate became heated and one of the partisans, Wm. Walls of Holly Grove, attempted to strike one Dillard. But Dillard pulled his gun and shot Walls, who fell to his knees, pulled his revolver and shot Dillard twice, after which Walls fell back dead.

The mob rushed in on Dillard, but his friends surrounded him and, with pistols and knives, declared their intention to defend him. Sheriff Robinson attempted to arrest Dillard, but was shot in the thigh. The mob then closed in on Dillard and beat him terribly. A stray bullet killed a spectator. Dillard was finally spirited away, and the mob is after him.

—News dispatch, c. 1890s

Now *that's* politics. Imagine getting worked up enough to have a fist fight, much less a shoot-out, over any of the platitudes and pabulum being put out by Gorebushbradleymccainforbesetal2000. I mean, do your neck hairs bristle when Shrub Bush scorches the hustings with such incendiary rhetoric as "I believe all public policy should encourage strong families"? Does your blood rise and your fists ball when Al Gore issues his clarion call for an "N11 National Traffic Hotline"?

Politics should matter. I know that's a radical thought, perhaps hopelessly idealistic in this age of carefully calculated political centrism, when the money backers demand candidates who are inoffensive (especially inoffensive to money interests), and when the army of consultants that directs every campaign insists that the way to win is not to lose. So both parties are scuttling cautiously along the pollster-tested center line like a couple of sand crabs, going sideways for fear of being perceived as either moving forward or backward.

Of course the Republican presidential nominee won't thump the tub this fall about the class war being waged against the middle class and poor folks by America's moneyed establishment—but neither will the Democratic nominee. *Of course* the Republican won't storm Wall Street's barricades of privilege to assail the greed of corporate downsizing and outsourcing of American jobs—and neither will the Democrat. *Of course* the Republican won't stand on the steps of the Capitol to decry the thievery of America's democracy by Gucci-wearing, PAC-peddling, Binaca-breathed corporate lobbyists—nor will the Democrat.

What a difference a generation makes. I can imagine teenagers today, as they come of voting age, gawking in disbelief as their parents tell them that there actually was a time when a Democratic presidential nominee was a species discernibly different from the Republican, when the Democrat was not skittish about kicking corporate ass, and when the Democratic Party didn't need a consulting firm to figure out who it was for . . . and who it was against. This is a party with a heroic history of siding unequivocally with the common people against the bastards, a party that once even voted by a four-to-one margin at its national convention to disown any political candidate within its own ranks "who is the representative of or under obligation to J. Pierpont Morgan . . . or any other member of the privilege-hunting and favor-seeking class."

Today, the Democratic Party itself, as well as its top candidates, *boast* of being under obligation to Morgan—or, more specifically, to J. P. Morgan Inc. and Morgan Stanley, the two Wall Street firms spawned by old J. Pierpont. Democrats go shamelessly and often into these houses of greed, obsequiously seeking campaign funds in a straight-up exchange for their populist principles and constituency. So far, Al Gore has bagged $22,000 just from the two Morgan firms, Bill Bradley has been blessed with $111,000, and the Democratic Party is obligated to the tune of $104,000.

This is an appalling perversion of everything that is *important* about the Democratic Party. If William Jennings Bryan were alive to see this, his eyeballs would explode and his hair would burst into flame! He would note, correctly so, that the party's only reason for existence is to serve those who want to challenge the haughty rule of Morgan Inc. and the other members of the privilege-hunting, favor-seeking class. It's fine for the J. P. Morgans to have one party, but if the Democrats, too, are inside the houses of Wall Street, where does this leave the vast majority of us who are outsiders?

Since Labor Day of 1996, it's been my good luck to be able to spend two hours every weekday talking with the American people on my call-in radio show, *Hightower's Chat & Chew*. With cohost Susan DeMarco, piano player Floyd Domino, and our occasional guests at the Round Table inside Threadgill's World Headquarters (the legendary Austin restaurant from which we sling our radio signal and our B.S. coast to coast), I've had a steady stream of feedback from folks about what's going on where they live, far away from Wall Street.

I know, talk-radio listeners are said to be a bunch of know-nothing right-wingers spewing thirty-two flavors of pure ditto-head venom, but that's not been our experience at all. I hasten to add that we're mostly on commercial AM stations, so our listeners cannot be accused of being a special crowd of effete liberals having a mocha-skinny-raspberry latte with their brioche while waiting for NPR's stock market report. Sure we get the odd spewer every now and then (as well as the odd NPR latte-sipper), but we're impressed day in and day out by how smart and informed the rank and file American people are . . . and how good-spirited and funny they are.

These regular, workaday Americans are not the slightest bit moved by this year's mainstream candidates for president or Congress. What they want is a gutsy, even brawling politics with unscripted butt-kicking candidates who'll stand up for the majority in our country who are getting stomped on by Wall Street and pissed on by Washington. People want a politics with meaning and passion, that's worth getting embroiled in a fistfight. They want a politics that rallies them, in the stirring words of FDR in 1932, to join in a "crusade to return America to its own people."

That would be a politics that would bring hordes of people to the polls. But in the politics of 2000, people don't matter.

Steve Sovern found that out a few years ago when he ran for Congress from Cedar Rapids, Iowa. A Democrat, he was a promising candidate with a terrific group of volunteers and an enthusiastic base of support. The party brought him to Washington for a two-day candidate's workshop put on by the Democratic Congressional Campaign Committee. Steve says he was excited to be among some seventy other grade-A Democratic candidates attending this how-to-win workshop: "I looked forward to returning to Cedar Rapids filled with ideas, ideals, issues, and inspiration." He came to the meeting all bright-eyed and bushy-tailed with his notepad and tape recorder, ready to absorb all the wisdom the party could offer.

"Understand how the game is played," offered a big-time media consultant as the workshop opened. "Game?" thought Steve, as it quietly dawned on him that this might not be about ideals and issues. "Money drives this town," intoned a DCCC staffer, followed by another consultant who informed the budding members of Congress: "You have to sell yourself to Washington first," by which he meant the lobbyists who control the PAC funds. Rep. Peter Hoagland, then a lawmaker from Nebraska, came in to assure the group that "raising campaign money from Washington PACs is much easier than from individuals because it's a business relationship." Steve's eyes squinted as he thought, "Business relationship?" The DCCC staffer clarified the point, in case any of the seventy innocents didn't get it: "These people are paid to give you money. You have to *do* certain things, but they *want* to give you money."

What if you don't want to take their filthy lucre, which Steve did not? Congressman Hoagland: "Some of you may be under pressure to repudiate PACs. I strongly suggest you not take the hook. Restrain yourself, don't let zeal for reform influence you." Hmmm, thought Steve: "Let lobbyists' money influence you, but not zeal for reform?"

To put theory into practice, day two of the workshop began with a "mating dance" brunch. The DCCC invited a flock of PAC directors to eat croissants and look over the seventy congressional prospects, who in turn were expected to preen, strut, and do whatever it takes to mate monetarily with the PACs. Steve reports that the candidates wore blue name tags, while the PACs sported red ones. Rep. Beryl Anthony of Arkansas led the dance, informing the candidates that the assembled PAC directors were their friends, that PACs represent "little people." Steve says, "I saw the Phillips Petroleum PAC representative smile with approval. I wondered if he was representative of the 'little people' to whom Anthony referred." The congressman then urged the PAC reps to visit with each of the candidates while they were in town, because he was sure the money interests would find matches among the lawmakers-to-be that will "make your board of directors proud of you."

Left out of the equation, said Steve, "were the people I sought to represent." Instead, all the instruction was on raising money and hiring Washington consultants to run their congressional campaigns. "You can't hire local people—forget it!" bellowed a PAC director. Congressman Hoagland underscored the point: "[You] must hire world-class people and not local people. *That's why you have to raise a lot of money.*"

Don't even mess with volunteers, the eager candidates were told by a PAC director: "They can't do polling, radio, direct mail, or TV." Steve was stunned: "At the moment he spoke, my campaign had scores of volunteers who still believed in a government 'of the people,' phoning neighbors to talk about the campaign and issues that concerned them. Other volunteers were stuffing and stamping envelopes for a direct-mail response to those concerns."

At this point, he had absorbed all the cynical, manipulative, money-driven expertise he could stand, so he rose to his feet and told them so, pointing out that what they were telling the candidates is exactly what people hate about politics, that this approach is a dangerous turnoff to turnout, and that it ought to be Democrats who lead the crusade to end the kind of politics they were being coached at this workshop to use. Steve says, "There was an uncomfortable silence after my comments." Then a PAC director said: "Well, I guess we don't have to worry about contributing to *that* campaign." There was a spattering of nervous laughter, then the workshop proceeded as though nothing had happened.

Sure enough, the PACs did not contribute. Steve says he was even cut from the DCCC mailing list after the workshop, no longer sent any issue papers or legislative updates. Instead, the Washington money, expertise, and even DCCC staff went to another Democrat who had already lost twice in this congressional district but was willing to "play the game." With his Washington lobbyists' PAC money, the two-time loser was able to overwhelm Steve in the primary, then proceeded to lose for a third time to the Republican in the fall.

FIRST, KILL ALL THE CONSULTANTS

Here they come, tromp-tromp-tromping over the horizon, the mercenary army of professional political consultants, now more than thirty-five thousand strong! They are coldly efficient at what they do, and they control practically every campaign in America, from city council to president.

Of course, political consultants have been around since politicians first popped up. The earliest recorded evidence of these creatures was Quintus Cicero's tract, the *Handbook of Electioneering*, which he wrote to guide the 63 B.C. campaign of his famous orating brother Marcus Tullius Cicero, who was seeking a consulship to Rome at the time. (However, some date the craft much further back, crediting the snake that advised Eve with being the first consultant—which shows what trouble they can cause.) Only recently, though, have these political pros become so pervasive and dominant. Whereas electioneering even twenty-five years ago was handled by the candidate, a campaign manager, a press secretary, maybe two or three other paid staffers, and a host of committed volunteers, today there are paid specialists to run every aspect of the campaign:

Strategic planner	Debate simulator/coach
Campaign director	Telemarketer
Staff manager	Delegate counter
High-dollar fund-raiser	Speechwriter
Low-dollar fund-raiser	Radio ad producer
Event planner	TV ad producer
Scheduling coordinator	Radio/TV time buyer
Poll-question writer	Direct-mail writer
Poll taker	Direct-mail list buyer
Focus-group coordinator	Media relations director
Voter targeting director	Travel aide
Weasel coordinator (just kidding)	Opposition-research director
Field-staff director	Issue-development director
Dress and color adviser (not kidding)	GOTV-director

More than fifty separate job categories exist for political professionals—including consultants who specialize in finding and selecting candidates to run for particular offices. Yes, it has come to this low ebb: Consultants choose the candidates! It will not surprise you, I'm sure, to learn that their chief criterion in choosing a "good candidate" is that the person have an aptitude for fund-raising—gotta keep the army fed. And it's a hungry army—one survey found that of the $542,000,000 spent by all congressional candidates in a recent general election, $248,000,000 of it went to these hired guns. There is so much paid staff that just keeping in touch is a problem—one of the odder artifacts unearthed when sifting through the statistical rubble of Bob Dole's 1996 presidential organization was this: He spent $14,000 on beepers.

The impact of this mercenary invasion of American democracy has been devastating, reducing elections to computerized, cynical exercises in which the people are irrelevant, and such niceties as issues, ethics, and the future of the nation are beside the point.

Candidates don't need their own core beliefs, or goals for America, when their handlers can provide market-tested beliefs and goals for them based on the results of a very nineties electioneering mechanism called the focus group. Borrowed from Madison Avenue, this process involves bringing a dozen or so voters into a room for a few hours of professionally structured conversation around such profound political questions as: "If George W. Bush were an animal, what would he be?" Miles Benson of Newhouse News Service sat through some focus groups last year and reports that participants "are hooked to computers and handed a device with a dial to twist to register the intensity of their reactions, positive or negative. These responses are displayed instantly as trend lines on a graph, with a computer isolating the effects of various words and ideas and showing precise differences in the reactions of Democrats, Republicans, and independents." Benson writes that consultants watch the group while hiding behind see-through mirrors, recording facial expressions and body language. Out of this voyeuristic exercise come the candidates' campaign themes ("compassionate conservative"), positions on issues, phrases for attacking opponents, and other manipulative language designed to sell product A over product B. This is why so many candidates come off sounding like a breath of hot air.

The official creed of consultants is: Whatever It Takes! The point is to win. Period. Consultants live and die on their won-lost record, so distortions, innuendoes, outright lies, dirty tricks, spying, negative ads, gay-baiting, hate mailings, and so forth are just part of the accepted weaponry of modern campaigns. As a consultant once told me, "We always stand on principle. And stand on it and stand on it, so it won't ever rise up and get in our way."

The most common weapon in the consultant's arsenal is the attack ad, which we've all seen and learned to loathe. Humorist Dave Barry explained these in a column last year: "In America, the only way you can get elected to high office is to hire expensive consultants who conduct expensive polls to find out what the voters think, and then, having found out that the voters think that all politicians are slime, make expensive TV commercials wherein you show a hideously unflattering photograph of your opponent and have a snarling announcer say something like: 'Harvey Hackenslit would have you believe that he has never eaten live human babies. Who's he trying to fool?' "

A preacher in the Methodist church I attended as a boy used to teach us kids that "you don't make your house any prettier by burning down your neighbor's." Apparently, consultants attended a different church, for negative campaigning—going after their opponents with lies, hammers, tongs, blowtorches, chain saws, and nuclear explosives, all designed to pervert positions and burn down reputations—is considered a legitimate part of the game.

I've had my own political house singed. Running for reelection as state ag commish in 1990, a last-minute negative TV ad smeared me . . . and hurt me. It came from my GOP challenger, whose campaign was being coordinated by Karl Rove, a fellow who now is consultant-in-chief on the George W. Bush presidential bandwagon. The ad showed a flag burner torching Old Glory and tossing it on the ground to burn. The camera panned in on the flag, then, arising out of the flames came my picture, along with the somber voice of a narrator declaring that Jim Hightower supports flag burners. I did not, but the impact on voters, though, was visceral and damaging—"My God," I could hear the viewers muttering to themselves, "I kind of liked ol' Hightower, but I had no idea he was a flag burner."

A 1998 poll of two hundred political consultants found nearly unanimous agreement that they found nothing wrong with such negative campaigning. Syndicated political columnist David Broder reports on an article written by two consultants with a firm called Campaign Performance Group: "Fear, anger, envy, indignation, and shame are powerful emotions in the political arena. . . . Go the distance. . . . Negative campaigning is rarely pretty. Sometimes it doesn't feel very good either. But once you've made the decision to inform the voters of your opponent's shortcomings, stick to your guns. . . . Remember, you're playing to win."

Then there are dirty tricks, which range from sophomoric pranks (like the "black fax," which involves faxing black paper to an opponent's fax machine in the wee hours when no one's around, thereby burning out their ink cartridge and filling their fax room with a pile of black paper) to the dangerous. Years ago, my friend José Angel Gutiérrez led a third-party insurgency to defeat the old Anglo power structure in Zavala County, Texas. Angel himself became county judge—a mighty powerful position in Texas, controlling road money, patronage, and a lot more. At reelection time, though, he kept coming across rattlesnakes in the most unusual places—like his desk drawer, his mailbox, and his wastebasket.

Once known as backroom hatchet men, today's consultants are as out-front and as quoted as the candidates, sometimes more so, taking credit for everything from the campaign's strategy to the candidate's speeches. They've become media stars—which tells us all we need to know about the vacuousness both of politics and of our country's celebrity system. Case in point: Dick Morris, who has no credibility and nothing to say, yet says it over and over again on national television yakety-yak shows. He's the party-hopping consultant who has no ethical problem with having been a gunslinger for Bill Clinton, then for Trent Lott, then back to Clinton, whom he coached on how to become more Republican than Bob Dole in his '96 reelection bid. The whorish Morris fell into complete personal and professional disgrace that year after his ongoing affair with a Washington prostitute of the sexual variety was exposed. She told the media that he revealed White House secrets to her while sucking her toes in a $400-a-night hotel. That's kinky on several levels. Yet, like a bad tamale, this gasbag keeps coming back—he got a book contract, writes a newspaper column, was on TV more often than Lucianne Goldberg (herself a former GOP dirty-tricks consultant) during the Monica Lewinsky unpleasantness, and still today is a sought-after television commentator, actually asked to give the public his insights into the ethics of other political players.

This would be inexplicable, except that it's not unusual. The media has bought wholly into the consultantization of our politics, reporting on the game rather than the substance, so it routinely interviews consultants in lieu of candidates, it evaluates the relative "seriousness" of candidates based on which set of consultants they hire, it relies on consultants as primary background sources for its election coverage, and it reports straight-faced the polls and political spin of consultants.

There's a term that applies to the media's tedious and essentially empty coverage of America's elections: teptology. It means boringly detailed discourses on trivial subjects. That's what we get when the media bothers to cover elections at all, which increasingly they don't. Rocky Mountain Media Watch, a fine watchdog group that monitors the decline in electoral coverage, analyzed 128 newscasts by local television in twenty-five states just before the '98 elections. Viewers were four times more likely to see a paid political ad than a news story about the campaigns. A third of the newscasts carried not a single political story. The three major networks were just as sorry— from Labor Day to Election Day in '98 they carried only 72 campaign stories (down from 268 four years earlier). In that same period, the nets carried 426 Monica Lewinsky stories.

This is the same media that runs editorials on Election Day chastising candidates for not talking more about issues and scolding people for not paying more attention and not turning out to vote.

The system is strictly an insider game in which the media and consultants not only know each other, they *are* each other—media types routinely cross the street to become consultants or campaign staffers, while consultants and staffers just as routinely cross the other way to become the media. Bob Beckel, for example, was a hired gun brought in to direct Walter Mondale's 1984 run for president against Ronald Reagan, a lamentable effort that resulted in Mondale winning only his home state of Minnesota. Shortly afterward, however, Beckel had his own political TV show! My friend and longtime political reporter Ken Bode said to Beckel, "Geez, Bob, imagine if you'd won two states—they would've given you your own network." Our laughter has now turned into reality, not for Beckel, but for Roger Ailes, the former GOP and Reagan operative-for-hire who has been ensconced by Rupert Murdoch to run the news division of Fox Television Network.

Those in this political class have turned politics into mechanics, turning off voters who would be a lot more interested if an election was about policies that might improve their lives. But, hey, shout the pros to the American majority: This is not about you! We don't even want you voting, because you're not in our databases, and when you vote the results are unpredictable and . . . well, messy.

It's the dirty little secret of today's money-and-consultant-based politics that a low voter turnout is desirable. This is because consultants for both parties maintain massive databases of voting records for every U.S. household. They know who in the household has voted, how often they've voted, how they're inclined to vote, and what their hot-button issues are. Since most people have been turned off by politics and government, and therefore don't often vote, the focus of campaigns is on the few who most regularly go to the polls—including union members, pro-choice women, and environmentalists for Democrats; antitaxers, antiabortion stalwarts, NRA members, and the extreme religious right for Republicans.

These "voters who really matter," in the parlance of the political pros, are the domain of Get-Out-the-Vote consultants. They pore over miles of computer printouts, targeting their core constituencies as well as the persuadables and the swing voters. *The Wall Street Journal* reports that they are assisted in this narrowing of the political focus by specially designed computer programs with names like "Turnout Advantage," "Smart Select," and "Vote Predictor." As a Democratic GOTV specialist told the *Journal,* "You're trying to sort out the grass from the weeds, collect the most data and figure out how many voters you can get out of these little clusters."

To help motivate their targeted "base," both parties play legislative games in Washington, forcing votes on what are called "hand-grenade issues" that won't pass but will provide electoral ammunition. Republicans, for example, keep returning to partial-birth abortion bans, prayer in the schools, abolishment of the income tax, a constitutional amendment against flag burning, and piffles like majority leader Trent Lott's "Ten Commandments Defense Act" (don't ask).

With their key voters identified, the consultants then apply the mechanics of GOTV, including phone banks, targeted mailings, phone banks, door drops, phone banks, absentee-voting and early-voting drives, phone banks, rides-to-the-polls, phone banks, voting-day checkoff lists, and more phone banks. The calls can be annoying. A Republican in Palos Verdes, California, fed up with all the GOTV calls to her in the '98 election, proposed in a letter to the *Los Angeles Times* that political operatives be banned from telephoning without prior written consent from the voter: "I got five calls a day for a week, then one evening a call every three minutes for an hour and a half—and my number is unlisted!" At least she was wanted—unlike the majority.

In case you're under any delusion that this will all go away, I'm sorry to report that the consulting industry is so entrenched that it has its own magazine (*Campaigns & Elections*), its own Grammy-style awards (the "Pollie"), and—horrors—its own PR/lobbying organization, called the American Association of Political Consultants. Based on Capitol Hill (where else?), AAPC's mission statement lists such goals as "enhancing the political process and improving public confidence in the American political system," and "reaching out to involve and educate young people in the art of political consultation and in the benefits it brings to the practice of democracy."

Please AAPC, back off. Leave our young people alone. Do not molest them any further with your obscene talk about any benefits that this bloodsucking coven of consultants brings to our democracy.

If AAPC is not a clear sign to you that the ideal of citizen government is headed straight to hell in a consultant's rocket-powered alligator briefcase, be forewarned that there's something called the Graduate School of Political Management at George Washington University. "Professional campaigning is a multi-billion dollar business, which is becoming increasingly sophisticated and technology driven," enthuses the GSPM Web site, apparently oblivious to the fact most Americans find this a deplorable development that needs to be fought, not taught. Nonetheless, they are churning out a whole new generation of political professionals (pol-pros) bearing master's degrees that proclaim them to be proficient at subverting democracy. Among the socially useful jobs that the GSPM girds its students to perform are campaign manager, fundraiser, lobbyist, and corporate public affairs officer. Classes include "campaign advertising and promotion," "issues management," "managing government relations," "lobbying the budget process," and "executive fund-raising."

Gosh, think how great this country might have been if—instead of Jefferson, Paine, Washington, Madison, and the other citizens who came up with all that "We the People" stuff—there had been some GSPMA degree holders to do the job for us.

THE NONEOFTHEABOVES

In the nineteenth century, British economist Walter Bagehot said: "The cure for admiring the House of Lords is to go and look at it."

The American majority has taken a long, hard look at the Democrat-Republican, two-party house of cards—and they are cured. You'd never know this, though, by listening to or reading the establishment media's farcical coverage of election results. "America Moves to the Right," screamed a headline the day after Newt Gingrich's Republicans won control of Congress in 1994; "New Conservative Tide," announced another; "Voters

Endorse Newt's Contract," asserted still another. But look out! Only four years later, voters were stampeding again: "America Seeks Middle," "A Move to Moderation," "Voters Choose Centrism" blared headlines the day after the 1998 congressional elections.

Boy, the people must be exhausted after having dashed so far to the right, then turned right around and bolted *en masse* back to the center. One could get tennis-neck watching the electorate dart back and forth—except that about 94 percent of folks didn't dart anywhere.

Let's do the math (it's only one paragraph, so you can do it, I know you can; come on, let's try). First, the Republicans. In 1994, about 22 percent of eligible voters went Republican in Newt's "big sweep"; in 1998, about 18 percent of voters went Republican; so, only 4 percent of eligible voters darted from the GOP. Did they dart to the Democrats? No: In 1994, about 19 percent of eligible voters went Democratic; in 1998, about 17 percent of voters went Democratic; so, even though the media pitched the '98 election as a "Democratic comeback" against Newt, they actually lost 2 percent of eligible voters from their column. In addition, third-party candidates got about 1 percent of the vote in both years: Therefore, the media-induced image of electoral masses surging here and there comes down to only 6 percent of eligible voters going anywhere.

Now, here's THE BIG STORY missing from the media's election coverage: The fastest-growing party in America is not the Republicans or the Democrats but the NOTA Party—the *Noneoftheabove* Party. All those numbers in the paragraph above come down to the startling fact that 58 percent of voters in 1994 could not stomach getting in the polling booth with either party, while in 1998, the Noneoftheabovers had grown to 64 percent. Need a chart to visualize all these numbers? Here:

PERCENTAGE OF ELIGIBLE VOTERS
WHO VOTED, BY PARTY

Year	Republican Party	Democratic Party	Third Parties	NOTA Party (*i.e.*, did not vote)
1994	22%	19%	1%	58%
1998	18%	17%	1%	64%
SHIFT	–4%	–2%	same	+6%

Source: Curtis Gans, Committee for the Study of the American Electorate.

In 1964, I got some 760 votes in a race for student body president at the University of North Texas. That was about 10 percent of the students in the school, and I thought, sheesh, how embarrassing. And I was the *winner*! But these days we're electing national lawmakers and governors on margins almost as low as my collegiate election. Consider "Shrub's Story." The upwardly mobile Texas governor was reelected in '98 by what was hailed nationwide as a "breathtaking landslide," with Texas voters "overwhelmingly" endorsing his political management of the state. Instantly, he was propelled into the front ranks of presidential aspirants, based on this demonstration that he is "a formidable vote-getter."

Unmentioned was the fact that the turnout in his election was a dismal 26 percent—lowest in the nation. He ran against a Democratic Party that had essentially abandoned its own gubernatorial nominee. Roughly 16 percent of eligible voters is all that George W. Bush could muster to stand with him. It's not so much that he increased the usual vote that Republican candidates for governor can count on, but that the Democrats had collapsed, unable to draw more than about 8 percent of the eligible to vote for them.

Bush was not alone among politicos in the last election who claimed to be exhilarated but were really just breathing their own exhaust fumes. "Democrats Exult in Broad Victory," declared the *Los Angeles Times* after the party cut into the GOP majority in Congress. Yet, the Republicans still controlled the House and Senate, and the Democrats actually had a lower percentage of voters going with them in '98 than in '94. Worse, the party-of-the-people continued to sag with its natural constituency of working-class folks—it only led Republicans among voters with a high school degree by two percentage points, and it lost among voters with some college but not a four-year degree. This is not happy news for Dems at all, since Americans with less than a four-year degree comprise 75 percent of all adults. Indeed, the party's only significant gain was among voters with incomes of more than $75,000 a year—a pool that includes less than 5 percent of the people. How many brains does it take to figure out you dive in the deep end rather than the shallow?

The media—clueless to the bone—hailed the '98 national vote as the public's demand for don't-rock-the-boat centrism. Again, the *LA Times*: "The nation's voters are looking for moderation. . . ." Really? Then what was that Jesse "the Body" Ventura thing in Minnesota all about? Whatever you think of Ventura since his '98 election, it's clear that the people who put this pink-boa-wearing, shaved-head, kick-ass professional wrestler and Reform Party upstart in the Guv's chair had something other than moderation in mind. But the political pros and media pundits gawked at him like he was a billy goat in a tutu: "This is the most bizarre result of the evening," gasped the election analyst at CNN.

Compared to what? Strom Thurmond and Jesse Helms still sitting in the U.S. Senate, despite being dead for years? A cockroach like Bob Barr and a purse-lipped, pucker-assed prude like Bill McCallom getting reelected to the Congress? Indeed, how about the fact that special-interest money gives incumbents such an advantage that house members are *four times more likely to die in office* than to be defeated. Isn't that bizarre?

Since Jesse wasn't a product of the money/consultant system, however, the media simply couldn't fathom his rise to high office. "Ventura's plain talk and populist ideas brought a near-stampede to the polls, many of whom told exit pollsters they voted only because 'Jesse' was in the race," marveled a *Los Angeles Times* election analyst, adding in befuddlement, "How exactly Ventura managed this is still being dissected." Managed? Dissected? Hello, pundit, please call home after your next orbit around Mars. The point is that Ventura *didn't* manage it—it's who he is, and dissecting that is like dissecting humor. More media: "Selling himself as outside the mainstream, he nonetheless came across as an 'Everyman' and had broad appeal across class and party lines." Good grief, get a grip. "Everyman" *is* outside the mainstream, at least as it's defined by those who draw the class and party lines. One more: "He effectively presented himself as a contrast to politics as usual." He didn't "present himself" as a contrast—he *was* a contrast!

Because he was unmanaged and outside the mainstream, not only did he win, but Minnesota's turnout was the highest in the nation at 60 percent. Ventura was especially strong with young people, blue-collar and Democratic voters, and mad-as-hellers who had not voted in years.

Jesse's election was the most publicized voter rebellion of '98, but hardly the only one. If you want a contrast to politicians-as-usual, you couldn't do better than Fred, a seventy-nine-year-old retired dairy farmer in Vermont. Fred Tuttle decided to run for the Republican nomination to the U.S. Senate against one Jack McMullen. The Vermonters who voted for Fred were definitely making a statement against today's politics of cynicism, which McMullen represented perfectly.

McMullen is a multimillionaire Boston consultant who decided he would buy himself a Senate seat, so he registered his Vermont vacation home as his new permanent residence in 1997, garnered the support of the state's GOP establishment, and set out to defeat incumbent senator Pat Leahy. Of course, to get to Leahy, he first had to hop the hurdle of the September '98 Republican primary, but Jack was spending $300,000 of his own money on the primary, airing a blitzkrieg of television and radio ads and running an all-out modern campaign designed by the best pros—so he was confident. Besides, his only opponent was some old coot in overalls.

Tuttle, who wears a cap that says "Fred" on it, had already had fifteen seconds of fame, having been the main character in an independent film called *Man with a Plan* (still available on video), written and directed by his neighbor, John O'Brien. In the film, Fred's character gets tired of being a broke dairy farmer and decides to run for Congress, because the job pays well. His motto is "I've spent my whole life in the barn, now I want to be in the House," and he has a bumper sticker on his manure spreader that proclaims: "Spread Fred."

Meanwhile, back in real life, Fred and his filmmaker neighbor were upset that a Massachusetts millionaire was prancing into their state with an overdose of cash and arrogance. To twit this twit (and to gin up a bit of publicity about their movie), they decide to enter Fred in the primary against McMullen. To make a wonderful story short, Fred caught on— and "Spread Fred" bumper stickers became a cry of Vermont rebellion against today's whole sick system of politics. Tuttle spent only $216 on his campaign—$16 for the filing fee, and $200 to rent Porta Potties. The portable toilets were an unexpected, out-of-pocket expense necessitated when a crowd of two hundred people showed up for Fred's "Nickel-a-Plate" fund-raising dinner at his farm. Come election day, Fred drubbed McMullen, 55 percent to 45 percent.

He's not in the Senate, because ... well, basically he endorsed Leahy, saying the senator was a good man doing a good job. Besides, Fred said, "I can't go to Washington, D.C. Too many people down there."

The cognoscenti don't like to talk about it, but centrism, moderation, middle-of-the-road and status quo generally get a swift kick in the butt whenever people get a sense that their votes can matter, when an ax handle is put in their hands to smash the machine. Jesse and Fred were part of this recurring political phenomenon in 1998, but there were plenty of other ax handles available, too, thanks to ballot initiatives.

- Voters in Arizona and Massachusetts gave a resounding YES! to *public* financing of their state elections, crimping the power of corporations to buy government policies. (Arizona's initiative even included a tax on lobbyists to help pay for the public election fund.)
- By a stunning 66 percent margin, the electorate in Washington State said YES! to a "living wage" initiative that effectively sets the wage floor there at $6.50 an hour, even indexing it to inflation.
- In Colorado, an initiative to regulate the massive (and massively polluting) corporate hog factories that are stinking up the place pulled a YES! from 64 percent of the voters; South Dakota went even further to stop the spread of these corporate stinkers, with 59 percent of the voters there saying YES! to a constitutional amendment that flat-out bans them from the state.
- In open defiance of the loopy national drug czar and of demagoguing politicians who are denying the medical use of marijuana even to terminally ill patients, voters in Alaska, Arizona, Nevada, Oregon, Washington State, and the District of Columbia said a great big YES! to initiatives authorizing marijuana for medical cases in their jurisdictions.

Then there's Newport, Maine. Desiree Davis, thirtysomething, enjoyed mowing her lawn topless. But neighbor Mary Thompson didn't like it, so she collected 125 signatures to put the issue on the November '98 ballot. A spirited public discourse ensued, including the printing by Desiree's mother of T-shirts declaring the wearer to be an "Official Member of the Topless Lawn Mower's Club." (Yes, if you were really a topless mower member you would not be wearing a T-shirt, but it's the political statement that matters here.) The debate was held, the vote was taken, and Newport went on record 775 to 283 to let it all hang out when mowing your yard. No reports yet as to whether tourism is up in Newport during mowing season.

Now comes Election 2000, a space odyssey so far out that even Stanley Kubrick would have had a hard time imagining it. Fueled by an unprecedented level of corrupting cash, the political system has disconnected itself from the body politic and is accelerating away from us at approximately the speed of light, creating a deep and dark divide between what the people want from politics and what they'll get.

The result is not so much an election process as it is a burlesque. Consider this election report from the *Chicago Tribune:* "People formed long lines at some of the 5,700 voting stations, but most said they were voting only because they had been ordered to . . . and few seemed to have any idea whom they were voting for. There had been no campaigning, and candidates had been selected in advance behind closed doors— ensuring a satisfactory result regardless of who was chosen. Even the candidates seemed somewhat nonchalant about the process. [One] said he wasn't sure exactly what entity he was running for or even for how long he would serve. 'If I get elected, I'm sure I'll find out, and I'll let you know.' If elected [he] said his goal is to 'represent the people's will.' But he acknowledged he didn't know what the will of the people was."

The *Tribune* was reporting on an election for district legislature in Beijing, China, but it's not that much farther out than our own space odyssey. Most of our candidates, too, are selected in advance behind closed doors, ensuring "a satisfactory result" for the moneyed interests that do the selecting, no matter which ones ultimately are chosen in the formal balloting. While our candidates generally do know what office they're seeking, most are as lost as their Chinese counterparts on what the will of the people might be.

In a way, our current system is more cynical than the Chinese's, for it is much more widely hyped, providing all the trappings of a democratic process, yet withholding the substance. In the coming year, we'll get campaigning out the kazoo—bunting everywhere, cheering supporters artfully arranged at every campaign stop, caucuses and primaries, nominating speeches, balloons and confetti, polls, an assault of ads, televised debates (no third parties, please), campaign slogans and throbbing theme songs, an overdose of punditry by the puffheads of the media, and of course the election itself— even as the system draws the ring of actual participation tighter and tighter around a closed circle of special interests. Issues of consequence to ordinary folks will be ignored, deliberately avoided by tacit agreement of the two parties, or crassly used as ad fodder by candidates who will do nothing about them once in office, further trivializing the debate and putting more mock in demockracy.

This insidious system begs for ridicule. Last year, as part of the hype for his gubernatorial inauguration, which his consultants carefully orchestrated as a prelude to the formation of his presidential exploratory committee, George W. Bush included a pitch to the politically significant Latino voters by adding this slogan to his ceremonial banners: "Juntos Podemos," which translates as "Together We Can." Unfortunately, the *Houston Chronicle* reported it as "Juntos Pedemos," which translates loosely as "We fart together." For many Americans, Latino or otherwise, that's a fair summation of what today's political system delivers.

"I won't vote," Manuel González told the *New York Times*. A superintendent at a store called Sunny Fruits and Vegetables in the Bronx, Manuel speaks for the multitudes when he says, "Doesn't count anyway—the politicians do what they like. It's not a people's country. It's a money country."

Tragically for America, Manuel is right. He can vote for Bushgorebradleymccainforbesadnauseam and nothing in his life will change. I happen to think he *should* vote—go third party, write in Daffy Duck, anything to show that he's there, that he casts an American's protest against the two-party con, that he won't be run out of the voting booth by the bastards— yet, there's no denying the angry truth of his statement: The politicians do what they like . . . it's a money country.

What kind of "election" is it that does not address, much less treat, the needs and aspirations of the millions and millions of Manuels who, after all, *are* America? What kind of democracy is it that can be perfectly satisfied, even glad, that Manuel won't vote? Indeed, despite there being an open presidential seat, despite the control of Congress being up for grabs, despite this being the first election of the third millennium—more Americans watched this January's Super Bowl than will show up for November's national balloting. We're staring at an electoral train wreck in the making, with the likelihood that fewer than half of the country's voters will be motivated to bother, and with the live possibility that this year will produce a lower national turnout than the scintillating Clinton-Dole matchup of '96 (third lowest in history), the thrilling Coolidge-Davis contest of 1924 (second lowest), and even rival the clunker of 1824 (lowest ever) when John Quincy Adams stumbled into the White House.

The good news is that there will be important exceptions to the general disinterest in campaign 2000—scattered rebellions by voters who find more ax handles like Jesse, Fred, and various ballot initiatives, as well as increasingly energetic campaigns by third parties. Whenever and wherever people find an election that matters and find that their participation will make a difference, they'll jump on it like a hungry grackle on a grasshopper, which puts the lie to the convenient wisdom of the conventionalists that voters simply don't care, are lazy louts, or are just happy with the way things are going. The "happy" theory is a recent favorite of some pundits and editorial writers, and all I can say to them is, if your IQ ever reaches fifty . . . sell!

Even the bad news—the mass nonparticipation of voters— is potentially good news, because such a mass will not be still for long. Like floodwaters swelling behind a dam, America's Noneoftheabove majority will find outlets. This is *the* political story of the millennium, not Bush, Gore, or whoever. None-oftheabovers are the largest, fastest growing, and most important political force in our nation. But where will they go? They are nonideological and multi-ideological (sometimes in the same person), and they've been somewhere between intrigued and inspired by an odd-bedfellow range of recent political rebels, from Jesse Jackson to Jesse Ventura, Jerry Brown to Ross Perot, Ralph Nader to Pat Buchanan. They are a populist force with the power to realign the old right-to-left, theoretical configuration of politics, supplanting it with a more vital (and radical) top-to-bottom, real-life politics based on people's desire to take their country back from an aloof and arrogant power structure (often referred to colloquially and collectively as "The Assholes").

Two things for sure: (1) This mass will move; and (2) it will be messy. It will not move as one body, certainly not at first, but the anger and aspirations of so many cannot be contained, so the most dramatic and defining political events in the opening decade of the new century will flow from efforts by None-oftheabovers to assert themselves. It will be messy because there is no road map for a flood—it cuts new channels, overflows boundaries, and swamps old structures. So far, it has been breaking out in spurts and rivulets, such as assorted third parties, maverick campaigns, and the term-limits movement.

But here's another messy reality that warrants reflection by those elites who imagine there will be no price to pay for having stiffed the majority, both politically and economically, lo these many years: The ballot is not the only form of political expression. For example, meet the militia. Yes, yes, it's considered politically proper to dismiss this skulking movement as a collection of paranoid gun kooks, zoned-out survivalists, and raw racists—but it's also politically stupid to dismiss such an explosive movement out of hand. The kooks, survivalists, and racists are there all right, yet the rank and file of many militias is made up of people we know . . . or once knew. They're the family farmers of the eighties and nineties who were suckered by governmental policies that got them way overextended on farm credit while at the same time pushing massive overproduction that busted their crop prices, then allowed the bankers and hustlers to waltz in and merrily rip their land, livelihood, and pride from them. They are also former U.S. autoworkers who saw Washington wink while General Motors dumped seventy-three thousand of them on the trash heap of global greed in the late eighties and early nineties, while simultaneously creating approximately seventy-three thousand jobs in Mexico, Brazil, and other wage-busting outposts.

These were middle-class people who did what the system asks: be skilled and productive, work hard, be loyal, have a family, fight your country's wars, go to church, obey the laws . . . go vote. They'd earned a slice of the pie, working up to $30–$40,000 a year. Then, from far away, some incomprehensible force suddenly reached down their throats, grabbed 'em by the balls, and yanked their whole beings inside out. Where was the system, they wondered, that had told them that if they followed the straight and narrow they'd live the American Dream? The system was over on the side, smirking at them and coddling the brutes who'd done the yanking. What does either party have to say to these roughed-up, bedrock Americans? Where was either Clinton or Bush in '92, or Clinton or Dole in '96, as hundreds of thousands of them were getting stomped? Silence. Now, in 2000, Bush, Gore, & Gang don't even know they're still out there. "Oh, yeah," they might say if pressed, "I remember something on television some years ago about a farm crisis and some downsizings." Where do they think these people went? They don't think about them at all. These are America's disappeared.

But they *are* there, and if no one is beating a political path to their doors, it need not be a surprise that they'll try to forge their own political paths, even if that means arming themselves for . . . what? Who knows, but there it is. This is what is at stake when the majority is shunted aside by the two-party system to become Noneoftheabovers. The populist movement is upon us as both the Republicans and Democrats narrow their attention even tighter on the affluent minority. But will this populism break out as a progressive and inclusive movement, as is possible? Or will it turn ugly, devolving into a reactionary, insular, bitter, brutish, and ultimately self-consuming rage, which is also possible?

At present, there is a huge hole in America that has to be filled. The top 20 percent of Americans—who own 96 percent of all stocks and bonds, who have 85 percent of all the net worth, who made 89 percent of all the gains in the stock market run up of the nineties—now own the two big political parties. There has to be something for the 80 percent of Americans. Just as a shadow is not something, but the lack of something; just as loneliness and hunger are not something, but the lack of something; neither is Noneoftheabove something. It is the lack of a political say in America. If this pent-up majority is not to turn ugly, a new politics has to be forged that opens a broad new channel so these good people have a real say in the way things are being run and the way things are being shaped for the future. Ordinary people have to matter again.

GO, GRANNY, GO!

Bo Pilgrim is a big-time chicken processor in East Texas, but he wasn't known to the average Texan until 1989, when he committed such a faux pas inside our state capitol that he was widely excoriated in the media as a political embarrassment. Now you've really got to go some to rise to the level of "embarrassment" in Texas politics, where we often elect embarrassments to high office just for their amusement value (I'll not stoop to naming any names here, but someone with the initials P.H.I.L.G.R.A.M.M. qualifies).

Bo earned his niche in the Lone Star Hall of Embarrassments during the state senate's consideration of a worker's compensation bill that he did not want to see passed, for he feared it could take a dime or two from his chicken-plucking profits. So, just two days before the noble senators were to vote, and while they were debating the bill, Mr. Pilgrim went to Austin to put in his two-cents worth, just as any ordinary citizen might. Only his wasn't two cents. He stood in a corner just off the senate floor, signaling first to one senator then to another, calling them over one by one to have a brief word with him. Then he would put a $10,000 campaign check into their hands, along with some materials about the legislation.

During the day, as the debate droned on, Pilgrim disbursed nine $10,000 checks, all to senators who had been identified as swing votes on the issue. One senator rejected Bo's offering outright, and another spoiled the party by not only returning his check promptly, but also blowing the whistle, which led to quite a press scramble to have the other bribees explain themselves. One had already rushed to the bank and deposited his! Another said with a forced smile that, Golly, he didn't even realize there was a check in all those materials he'd been given by Mr. Pilgrim. And another, when asked if the contribution seemed unseemly, responded: "Unseemly . . . that's in the eye of the beholder." He kept the money.

The fun part of such audacious bribery is that it's not illegal! Texas being Texas, our legislators have never been strong for interfering in the free flow of money into their pockets, so Pilgrim's check-weaving routine was technically legal. Still, it was tacky, and the news about Bo and his Little Bo-Peeps set off a full round of indignant editorials and stern scoldings by the media and assorted establishmentarians. However, the real embarrassment was not that money had changed hands over a legislative vote, but that it had been handled so sloppily. "Goodgodamighty," bellowed the professional lobbyists privately. "Don't this Pilgrim boy know how to play the game? You deliver the check before or after the vote, you dummy, *not during it,* and damn sure not on the floor of the senate with God and the Associated Press watching the whole damned deal go down. We need to take up a collection and buy him a brain cell." All in all, it was an edifying moment in Texas civics for the schoolchildren of our state.

The embarrassment of Bo Pilgrim came back to me in early January, 1999, when I first heard about quite another kind of pilgrim. Doris Haddock is her name, known to her family and now to countless numbers of us who have been touched by her great spirit as Granny D.

At eighty-nine years of age, she embarked on an extraordinary pilgrimage. Beginning New Year's Day of that year at the Rose Bowl Parade in Pasadena, California, she set out to walk the entire breadth of this great country, all 3,000 miles of it, to the Nation's Capital. This was not a fitness feat she was striving for, but a political feat of prodigious proportions. Her mission was nothing less than to put a stop to today's uptown Bo Pilgrims—the slick, suave, sophisticated versions of the chicken plucker, the ones in the corporate suites and lobbying offices who are using their checkbooks to buy legislation, too, and—through their massive soft-money contributions, PACs, bundled checks, and other devices—to drown out the voice of the people in American politics. "Call me crazy, call me God-sent," proclaimed this feisty octogenarian as she began her cross-country journey, "but I am on a crusade to create a groundswell for campaign finance reform, to eliminate the cancer of corporate money that's killing our democracy."

At least a few thought she was crazy—and they were in her own family! Actually, her two children, eight grandchildren, and eleven great-grandchildren ranged from supportive to enthusiastic about this idea of hers, but there was a natural concern that it was quixotic and not all that safe. Still, they knew and trusted her, they knew her seriousness, so they helped her do it. "I believe the people who make progress for us are crazed. You can't send an eighty-nine-year-old woman into the desert without thinking that," her son Jim told the Los Angeles *Daily News*. "But there's a difference between crazy and insane," he said.

Bingo! Thomas Paine was a crazy. Sojourner Truth and Frederick Douglass, too. Mary Helen Lease ("The Kansas Pythoness") and "Sockless Jerry" Simpson of the great populist movement, Eugene Debs and Mother Jones of labor—crazies, one and all. Yet these and so many, many more are the ones who've stretched the reach of our democracy, not the presidents, tycoons, and other "Great Men" of the time, nearly all of whom have fought ferociously to suppress the free thinkers, iconoclasts, political mavericks, visionaries, organizers, and other democrats—like Granny D.

Who is this lady? A widow who has lived a long time in Dublin, New Hampshire, population 1,400. She was a secretary and office manager for a shoe company before retiring some years ago. She is informed and well-spoken, polite, patient, and respectful of others. But don't mistake politeness for meekness—after all, this is the "Live Free or Die" state, and Doris Haddock has always been a reformer, and often an agitator. In the 1930s she performed one-woman feminist plays, so you know she's not afraid to speak her mind.

In 1960 she took on her first national crusade. It was against an insane scheme by Edward Teller, father of the H-bomb, to use thermonuclear weapons to (hold your breath now) dig canals. Like the Panama Canal, only he figured nuclear blasting could re-engineer the landscape all over the planet. All he needed was a chance to show his stuff. Through her church, Doris and her husband, Jim, learned that Teller had targeted a place that, ironically, was named Point Hope, way up in northwest Alaska, inside the Arctic Circle. It was a remote village of poor and powerless Eskimos, and Teller planned to demonstrate the efficacy of his nuclear relandscaping dream by detonating six bombs to create an artificial harbor there. Never mind that the Eskimos wanted neither the harbor nor the radiation that would result.

Doris was determined that this brilliant idiot had to be stopped. With Jim, five other people, and a really big dog crammed into a VW minibus, she took off for Point Hope. This is a terrific tale (check the 1993 book *The Firecracker Boys* by Dan O'Neill), but I'll flip to the ending for you: Doris and her hardy band of Volkswagen activists succeeded in stopping Teller after a three-year campaign that went all the way to JFK in the White House—a result that no one outside her group would've thought possible. Granny D might be idealistic, but she's no naïf when it comes to taking on the system.

Why walk? Because of Jack Kerouac, Willie Nelson, Mildred Norman, and an old man on the road. And because she doesn't have much time left. In January, 1998, not long after her best friend had died, Doris was being driven by her son to see her sister in Florida. Along the way, in a melancholy mood, she noticed an old man standing by the highway as they roared past. He was "wearing a black watch cap and a full-length Macintosh, leaning against his cane," she later wrote in a personal remembrance. "He was miles and miles from any town or house. 'What's he doing way out here?' I asked my son, Jim. 'He's on the road again, mother,' he replied." She and Jim then talked for a while about the road, about Kerouac's book and Willie's song. "It occurred to me that I should go on the road for the political issue I cared most about: campaign reform." This had been her crusade recently in Dublin, where she had been speaking out and getting signatures for Common Cause's petition drive to pressure Congress on the issue. "I looked at my son as he drove us along," she writes, "and I knew I was about to change our lives when I spoke. I told him that I would walk across the U.S. for campaign finance reform. I said I would talk about how our democracy is being purchased from underneath us. I would help round up votes for reform in congress."

"Oh, boy," sighed Jim.

Shortly after, Jim went from sighing to coaching, realizing that his mother was determined to do it and had to be prepared. To walk across America in a year required doing 10 miles a day. So she began training on the streets and hills of Dublin, working her way up to 10 miles while carrying a 25-pound backpack. What a sight! Then eighty-eight, five feet tall, stooped a bit from the years—she would walk and walk, all through 1998, and she would spend nights sleeping on the ground, getting used to a year on the road. She learned about another remarkable woman, named Mildred Norman, who had walked seven times across the country during the McCarthy period and the Cold War, talking about the need for peace. Mildred began each of her treks by walking in the Rose Bowl Parade, but when the parade stopped, she just kept going. Her plan was simple—walk until given shelter, fast until given food. The simplicity of it appealed to Doris, so she adopted this basic plan.

Working with the auto club, she mapped out a route, which a geologist acquaintance revised to avoid the cold and any steep climbs. Jim got airline tickets to fly them to LA, and daughter Betty got a cell phone for her. She decided she needed a road name, too, and she chose Granny D, which one of her granddaughters had always called her. She was ready.

On Christmas day, she and Jim flew nonstop to the West Coast. She had a window seat and gazed out on America for five hours. "It is a very large place we have here," she said to herself.

Staying in Santa Monica, she went down to the beach, because she wanted to wade a bit in the Pacific waters. As she did, she thought, "I'm going to walk over to the east and put my feet in the Atlantic." It was a calming way to simplify the enormity of what lay just ahead. There were a lot of people on the beach that morning, so she decided to practice her technique for getting signatures on her petitions. It was her plan as they traversed the country to sign up as many ordinary Americans as possible on a simple, straightforward petition. "We the People of the United States Beseech Our Government to Enact With All Speed Meaningful Campaign Finance Reform." The petitions would put the lie to the claim by pundits and politicians that the people don't care about reforming the corrupt system. But as she stood there, offering her petitions, no one stopped. "An old woman at the beach is evidently quite easy to walk by," she later wrote—"but they were all polite."

A young woman who had been watching came over and asked Granny what reform meant to her. She explained, and the woman signed, then offered a bit of advice. She said she thought at first that Granny D was talking about a local issue, so people weren't sure what it was about. "Add the word *national*," she advised. "Say national campaign finance reform, and people will get it immediately." Sure enough, the extra word was all that was needed. People stopped to sign, and the helpful young woman stayed on for a while as Granny's barker: "This woman is walking across the United States for national campaign finance reform. Support her by signing her petition." It was the first of countless encounters with the wonderful people of America who do indeed care very much about reform and would lend helping hands to Granny D for the next 3,000 miles. On January 1, she put on her special reinforced corset for her back, her hiking boots with steel supports, her orange vest proclaiming "Granny D—Pilgrim for Campaign Finance Reform," her backpack, and her floppy, broadbrimmed straw hat—then she followed the Parade of Roses past Sierra Madre Boulevard . . . and headed east.

She was never alone. Stepping out of Los Angeles with her the first day was Ken Hechler, himself eighty-four years old. Once a speechwriter for Harry Truman, Hechler is a terrific, hell-raising political leader and reformer from West Virginia, having served as its representative in Congress and presently serving as its secretary of state. He had seen a brief item about Doris Haddock's intention to walk for reform, and he decided to help her—he has walked with her for some stretch of the road in every state. Ken also is running for Congress again— "If Granny can walk at eighty-nine, I can run at eighty-four," he told me.

Common Cause also adopted Granny, notifying its membership that she was headed their way. So Common Causers, which Granny herself was back in Dublin, have been key supporters all along the way. Two were there at the start—Ralph and Maria Langley, a retired couple from Upland, California, who showed up in their Cadillac to escort her across the state and into the Mojave Desert. They would drive alongside her as she walked in the mornings, then drive ahead of her while she rested in the afternoons to alert the media and local officials in the next town that "Granny Is Coming!" It was hard traveling at first, for the press coverage was sparse, the helpers few in number (though strong in energy and heart), and the road was ever so long. "At some level, I thought the whole thing was ridiculous," Doris confided.

But things quickly picked up as people heard about her. That's all it took—let people know that some woman is on the road fighting the Washington bribe artists, and they'll say, "Where do I sign up?" The first big media break was Michael Coit's article in the *Los Angeles Daily News*, which went on the AP wire and put Granny's trek on the national radar. That's how I learned about her. My "Chat & Chew" radio talk show began on January 14 to have a weekly chat with Granny D, usually via her trusty cell phone, and we've continued with her for the whole trip. Not only was she a delight for our listeners, but they were thrilled to learn that she would be passing through their town, and they turned out to welcome her, walk with her, put her up for the night, buy her a hot meal, arrange for her to speak to local groups, circulate her petitions, and generally be a part of this gutsy lady's pilgrimage.

The routine was for her to be up and out early (6 A.M. in the summer months, to try beating the worst of the heat), walk the 10 miles of the day (taking rests as she needed them), mark the spot where she left off, then be driven by volunteers for a lunch, nap, event, or whatever people had arranged for her in a nearby town. After an overnight in a home, B&B, motel, or the best deal she could get, she'd be driven out to her marker the next morning to start another 10-mile leg. No fudging for Granny—her odometer is true.

What a trip. Cars, pickups, and eighteen-wheelers would honk at her little group; some would stop to sign the petition or join the troupe for a while; "Go, Granny, Go!" became the common greeting; mayors and high school bands would meet her at the city limits; parents brought their children out to walk with her; town after town proclaimed "Granny D Day"; she got enough keys to the city to start a locksmith shop; she was welcomed into a Tucson biker bar (where she was told that the word would be spread among bikers to keep an eye out for her on the road and assure her safe passage); she lectured at colleges, rode in rodeo processions, threw out the first pitch in a minor league baseball game, spoke from the steps of state capitols, got blown down a couple of times by the wind in West Texas, did innumerable interviews, and, among other sights, she saw a rattlesnake.

Not all snakes are in the wild, though. Some are in the U.S. Senate. One of the most fun moments came early in the journey, in front of the Phoenix office of Sen. Jon Kyl. This Republican has been a vituperative voice against reforming the corrupt money system, and Granny D wanted to have a public discussion with him about it—not a formal debate or staged confrontation, but a civil and civic conversation. An hour would be nice, but less would be acceptable too. Arizona Common Cause tried for weeks to set up a meeting, but the senator's schedule was just awfully tight, don't you know, what with him being so very, very busy with many, many important matters demanding his attention . . . and garbage like that. Yet Granny kept coming, 10 miles a day, getting closer and closer to Phoenix, and getting more media attention the closer she got. Finally she was there, and word was hastily sent to her that the senator could spare ten minutes for a private hello in his office. No deal, said our crusader, sending word back that she would arrive at his front door, with the media present, and invite him to come out. She and the local media arrived, and our "Chat & Chew" radio crew also took our national audience live to the action via the cell phone—but no Jon. We imagined him not only locked inside his inner office with the lights out, but also hiding under his desk. "I think he's afraid of Granny," our champion said with a smile so impish that it could be seen on radio.

A side note to the Kyl episode: Common Cause alerted my radio producer that the ABC, CBS, and NBC affiliates in Phoenix were not intending to cover her arrival on the senator's doorstep, since he had said he wasn't going to appear. Hello, Pulitzer Prize committee, has news judgment been outlawed in Arizona? Here's a money-drenched senator hiding in his own office from a little old lady who wandered in off the desert so she could ask him to give reform a chance. Wouldn't viewers find Kyl's hide-and-seek behavior amusing, odd, silly, impolite . . . *newsworthy*? We gave out the phone numbers of all three network affiliates in Phoenix and unleashed our radio audience to call them. The stations all came, and they ran the story on that night's news. Sometimes people have to free the "free press" from itself.

Granny just kept going. Dallas was her halfway point, and a local reporter, Jacquielynn Floyd of the *Morning News,* joined her for one morning's walk:

A morning with Doris offers instruction in determination, endurance, and passion for a cause. More than anything, it demonstrates just how far 10 miles is. . . . We were a jolly little parade when we set out from a Mobil station; Doris, her support van, a few hardy tagalongs, and a police car with flashing lights. Well-wishers honked and waved; one man showed up with a bouquet of flowers as a send-off. . . . And so we walked merrily along the first few miles, waving to bystanders. . . . Part of the party peeled off after mile four, and some took a break to ride in the van. . . . Between miles six and seven, I turned kind of queasy, doubtless because of the whopping dose of caffeine it had taken to get out of bed at 4 A.M. . . . By mile eight, my dogs were barking fiercely, and I secretly marveled that the human body could excrete so much sweat. Doris never complained— she never does, her entourage says—so I kept my mouth shut. Mile nine felt like a forced march at bayonet point. Nobody but Doris had the energy left to lift a hand and wave. . . . We collapsed gratefully at the 10-mile mark. . . . I was footsore and exhausted, but proud of making the whole hike. But on Saturday morning, I'll be fast asleep. Doris will be on the road again.

The real story is not her march, but her message, and the fact that it resonates so clearly with such a broad majority of Americans. The need for reform really doesn't take much explaining, whether talking before a local chamber of commerce crowd, in a union hall, on a college campus, in a church, or with folks sitting in a booth at a café. Also, Granny says it so plainly—asked by a reporter what kept her moving, she replied, "I have eleven great-grandchildren, and I want them to grow up in a democracy." At that Tucson biker bar that embraced Granny, the manager (known simply as Kuzzton, and who is going to ask him if that's his first, last, or nickname?) said that he's not surprised that she could come in there and strike up a conversation with the regulars about something supposedly so boring as campaign financing: "Most of the customers know that issue real well. It seems like it takes too much money to get elected, and a regular person can't do that."

Not that everyone sends Granny hugs. Her Web site (still operative at www.grannyd.com) has drawn some unpleasant communications from assorted boneheads, but the polite New Englander is more than a match for them:

BONEHEAD #1: You are a fraud. Your Web site is a fraud. Al Gore, Bill Clinton, Bill Bradley, and you are all frauds.

GRANNY D: Thank you for taking time to write to me. Sometimes when I get up in the morning I indeed wish that I were a fraud! But my old muscles and bones tell me that I am the real thing.

BONEHEAD #2: [You are] a leftist.

GRANNY D: Yesterday I was a leftist, but this morning I was a rightist, because the traffic was safer there. Tomorrow, we'll see.

BONEHEAD #3: Get lost!

GRANNY D: Thank you for your brief note. If you knew how many wrong turns I take, you would be cheered no end.

As I write this, Granny D is in Kentucky, 2,500 miles into her journey. Her intention is to arrive on the Capitol steps, January 24, 2000—her ninetieth birthday—where she'll present petitions to some members of Congress and have some sort of rally/press conference/speech. In the better world that Doris Haddock is doing so much to help build, however, she would not be on the outside of the Capitol building, but be brought inside to the House chamber, escorted up to the speaker's podium from which Presidents deliver their State of the Union ramblings, and from there be asked to speak to a joint session of Congress in a nationally televised address. I know what she would say, because she has said it again and again from sea to shining sea, and I've never heard a better speech in my life, delivered with such honest passion. Here is the speech, only slightly condensed, as she delivered it last year to the national convention of the Reform Party in Dearborn, Michigan:

Ladies and Gentlemen,

I have been involved in reform fights through most of my adult life, but I have saved the most important for last.

It is my belief that a worthy American ought to be able to run for a public office without having to sell his or her soul to the corporations or the unions in order to become a candidate. Fund-raising muscle should not be the measure of a candidate—ideas, character, track record, leadership skills: those ought to be the measures of our leaders.

It is my belief that the hundreds of thousands of our dead, buried in rows upon rows in our national cemeteries, sacrificed their lives for the democracy of a free people, not for what we have today. It is up to each of us right now to see that these boys and girls did not die in vain.

With the support of my dear children, grandchildren, and great-grandchildren, I began my trek and I will see it through. I am doing it to bring attention to the fact that ordinary Americans like me care desperately about the condition of our government and the need for campaign finance reform.

I have traveled as a pilgrim, and Americans have taken care of me through each of my 1,800 miles. If you knew, as I know from these last seven months, what a sweet and decent nation we live in, you would be all the more determined to raise it out of this time of trouble—this sewer of greed and cash that we have slipped into.

Friends, I have walked through a land where the middle class, the foundation of our democracy, stands nearly in ruins. Main streets have given way to superstores. Towns have died. Family farms, family businesses, and local owners have given way to absentee owners and a local population of underpaid clerks and collection agents. People are so stressed in their household economies, and in the personal relationships that depend on family economics, that they have little time for participation in the governance of their communities or of their nation. They struggle daily in mazes and treadmills of corporate design and inhumane intent. They dearly believe their opinions matter, but they don't believe their voice counts.

They tell me that the control of their government has been given over to commercial interests. They cheer me on, sometimes in tears, but they wonder if we will ever again be a self-governing people, a free people.

With the middle class so purposefully destroyed—its assets plundered by an elite minority—it should not surprise us that the war chests of presidential candidates are grotesquely overflowing. . . . The privileged elite intend to elect those who have helped them achieve this theft and who will help them preserve their position of advantage.

That is what accounts for the avalanche of $1,000 checks into presidential campaigns.

Walk through [any] city and mark the doors of the families who cannot afford to give $1,000 to a presidential candidate or to a senator or two. For those who live behind these millions of doors we do not have a democracy, but an emergency—a crisis that deeply threatens our future as a free people.

The thousands of Americans I have met are discouraged, but they are not defeated—nor will they ever be. They know that the government and the social order presently do not represent their interests and are not within their control—that American democracy is nearly a fiction. But the flame of freedom that no longer burns in public, burns securely in their longing hearts.

It is said that democracy is not something we have, but something we do. But right now, we cannot do it because we cannot speak. We are shouted down by the bullhorns of big money. It is money with no manners for democracy, and it must be escorted from the room.

While wealth has always influenced our politics, what is new is the increasing concentration of wealth and the widening divide between the political interests of the common people and the political interests of the very wealthy who are now able to buy our willing leaders wholesale. The wealthy elite used to steal what they needed and it hardly affected the rest of us. Now they have the power to take everything for themselves, laying waste to our communities, our culture, our environment, and our lives, and they are doing it.

What villainy allows this political condition? The twin viral ideas that money is speech and that corporations are people. If money is speech, then those with more money have more speech, and that idea is antithetical to democracy. It makes us no longer equal citizens.

Business corporations are not people. They are protective associations that we, the people, allow to be chartered for business purposes on the condition that they will behave.

We must look to whether we can still afford, as a people and as a planet, to give these little monsters a birth certificate but no proper upbringing, no set of expectations, no consequences for antisocial behavior.

We are simply tired of the damage they do, and we are tired of cleaning up after them. If they are to be allowed to exist—and they are indeed important to us—they must agree to be responsible for their own activities, start to finish, without requiring public dollars to be used to clean their rooms up after them. The era of corporate irresponsibility must be ended immediately, particularly in regard to the degradation of our political and cultural and natural environments, while we still have the power to act. Parents know that there comes a time when infantile behavior persists, but the child is too large to do much with. We Americans still can act in regard to the corporations we have given birth to, but not by much of an advantage. Our advantage will evaporate early in the twenty-first century if we do not act soon.

Friends, does it matter if it is Rupert Murdoch or Michael Eisner, instead of Marshall Tito or Nikita Khrushchev, who owns everything and decides everything for us, even if, through the stock exchange, we all have a powerless piece of this new mass collective? The soul of democracy is diversity, not concentration. Diversity requires the human scale, not monstrous scale.

General Eisenhower said, "Pessimism never won any battle." He was right. Pessimism visualizes defeat. What we visualize, we bring forth. Carl Sandburg wrote: "Nothing happens unless first a dream."

To the reformers, then: Learn optimism if you would have the endurance to succeed, and endurance is required.

Where to find optimism? Well, I have found it for you out on the road, and I give it to you now. It is this:

I give you the Americans I have met. Without exception, they deeply love the idea of America. It is an image they carry in their hearts. It is a dream they are willing to sacrifice their lives for. Many of them do. There is no separating this image of democracy from their longing for personal freedom for themselves, their family, their friends. To the extent that our government is not our own, we are not free people. We feel a heavy oppression in our lives because we have lost hold of this thing, this self-governance, that is rightfully ours because it is our dream and our history. But the spirit of freedom is strong in the American soul, and it is the source of our optimism and joy, because it will always overcome its oppressors.

On the road so far, these Americans have taken me into their homes and fed me at their tables—shown me the children for whom they sacrifice their working lives and for whom they pray for a free and gentle democracy. And I will tell you that I am with them.

Yes, it is a long road ahead. But what nation can look at their neighbors with such pride as can we? Who thinks they can stand in the way of our need to be free, to manage our own government, to be a force for good in the world, to protect our children and our land, to sweep away before us anyone who tries to turn our sacred institutions of civic freedom to their greedy purposes?

On the road so far, I have seen a great nation. I have felt it hugging my shoulders, shaking my hand, cheering from across the way. I am so in love with it.

Thank you all.

PART TWO

SOME SAY WE NEED A THIRD PARTY, I WISH WE HAD A SECOND ONE

SOME SAY WE NEED
A THIRD PARTY, I WISH
WE HAD A SECOND ONE

Tolstoy's dying words reportedly were: "I don't understand what I'm supposed to do."

It occurred to me that maybe this is the problem with the Democratic Party—it's been so long since its leaders actually included the *demo* portion of the party in their thinking that they've forgotten how. Not that it would seem all that difficult, but sometimes even the obvious needs addressing. For example, *Funny Times*, one of the most useful newspapers of our age, recently compiled a list of instructions that can be found on various packages and products, including these treasures:

- On a frozen dinner box: "Serving suggestion: Defrost."
- On the package for an iron: "Do not iron clothes on body."
- On a packet of peanuts: "Open packet and eat contents."
- On a helmet-mounted mirror for bicyclists: "Remember: Objects in the mirror are actually behind you."
- On a camera: "This camera only works when there is film inside."
- On a chain saw: "Do not attempt to stop chain with your hands."

Equally obvious would be a how-to instruction for building a real *Demo*-cratic Party: "To have a people's party, go to the people." *Not just to the bean sprout eaters, but to the snuff dippers as well,* talking about the gut-level issues of economic fairness and social justice. For example, working people *are* overtaxed—the income tax is the least of it for most folks, who are socked again and again by grossly regressive federal payroll taxes, state and local taxes of all sorts, ever increasing sales taxes, and more and more "fees" attached to everything from plane tickets to using a national park. It's not enough just to complain that Republican tax cuts are a giveaway to their fat-cat contributors (which they are), for that doesn't do anything for the working stiffs who really need the tax relief. How about going to the people with a real populist tax-cutting program for the middle class, including a proposal to stop taxing work (wages), instead taxing international currency speculation and short-term stock market transactions?

What about the fact that the genetic manipulators, led by Monsanto, have messed with our food supply and with Mother Nature in a massive and most alarming way, and that our watchdog agencies have conspired with the manipulators to hide it from us? This would make a lively campaign issue, and it's a growing national concern that would allow a people's party to get on the side of the people. And while we're at it, why not start talking about the American government's dirty little wars—like its destructive, money-gobbling drug war that's been an embarrassing failure at stopping the flow of drugs but is spectacularly successful at stomping on people's liberties; or the war against the family farm, using both the actions and inactions of government to squeeze efficient, productive people off the land; or the war against unions, writing the rules of collective bargaining in such a way that the union-busting tactics of a century ago are back, and legal; or the war on privacy, using "terrorism" and "drugs" as the alarm buttons to allow all levels of police deeper into our personal lives.

These issues are part of the election that *could be* if we had a no-bullshit Democratic Party that really wanted to stand up for America's workaday majority, kick Republican butt from coast to coast, and realign American politics for the next century. At the heart of this populist politics is the recognition that there has been a radical and totally undemocratic remaking of our economy in the past few years, deliberately wrenching it to serve the few, then pretending to the many that the changes are the result of immutable forces that have brought a halcyon epoch of prosperity for all. Political leaders of both parties, including the leading contenders for the 2000 presidential nominations, are full participants in the pretending. But who are they fooling? The wrenchers and pretenders can put all the cologne they want on this skunk, but it won't cover up the stink.

MUGGING THE MIDDLE CLASS

You pay a price for going against your political roots, whether you're the Democratic Party . . . or a boy of eight.

That's how old I was when I made my first foray into partisan politics. It was 1952, and a neighbor who ran an insurance agency in my hometown of Denison was a local coordinator for Alan Shivers, a candidate for governor. At this time, Texas literally was a one-party state, with both Democrats and Republicans confusingly (and uncomfortably) residing together inside the Democratic Party. Your actual Democrats were backing the crusading people's champion Ralph Yarborough for governor that year, while your faux Democrats (Republicans in hiding) were behind Shivers. A scion of one of the Anglo families that reigned rather brutishly over the old plantation system of the Rio Grande Valley, Shivers was the candidate of the state's financial powers. Members of this money caste later came to be known as

Shivercrats. It was not a term of endearment—a ditty from the fifties went:

> A buzzard is a dirty bird,
> A skunk a stinking cat,
> But the dirtiest creature on the earth,
> Is a God Damned old Shivercrat.

None of this meant anything to me at eight, though, for my attention was not on politics but on becoming the second baseman for the Tigers, my Little League team. I wouldn't have known Shivers from a 5-pound roll of bologna. All I knew was that my insurance agent neighbor was willing to pay me and my brother fifty cents *each* to put some campaign flyers in the screen doors of homes for several blocks around. Since I was paid only twenty-five cents to mow yards, being offered half a buck just to distribute a satchel full of flyers seemed like easy money, even if they were flyers for some guy named Shivers. Only in later years would I learn that he was for the bankers and big shots over the kind of people that made up my own family and most of my town—tenant farmers, railroad workers, small business people, and other working folks. Meanwhile, I had the flyers to get out and baseball to play.

It was an easy job until I came to a certain house on West Crawford Street. I went briskly up the sidewalk toward the high steps that led up to the front porch. It was when I started to take the steps that I first heard the growl. A very deep growl. A very serious growl. Instinctively, I froze, my eyes jerking up to the porch to encounter the biggest sheepdog I've ever seen—and one that was most unhappy to have me intruding on his turf. However, my daddy had taught me that dogs really are afraid of us humans and that I should have no fear of a barking bowser—just look the creature square in the eye and go ahead about my business. Despite a staccato surge of signals from my primitive brain frantically shouting "Run, you little bastard, as fast as your eight-year-old legs can possibly go!" I calmly recalled Daddy's doggie admonition, overruled my brain's primitive impulse, and proceeded to climb the stairs.

My foot had not touched the bottom step before that dog was down on me like a . . . well, like a big dog on a small boy. He knocked me down, bowled me over, sank a couple of teeth into my thigh, and sent me sprawling and squawking all across the yard, spraying Shivers's flyers hither, thither, and yon. Never has one boy scrambled backwards so quickly, fleeing to the safety of the street and doing a sort of gimpy-legged half-run, half-hop toward home. I never looked back, having forever abandoned the flyers, the satchel, the fifty-cent payday, *and* Alan Shivers.

Call it what you will, but I sensed in my very being at that moment that the gods were speaking to me: "Jim Hightower, don't you ever again go against your populist roots for money."

Maybe we need a big dog to bite the national Democratic Party. Maybe that would cause it to come to its senses and come home to its populist roots. Today's Democratic leadership—from Gore and Bradley to the DNC—has taken the money and willingly become Shivercrats. As a result, they now compete with Republicans to win a plurality of the minority of relatively well-off Americans who vote. And, to appeal to this minority, they campaign and govern on policies narrowly tailored to benefit the few, ignoring or actually stiffing the many, which further shrinks the Democrats' electoral base and makes them ever more dependent on the money powers, which demand an even narrower focus on their special needs, which . . . well, you see the downward spiral. Amazingly, this suicidal strategy is the product of smart people (too smart by half, maybe) who seem to have lost all traces of street savvy. They're like the fellow who received this less than glowing performance evaluation for his work: "This employee has the full six pack, but he's missing the little plastic thingy that holds it together."

IF THESE ARE GOOD TIMES,
WHY AREN'T I HAVING ONE?

To build a new majority politics means (Oh, the genius of it!) appealing to the majority. Where to start, where to start? One place is with the truth—start talking about the *real* economy. How about admitting what the majority of people already know since they're experiencing it: The middle class is getting mugged.

"Mugged?!" shriek the Perky Purveyors of Perpetually Positive Press about Prosperity. "Sweet Visa and Holy MasterCard, Hightower, don't you listen to the news, don't you know about the leading economic indicators, don't you follow the Dow, don't you feel the *buzz*, don't you know, for God's sake, that Starbucks is opening its two thousandth store this year—you call that getting mugged?" America is a sea of prosperity, we're assured, and everyone can dip their sterling-silver ladle in it at will. Hasn't *Newsweek* magazine informed us that "pampering is going mainstream," that "massage is now for the masses," and that things are so good for average middle-class folks that their typical day now includes buying a $3 cup of mochaccino coffee on their way to work, getting a $35 pedicure on their lunch break, then stopping by the Sharper Image store on the way home to pick up such self-pampering gadgets as a $249 "private masseuse" back massager. It has. These are the best of times. We know it because we're told it over and over. Check these recent headlines about the economy:

Consumers See Blue Skies Ahead

Dreams Really Do Come True

Go-Go Growth

Misery Just a Memory

How Long Can Americans Keep Splurging?

Why Life In the U.S. Has Never Been Better

A Nearly Perfect Economy

Like a fuzzy blue blanket, this constant overlay of economic superlatives creates a warm feeling of national comfort, a sense that except for the odd poor family all is right in the jolly kingdom of America. The blanket of good news also shields the comfortable from having to address the possibility that there just might be something fundamentally flawed about globalization, conglomeration, outsourcing, and the other processes of economic rapaciousness that are loose on the land. "Who cares if a few people lose their jobs," shrug the PPPPPP, "there are beaucoup jobs out there, Bubba, *if* you really want one, and, besides, all that globalization and whatnot sure seems to be working for everybody else, haven't you been paying attention to the economic reports?" To punctuate the point, they always turn to the one indicator that's been relentlessly perky: the Dow Jones Average.

"**WHERE TO NOW, MIGHTY DOW?**" This was the Associated Press headline March 30, 1999, when the Dow closed above 10,000 for the first time in history. The media pealed with joy! *USA Today* enthused that "10,000 is more than just a number. . . . It's like Mark McGwire beating the home run record, it's like the calendar turning to the year 2000, it's like McDonald's selling its first billion hamburgers. It's a cultural milestone." A market analyst for Prudential went over the top with the Dow: "It's exciting. It's America. We all should get up and sing 'God Bless America.'" The *New York Times* joined the cheerleading, saying flatly, "The Stock Market surely is America today," which surely is the millennial equivalent of the 1950s comment by GM's chief executive Charles Wilson that "What is good for General Motors is good for the country." *USA Today* went even further, elevating Dowism to the level of a mystical omnipresence, claiming that the whole nation "is riveted to every tick in the market" and "attuned to Wall Street," asserting that as the Dow rises, "a lot of people feel wealthier and inclined to spend more on cars, houses, and other goods."

The story of the Dow's awesome prowess was still reverberating in the media when, lo, it came upon us again, bringing glad tidings to all. Barely a month after topping 10,000 the Mighty Dow blew past 11,000—and once again the media was filled with tales of the nation's euphoria at this blessed event.

There were heretics, here and there, of course. *Newsweek's* Allan Sloan, for example, termed the Dow Jones average such a hokey indicator of real economic strength that rather than watching worshipfully for it to surpass 10,000 or any other arbitrary height, we should "obsess over something more important. Like why Buffy the Vampire Slayer has blond hair and black eyebrows."

Sloan aside, though, the media and the politicians broadly accept that the market is God and that the Dow is God's own messenger, conveying the Word that when the Dow is up, so is America. Harvard divinity professor Harvey Cox, writing last year in *Atlantic Monthly,* observed that "current thinking already assigns to The Market a comprehensive wisdom that in the past only gods have known. The Market, we are taught, is able to determine what human needs are, what copper and capital should cost, how much barbers and CEOs should be paid, and how much jet planes, running shoes, and hysterectomies should sell for. But how do we know The Market's will?

"In days of old," Cox continues, "seers entered a trance state and then informed anxious seekers what kind of mood the gods were in. . . . The prophets of Israel repaired to the desert and then returned to announce whether Yahweh was feeling benevolent or wrathful. Today, The Market's fickle will is clarified by daily reports from Wall Street. . . . Thus we can learn on a day-to-day basis that The Market is 'apprehensive,' 'relieved,' 'nervous,' or even at times 'jubilant.' On the basis of this revelation awed adepts make critical decisions about whether to buy or sell. Like one of the devouring gods of old, The Market—aptly embodied in a bull or bear—must be fed and kept happy under all circumstances. True, at times its appetite may seem excessive—a $35 billion bailout here, a $50 billion one there—but the alternative to assuaging its hunger is too terrible to contemplate."

Cox then tells of the power that what I call Dowism holds over our secular leaders of both parties in Washington: "If any government policy vexes The Market, those responsible for the irreverence will be made to suffer. That The Market is not at all displeased by downsizing or a growing income gap, or can be gleeful about the expansion of cigarette sales to Asian young people, should not cause anyone to question its ultimate omniscience. Like Calvin's inscrutable deity, The Market may work in mysterious ways, 'hid from our eyes,' but ultimately it knows best."

Indeed, the theology of Dowism, just as of other religions, is dependent on a hearty dose of faith over reason. Cox quotes an early Christian theologian who remarked: "*Credo quia absurdum est*"—"I believe because it is absurd."

Especially absurd is the new insistence by fervent Dowists that Wall Street has spread to every street, that there has been a miraculous democratization of stock market wealth to the broad populace. Therefore, what's good for the market *really is* good for America. So you've been downsized, so you're among the 80 percent of Americans whose incomes have gone down or barely kept up with inflation in the boom-boom nineties, so you and the spouse are working three or four jobs just to try to stay even—stop your bitching and start counting your stock market blessings.

In a front-page headline, the *New York Times* trumpeted: "Share of Wealth in Stock Holdings Hits 50-Year High." The *Times* had done its own analysis of American household wealth—a measure that counts everything you own, including your house, car, bass boat, clothing, furniture, velvet paintings of dogs playing poker, your collection of those tiny liquor bottles you get on airplanes . . . and your portfolio of stocks and bonds. Good gosh, gushed the *Times,* people's homes are no longer the number one source of their personal wealth; stock market investments are! Strip off those old "Share the Wealth" bumper stickers, for the dream has at last been realized. As the *Times* put it, "The size of their paychecks aside, many Americans are feeling richer as the value of their stock holdings rises. . . . Where skyrocketing real estate prices once provided reassurance to the middle class, soaring stock portfolios now do."

Before you "middle-classers" dash out to buy a $250 bottle of Dom Pérignon to celebrate your newly discovered stock wealth, let's all take a deep breath and stand back from the giddiness for a moment. The *Times* rushed to disseminate the Good News about household wealth without applying the first lesson of journalism, which teaches reporters to answer the six most basic questions in a story: who, what, where, when, why . . . and *huh?* In this case, your household's stock portfolio is averaged with those of Bill Gates, Ted Turner, Warren Buffett, and the other 1 million or so families at the very tippy-top of the economic pyramid. These elites are among the wealthiest 1 percent of Americans and need a special bank vault just to hold their stock certificates. The law of averages is such that if you've got one foot in a bucket of ice and the other in a bucket of boiling water, on average the temperature should be just right for you. Likewise, the *Times* can claim that "average" households now have 28 percent of their wealth in stocks, without noting that most people have NONE of their wealth in stocks.

In one of the weirder incidents involving the zeitgeist of the Dow, one Richard Grasso, the chairman of the New York Stock Exchange, was helicoptered deep into the jungles of southern Colombia last June to the village of La Machaca. There he met for an hour and a half with Raul Reyes, one of the top commanders of the powerful rebel group that controls better than a third of that nation. The rebels are pushing for social justice for the vast majority of Colombians who are impoverished, while the elites in Bogotá enjoy the good life of selective capitalism. What an odd meeting— there was Grasso, coming from the very pit of capitalism, still wearing his $150 shirt and the pants of his $1,000 suit (in a gesture to the informality of the occasion, he had tossed his tie and jacket), giving a big *abrazo* to this rebel leader, who was fully decked out in jungle camouflage. They had their conversation and, who knows, maybe even a round of s'mores at the rebel encampment; then Grasso left as quickly as he had come, later telling *The Wall Street Journal* that he and Commander Reyes had "talked about economics, capital markets, and how peace translates into economic opportunity for Colombia." Give Wall Street a Chance, was Grasso's Beatle-esque message: "I gave him a tutorial on what's happened in the U.S. in terms of this democratization of capitalism. One of the messages I wanted to emphasize is how . . . with indirect ownership, literally everybody in America is a stockholder."

LITTLE MISS ROSIE SCENARIO

If you are wont to believe the rosy economic assessments of today's authoritative voices, consider the following blasts from the past. These quotes show that there is nothing new about power elites who stand in the back of a wagon orating at length about how things are rolling along perfectly, while everyone in the crowd can see that the wheels have fallen off the wagon. Here is a sampling of public statements by the authorities of the day as the Great Depression unfolded.

SCENE ONE. In 1929, stock prices were soaring, media barons were hailing the prosperity of the Roaring Twenties, and the public was assured that there would be nothing but good times ahead:

"The economic condition of the world seems on the verge of a great forward movement."
—Bernard Baruch, American financier, *Financier* magazine, June 1929

"Stocks have reached what looks like a permanently high plateau."
—Irving Fisher, Professor of Economics,
Yale University, October 17, 1929

SCENE TWO. On Thursday, October 24, 1929, panic struck Wall Street as stock values plummeted $6 billion. But not to worry:

"The worst has passed."
—Joint statement by thirty-five of the largest houses on
Wall Street at the close of trading, October 24, 1929

"I see no cause for alarm."
—J. J. Bernet, President, Chesapeake and Ohio Railway,
Friday, October 25, 1929

"I do not look for a recurrence of Thursday."
—M. C. Brush, President of the American International
Corporation, Friday, October 25, 1929

"We feel that fundamentally Wall Street is sound."
—Goodbody and Company, market letter to customers, Friday,
October 25, 1929

SCENE THREE. On Tuesday, October 29, 1929, the bottom fell out of the stock market, hysteria gripped Wall Street, the nation trembled . . . but the authorities still viewed it all through rose- colored glasses:

"[The Wall Street crash] doesn't mean there will be any general or serious business depression."
> —*Business Week,* November 2, 1929

"The end of the decline of the Stock Market will . . . probably not be long, only a few more days at most."
> —Irving Fisher, Professor of Economics,
> Yale University, November 14, 1929

"Financial storm definitely passed."
> —Bernard Baruch, American financier, cablegram
> to Winston Churchill, November 15, 1929

SCENE FOUR. As the weeks and months passed, stock prices continued to plummet, farmers were bankrupted, banks went under, and bread lines stretched for blocks in the cities—yet the authorities pretended nothing bad was happening:

"In most of the cities and towns of this country, this Wall Street panic will have no effect."
> —Paul Block, Block newspaper chain, editorial,
> November 15, 1929

"[1930 will be] a splendid employment year."
> —U.S. Department of Labor, New Year's forecast,
> December 1929

"I see nothing in the present situation that is either menacing or warrants pessimism. . . . I have every confidence that there will be a revival of activity in the spring, and that during this coming year the country will make steady progress."
> —Andrew Mellon, U.S. Secretary of the Treasury,
> December 31, 1929

"Gentlemen, you have come sixty days too late. The depression is over."
>—Herbert Hoover, responding to a delegation requesting a public works program to help speed the recovery, June 1930

SCENE FIVE. The ultimate in authoritative prognostication came from the prestigious Harvard Economic Society. Here are some of its determinedly cheery insights offered in the Society's *Weekly Letter* as the depression turned ever more wrathful across the American countryside:

"With the underlying conditions sound, we believe that the recession in general business will be checked shortly and that improvement will set in during the spring months."
>—January 18, 1930

"Since our monetary and credit structure is not only sound but unusually strong . . . there is every prospect that the recovery which we have been expecting will not be long delayed."
>—August 30, 1930

"[R]ecovery will soon be evident."
>—September 20, 1930

"[T]he outlook is for the end of the decline in business during the early part of 1931, and steady . . . revival for the remainder of the year."
>—November 15, 1930

Note: In 1931, the economic squeeze of the depression forced the Harvard Economic Society to suspend publication of the *Weekly Letter*.

SCENE SIX. The depression was in full rage, but some folks still didn't get it:

"These really are good times, but only a few know it. If this period of convalescence through which we have been passing must be spoken of as a depression, it is far and away the finest depression we have ever had."

—Henry Ford, c. 1931

"I don't know anything about any depression."
        —J. P. Morgan Jr., American banker and financier, c. 1931

(Source: Christopher Cerf and Victor Navasky, *The Experts Speak*. Villard Books.)

Señor Reyes—I recommend that you plunge even deeper into the jungle and lock-and-load. Mr. Grasso lies, or (let's be generous) he embellishes like a vinyl-siding salesman. Six out of ten U.S. citizens own no stocks at all—not through a 401(k), a mutual fund, a pension plan, nothing. The Dow might as well be a pink- and purple-polka-dotted cow for all the good it's doing the typical household. And most folks who are "in the market" are barely there. In fact, 89 percent of all stocks are owned by only 10 percent of American households, and nearly half the stocks are owned by those 1 million families who comprise the wealthiest 1 percent of Americans.

Yet, Washington continues to bow before the Dow, with Republicans and Democrats alike proclaiming all of America to be "prosperous" so long as the market's investors are prospering. A rich example of this skewed perspective came to the fore in mid-May of '99 when Treasury Secretary Robert Rubin stepped down as pontiff of the Clinton administration's Dowist economic policies. Another media gush ensued, with adoring paean after paean hailing Rubin as the "Architect of Prosperity" (*New York Times*), and virtually every story cited the tripling of the Dow Jones Average as the high mark of his "wildly successful tenure" (*Washington Post*).

In a farewell Rose Garden ceremony filled with more adoration than the pope usually gets, President Clinton did not praise Rubin simply for his righteous due, which was that he steadfastly fattened the fat no matter what it cost others, but by asserting that Rubin was somehow a populist pontiff. Without so much as an embarrassed twitch, Clinton proclaimed to the assembled media that Rubin had come to Washington "to help me save the middle class." Middle class? Rubin, a money-scavenging investment banker who amassed a $100 million personal fortune at Goldman Sachs before coming to Washington to preserve and extend the wealth of his privileged peers, wouldn't know a middle-classer if he ran over one with his limousine. Apparently oblivious to the irony, Clinton pressed on with his characterization of Rubin's work as an exercise in grassroots economics: "He built a spirit and a belief that we could actually make this economy what it ought to be for our people. That will be his enduring achievement—along with the fact that everybody believed as long as he was secretary of the Treasury nothing bad could happen."

Was *Saturday Night Live* scripting this? Rubin was the guy who fought ferociously to kill any of the jobs initiatives that candidate Clinton had promised in 1992, who promoted high stock prices by encouraging lower wages for middle-class workers, who opposed any significant increases in the minimum wage, who pushed hard for NAFTA and the World Trade Organization, who breakfasted every week with Fed chairman Alan Greenspan and enthusiastically backed his wage-stifling monetary policies, who took billions of tax dollars that could have been used to rebuild America's manufacturing base and instead used them to bail out rich speculators who had made bad gambles in Asia and Latin America, who protected corporate welfare from any budget cuts while whacking away at health and housing programs that benefit working families, and who generally treated the middle class like a fire hydrant in a dog show.

Hanging a final accolade around Rubin's neck, Clinton praised him as "the most effective treasury secretary since Alexander Hamilton." Now this one seems to be a true fit.

Hamilton was the most aristocratic of all the founders, distrusting the common people and advocating that only the "rich and well-born" should govern. As the first treasury secretary, Hamilton insisted that the federal government's role was to protect and promote the interests of the propertied classes, including helping to make their investments profitable. This was no big surprise to those who knew the guy, since he had earlier tried to change Jefferson's three inalienable rights from "Life, Liberty, and the Pursuit of Happiness" to "Life, Liberty, and Property." He and Rubin are soul mates there! Secretary Hamilton also proposed America's first tax plan, putting the burden not on the rich and well-born but on the small farmers. He then goaded President George Washington into amassing an army (bigger than the one he had commanded against the British) to march on the small farmers of the Pennsylvania frontier to put down the "Whiskey Rebellion" that they had mounted against Hamilton's tax.

There was no Dow Jones average during Hamilton's tenure at Treasury, but as in Rubin's tenure the operating principle was that speculators got rich ... and the commoners got shtooked.

CONSUMER CONFIDENCE INDEX. Another happy statistic has gained prominence in recent years, popping up monthly with the intent of delighting us, much like a jack-in-the-box can cause two-year-olds to squeal with joy when the little clown head pops out. This little clown is called the "Consumer Confidence Index," and it practically always tells us that consumers across America are a happy lot, brimming with confidence about economic conditions and in a mood to spend, spend, spend. Apparently they think we have the gullibility of two-year-olds who think the clown really does live in the box.

Since 1985, the index has been computed and promoted by the very official-sounding Conference Board, and it is now dutifully reported each month by all the media, who treat it as though it is not only something real but also profound, as in this 1999 AP story: "The Conference Board reported today its index of consumer confidence rose 3.2 points to 132.1 in February from a revised 128.9 in January. Consumers were thoroughly pleased with the current economic situation, the report said." Feel better? It's that fuzzy blue blanket again being pulled over any unpleasant economic realities that folks might be experiencing. How can the economy have anything wrong with it if your fellow consumers are so upbeat? Hell, upbeat doesn't say it—they're at 132.1! So if you're feeling maybe a 107.8 or even 67.4, then there must be something wrong with you, Bucko.

What we have here is proof again that the media will report the wildest tales with a straight face as long as there are some decimals involved. Here's the inside skinny on the Consumer Confidence Index:

First, despite its ubiquity and authoritative tone, the index is not the bona fide calculation of any government agency, academic institution, or other independent entity. Rather, The Conference Board Inc. is a private business that is thoroughly dependent on delivering and publicizing monthly reports that please its corporate clients, which include an alphabet full of brand-name marketers, such as Aetna, BankAmerica, Chevron, Dow Chemical, Exxon, Ford, General Electric, Hewlett-Packard, IBM, JCPenney, Kmart, Lockheed Martin, Merrill Lynch, NationsBank, Philip Morris, RJR Nabisco, Sears, Texaco, United Airlines, Wal-Mart, and Xerox.

Basically, the Board is a service company for corporate executives, holding seminars and conferences for them, producing reports, doing management research, organizing executive "networking groups," and the like. Just as the U.S. Chamber of Commerce and other corporate service organizations have an unabashed procorporate agenda, so does the Conference Board, which has no representatives of consumers, workers, or other broad public interests overseeing its work. John Williams, an independent consumer research analyst who is the director of a watchdog organization called the Shadow Bureau of Government Statistics and who produces a no-nonsense newsletter of economic conditions called *Straight Shooter,* says bluntly: "The purpose of the Conference Board is to promote business, and it is dedicated to good news for business."

Second, the index is a lot less authoritative than its tone suggests. Each of its monthly releases to the media carry this notation: "The Consumer Confidence survey is based on a representative sample of 5,000 U.S. households." That's a most impressive number of citizens for the Board's surveyors to talk to each month . . . except that they *don't* talk to the people. The survey is simply a multiple-choice questionnaire that is mailed out to the five thousand households. Not mentioned in the monthly media releases is the fact that less than half of these households actually respond by the time the index is compiled, so it's really a *completed* survey of more like two thousand to twenty-five hundred households each month. Still, two thousand households could make a very valid survey *if* the Board used a representative sample of the U.S. population chosen by the scientific sampling techniques used by professional pollsters. It does not. Instead of mailing the questionnaires to five thousand homes chosen from all hundred million U.S. households, the five thousand monthly names are drawn from a preselected pool of less than seven hundred thousand households! January through December, the survey goes out to another five thousand addresses taken from this same tiny pool—which includes a mere six-tenths of 1 percent of us.

Nor are these seven hundred thousand chosen scientifically. Rather, the Board's surveyors send out assorted direct-mail solicitations asking, in effect, "anyone out there want to be in our survey pool?" If this strikes you as lacking somewhat in survey-selection professionalism, consider that some of those already in the pool get their golfing partners, their business clients, their brother-in-law Bob, and other acquaintances to jump in, too. No one gets paid to participate, but there are free products to sample from time to time, and there's the thrill of knowing that you're speaking for America, even if you really don't.

Then there's the matter of the questionnaire itself, which is not exactly a penetrating examination of any consumer's basic sense of economic confidence. It asks sixteen questions, nine of which are marketing queries, like what make of car you plan to buy in the next six months, what brand of refrigerator you're likely to purchase, and which airline you plan to fly on your vacation. The other six questions cover general opinions of whether overall business conditions are good, normal, or bad; whether there will be more, the same, or fewer jobs in the next six months; and whether stock prices can be expected to increase or decrease.

That's it. Yet, on the basis of these vague questions, the Conference Board issues not only its firm assertion that America's consumer confidence stands precisely at 132.1, but it also adds such sweeping rhetorical embellishments as "consumers were *thoroughly pleased* with the current economic situation." Apparently, if you torture the statistics long enough, they'll confess to anything.

Even if the Board did not embellish, there is a built-in positive bias to the survey because of the inherent optimism of us Americans. Our immigrant culture ("Seek a new beginning"), our enterprising nature ("I *can* make a silk purse out of a sow's ear"), our frontier spirit ("Go west, young man") all well up to produce an emphatic "Yes!" when we're asked, "Will tomorrow be a better day?" But there's more at work than human optimism in these survey findings—there's also the fact that people's responses to such questions can be influenced by what they are being told by the mass media. If the newspapers and broadcasts are blaring "Zip-a-dee-doo-dah,

Zip-a-dee-a/My, oh my, what a wonderful day" over and over, there's a tendency to go down the road humming that tune, too, because you can't get it out of your head. Are business conditions good? Zip-a-dee-doo-dah! Are employment conditions good? Zip-a-dee-a!

Professor David Fan of the University of Minnesota has done a "media climate index," which has been stunningly accurate at predicting the outcomes of consumer confidence surveys— whenever the news is saturated with sunny economic stories, you can count on the confidence index to be almost exactly as radiant. Even in the early years of the depression of the 1930s, when the authorities kept insisting that the overall economy was doing well, people agreed with that assessment, although they were personally devastated. As Studs Terkel revealed in his poignant and magnificent oral history, *Hard Times*, folks blamed themselves for losing the farm or being in a bread line, because officialdom said that prosperity abounded in the land, with everyone but YOU (you loser!) being in splendid shape.

Third, at least one industry insider says the Conference Board is a little loosey-goosey with its tabulations. Al Sindlinger, a pioneer of telephone surveys, is the fellow who came up with the very term *consumer confidence* way back in 1928. He conceived of a confidence index as a way of measuring the likelihood of consumer buying. Years ago, he first connected to the Conference Board through a contract he had to supply *Newsweek* with his data. The Board also had an arrangement with the magazine that allowed it access to Sindlinger's weekly survey information, and for a brief while he even furnished data directly to the Board. But he soon quit letting them use his information because, he says, "They always put a spin on it." He says that if his findings showed that confidence was up, the report would be zapped out to the media within hours, but if the numbers were down, they would put the report on hold until more surveying could be done, and they would tell him,

"Wait a couple of weeks, something must be wrong with the data." Sindlinger doesn't like what the Board's index has become: "It's no longer a measurement, but a promotion." As a professional, he is particularly appalled by the fact that the board "seasonally adjusts" their data, which he says allows them to rig already dubious numbers. The Board's numbers reflect nothing but people's attitudes or opinions, so Sindlinger asks, "How can an opinion be seasonally adjusted?"

Al Sindlinger continues to do his own consumer analysis, issuing weekly reports to subscribers via his "Sindlinger Fax." His reports offer a kitchen-table perspective of not only how people are feeling but how they're actually *doing*. And these days, Al is not using any glib phrases like consumers being "thoroughly pleased" with the way things are going. While about a third of the people he surveys are indeed bullish about their economic fortunes, he says another third are standing still, and the final third are in the negative. There's the two-thirds majority that's wondering when, if ever, the politicians are going to begin telling the truth about the economy and start fighting for those who are being mugged.

THE FLO CHART

Flo is a waitress at the Dine & Go Diner, where she works an early breakfast shift, six to nine. Then she goes downtown to the law offices of Meager, Wages & Miser, where she's a "legal aide" (much like a plow mule is a "farm aide"), doing grunt work ten to four for a bevy of insurance company lawyers. Ironically, Flo doesn't have insurance. She does have a couple of great kids, though—Kim, twelve, and Zach, seven—and she considers them her real job, though she is stretched mighty thin on time and energy and wishes she was with them more frequently. She's also taking a couple of night courses at the community college, trying to get ahead.

To know how the nation's economy is doing, we don't need to consult some trumped-up confidence index or the ethereal Dow Jones average but the Flo Chart: How's Flo doing? Hers is the heartbeat of America's majority—the 80 percent of folks who are paid less than $50,000 a year, the 60 percent who don't own *any* stocks and bonds, the 75 percent who don't have a university sheepskin hanging on the office wall . . . and the two-thirds who aren't voting because neither party is fighting for Flo.

The economic elites try to fool Flo by pointing to the glittering stock market; the media elites try to fool Flo by pointing to their smiley-faced consumer reports; the political elites try to fool Flo by pointing to the twenty million jobs created in the nineties. So why isn't Flo fooled? Because, to determine her economic situation, she analyzes data that the elites ignore. Calculated by universally accepted, scientific survey techniques and seasonally adjusted for inflation, Flo's leading economic indicator is called "Income." Or, in the more technical jargon that she sometimes employs: "How's my in-coming matching up with my out-going?"

When you're alone at your kitchen table doing calculations like that, it's hard to be fooled by a distant chorus telling you you're doing great. Even a few political leaders have figured this out. Rep. Jim Traficant, a working-class Democrat from Youngstown, Ohio, offered this pungent economic assessment during a one-minute address from the floor of the U.S. House: "Let us tell it like it is: When you hold this economy to your nosey, this economy does not smell so rosy. If [it's] any consolation to the American workers, I never heard of anyone in America committing suicide by jumping out of a basement window. I yield back all of the propaganda on this great economy." With important exceptions like Traficant, politicians of both parties gloat about America's amazing "job-creating machine," and the media cheerfully parrots industry's claim that so many people are now at work that they can't find applicants for all kinds of jobs, from low-tech hamburger flippers to high-tech computer code writers. For employees and job seekers, however, the issue is not getting a job (Flo has *two*), but getting a job that offers middle-class basics—decent income, health care, vacation time, and pension. Nor is this merely a crude issue of financial compensation; at the personal, social, and political levels, this is about workaday Americans being valued and getting respect.

You want statistics? Here's one that's as true as they come for measuring prosperity in America, and it's a ticking time bomb inside our champagne-popping, self-satisfied political system: In real dollars, average hourly wages in 1973 were $13.61. Today, they average $12.77. Far from gaining from the "Boom," *American workers are paid less today than when Richard Nixon was president*! We're talking about the income of the majority of our nation's people.

This decline comes at a time when people are busting their butts—working harder, longer, and smarter. Since Nixonian times, the productivity of workers has jumped by a third. Economics 101 teaches that more productivity equals economic gains for all. As recently as last year, the *New York Times* was still mouthing that economic platitude: "Only when productivity rises, can incomes and living standards rise for most Americans" it intoned in an article headlined "Productivity Sets Fast Pace." So—yoo-hoo, *New York Times!*—where's the "rising incomes and living standards" for the mostest of the people? You don't need Economics 101 to do the cognitive analysis of the discrepancy between theory and reality on this one. Anyone who can spell IQ knows that folks are doing more and getting less—at the same time that the Establishment is whooping and hollering about the fact that our overall economic pie is growing at an unprecedented rate and that more wealth is being generated than ever before.

The income drop for working families in these otherwise prosperous times would have been even more precipitous except for two factors. First, the flow of women into the workplace. Median family incomes have not risen since the Nixon years, but they would have plummeted disastrously, since real wages for 80 percent of American men are down. The chief stopgap against total family financial disaster has been that both spouses now work. Even with this, though, families are barely keeping up, much less getting ahead. Economist Lester Thurow reports that since the early seventies, "The proportion of year-around, full-time working wives has doubled for those with children and increased 50 percent for those without children. More female work should be leading to more household income. But it isn't." So Mom and Dad are scrambling to stay middle class, sometimes working a couple of jobs each, yet leaders of both political parties avert their eyes, pretending that this eight-hundred-pound gorilla is not sitting in the corner at the lavish party they're having to celebrate "Boom Times." The only acknowledgment they have given to these families' stress has been to chastise them for not spending enough time with their children. Duh.

The second factor keeping families out of the poorhouse (temporarily) is debt—mostly, debt that is being piled up on those friendly little pieces of plastic that pour into our mailboxes almost daily with the siren phrase, "Preapproved Credit!" printed so boldly on the envelope. Banks offer four billion credit cards every year, which is fifteen for every man, woman, and child in the country. About 60 percent of households now owe money on their credit cards, with the average debt being $7,000! If you're only making $25–$30,000 a year, that's a heavy load, and it's costing you $1,000 a year just to pay the interest. The result has been a doubling in the 1990s of families filing for personal bankruptcies. Congress did respond to this crisis, though. Not to help the families (you dreamer), but to protect the banks and other credit-card issuers by making it next to impossible for working stiffs to use the bankruptcy laws.

The twenty-five-year decline in the Flo Chart almost exactly tracks the twenty-five-year rise in the Democratic Party's fealty to Wall Street money. As the party's congressional, White House, and campaign officials bonded tighter and tighter with the corporate and financial elites, they distanced themselves further and further from Flo, effectively leaving her with no representation in matters of economic policy. The fact that Flo is being pounded economically is not a case of benign neglect but of the Democrats joining the Republicans to support policies that mug her, stealing her middle-class aspirations by aggressively holding down her income.

Let me be blunt: Low wages are the official policy of the U.S. government. If you're a manufacturer wanting to hold down wages here at home, the government will book you on a trade delegation to Asia, hook you up with a contractor that provides workers for as cheap as fifteen cents an hour, underwrite your foreign investment, suspend tariffs and quotas so you can ship your cheap-labor products to stores back here, and put out a press release saluting you for joining in a private-public partnership to foster "global competitiveness." If you're a minimum-wage employer, don't worry about any rabble-rousing populism from Democrats—they'll give you a wink as they hold any increases to a level way below poverty. Even at the higher wage levels, if you're a Microsoft, IBM, or Silicon Valley giant and want to put a drag on the salaries of your engineers, programmers, and other high-tech workers, count on the Democrats to join Republicans in helping you import an extra fifty thousand or so of these workers each year from Pakistan, Russia, and elsewhere, letting you pay them a third to a half less than U.S. workers, thus busting the American salary scale.

And if wages do show any sign of creeping up, count on Uncle Alan to step in and stomp on them. Alan Greenspan, as chairman of the Federal Reserve Board, is the ruling authority over our nation's monetary policy, and he hates wage increases. You see, if wages rise, they might possibly pinch corporate profits ever so slightly, and this might spook your big Wall Street investors, causing the high-flying stock prices of corporations to slip a notch. Since today's upper-class prosperity is built almost entirely on the bloated prices of those corporate stocks, both parties are determined that nothing should spook those investors, even if this means keeping Flo down. It's really a choice of who you want to help—the few who profit from stock prices, or the many who depend on decent wages. Both parties have made the same choice—Greenspan, first appointed by President Reagan and reappointed by Presidents Bush and Clinton, has been their bipartisan hit man on Flo. There's no relief in sight for the poor lady, either, since both Democrat Gore and Republican Bush have signaled that they want Uncle Alan back for yet another term. It's a convoluted process, but essentially Greenspan uses the Fed's power over interest rates to hammer Flo, much like some clod might use a sledgehammer to swat a fly. At the slightest hint (even if imagined) that it's possible sometime in the future for wages somewhere to rise even negligibly . . . Greenspan pounces. This guy hunts down wage hikes like Joe McCarthy used to hunt down commies, and he'll use every power the government has to keep working people's paychecks down. Last summer the cold-eyed, pursed-lipped Greenspan openly urged Congress to bring in more immigrants, using them as wage-busters: "I have always thought . . . we should be carefully focused on [what] skilled people from abroad and unskilled people from abroad . . . can contribute to this country. . . . If we can open up our immigration rolls significantly, that will clearly make [wage inflation] less and less of a potential problem."

Add to Washington's wage-busting policies the delight that Wall Street takes in corporate downsizing, and you have a surefire formula for holding wages (and people) down. The politicians who talk so loud and lovingly about America's job-creating machine go mute on the topic of America's job-*destroying* machine, which has been ruthlessly efficient. Challenger, Gray & Christmas is a highly regarded employment firm that tracks job cuts daily, and it reports that companies have been eliminating some sixty-four thousand jobs a month, most of which are the higher-paying jobs that come with health care, pensions, and vacation time. It gets little media coverage, but downsizing in the late nineties has been more rampant than it was in the eighties and early nineties, when it was a major media story and led to Clinton's '92 presidential victory. Remember his slogan, "It's the economy, stupid," and his pledge to create "good jobs at good wages"? Instead, he learned that if he just laid low, like Brer Fox, while corporations punted those jobs, Wall Street investors would cheer lustily and run up the stock price for the companies doing this "streamlining," then the media would focus on the lightning flash of the Dow Jones average, and he would get credit for presiding over a thunderous, stock-driven boom.

Clinton's self-congratulatory claims about job creation and prosperity for all call to mind "Boss Daley," the longtime mayor of Chicago, who once said with a slip of the tongue, "We shall reach greater and greater platitudes of achievement." The President and other politicians have averted their eyes from the massive loss of good middle-class jobs, hoping that if they don't see it, maybe no one else will either. But working families already know all about it, of course, since they know the people being punted . . . and fear they'll be next. Stephanie Schmidt, an economist with the Urban Institute, surprised herself when she did a paper titled "Workers' Beliefs About Their Own Job Security," published in 1999. She had assumed that all the upbeat reports on stock gains and job creation would have just about everyone loaded with optimism. *Newsweek* had even done a cover story called "The Year of the Employee." It went on at great length about "this white hot job market," claiming that people *want* to be fired because they get such "hefty severance packages." Besides, said the magazine, today's lucky job seekers can take their choice of job offers that not only include "stunning pay increases and gold-plated stock options" but also such perks as being allowed to bring your dog to work (complete with company-supplied Milk-Bones). "It's the revenge of the downsized," *Newsweek* prattled.

But Schmidt found that most working people must not have read that issue of the magazine. Instead, workers today have as much job anxiety—fear of losing their jobs—as in the bad old recessionary days prior to Clinton's election, and they're even more scared that if they lose their current job, they won't find another one as good in terms of pay and benefits. She also found that this insecurity is no longer the burden of blue-collar workers alone but now has permeated the white-collar world as well.

Lest you think such anxiety is mere paranoia, take a peek behind the glowing job-creation numbers that politicians and the media toss around. "Job Growth Remains Strong," blared the headline on an Associated Press story in May of 1999, reporting that 234,000 new jobs had been created the previous month. But what kind of jobs? Not high-paying manufacturing positions—indeed, twenty-nine thousand of those had been lost during the month. Instead, the bulk of the additional jobs were in the low-paying service sector, including eighteen thousand new hires by temporary help firms, twenty-three thousand in health-care services, and sixty-four thousand in restaurants and bars.

Yet, the public keeps being told not to sweat the loss of America's manufacturing jobs, because the future for the middle class is in high-tech "knowledge jobs," so "cross that bridge to the twenty-first century," as President Clinton says repeatedly. Al Gore flatly proclaims that 60 percent of new jobs will require advanced technological skills, and both George W. Bush and Bill Bradley echo the mantra that the "new economy" means you've got to be a college-educated techie.

But this is just another middle-class mugging. Education analyst Richard Rothstein of the *New York Times* reports that in the next decade, "employers will hire more than three times as many cashiers as engineers. They will need more than twice as many food-counter workers, waiters, and waitresses than all the systems analysts, computer engineers, mathematicians, and database administrators combined." He adds that "we already enroll enough college students to fill foreseeable vacancies in professional fields," yet, corporations and their political puppets are deliberately flooding the job market with overeducated workers—a cynical ploy that will turn the middle-class's high tech future into low-paid work. The real job market is decidedly low tech. Between now and 2006, according to Clinton's own Bureau of Labor Statistics, the thirty fastest-growing job categories include only seven that require even a bachelor's degree. Most of the other twenty-three jobs are decidedly low-tech, with *more than half of them paying less than $18,000 a year*. Here's the real "middle class" future, ranked in order of the occupations expecting the most job growth:

OCCUPATION	MEDIAN ANNUAL PAY	EDUCATION OR TRAINING REQUIRED
Cashiers	$12,844	Short-term on-the-job training
Registered nurses	$36,244	Associate degree
Salespersons, retail	$19,344	Short-term on-the-job training
Truck drivers	$25,012	Short-term on-the-job training
Home health aides	$15,184	Short-term on-the-job training
Teacher aides and educational assistants	$13,312	Short-term on-the-job training

Nursing aides, orderlies, and attendants	$15,184	Short-term on-the-job training
Receptionists	$17,628	Short-term on-the-job training
Child-care workers	$12,324	Short-term on-the-job training
Clerical supervisors and managers	$28,860	Work experience
Marketing and sales worker supervisors	$26,988	Work experience
Maintenance repairers, general utility	$25,220	Long-term on-the-job training
Food counter, fountain, and related workers	$12,116	Short-term on-the-job training
Food preparation workers	$13,728	Short-term on the job training
Hand packers and packagers	$16,120	Short-term on-the-job training
Guards	$17,472	Short-term on-the-job training
General office clerks	$19,344	Short-term on-the-job training
Waiters and waitresses	$14,092	Short-term on-the-job training
Adjustment clerks	$21,580	Short-term on-the-job training
Cooks, short order and fast food	$13,728	Short-term on-the-job training
Personal and home care aides	$14,820	Short-term on-the-job training
Food service and lodging managers	$23,816	Work experience
Medical assistants	$22,412	Moderate length on-the-job training

(Source: Bureau of Labor Statistics)

I AIN'T GOT NO HOME
IN THIS WORLD ANYMORE

When she was First Lady, Nancy Reagan received a letter from a single mom whose job paid so little she had to use food stamps to help make ends meet for her family. She was getting only $27 a week in stamps, which didn't buy a lot of groceries, but Ronald Reagan was on his high horse at the time railing that these "handouts" for food should be slashed (even while the Gipper was also demanding that much fatter handouts to Pentagon weapons contractors be grossly increased—a perverted policy of beating plowshares into swords). The letter writer was upset by the President's political rant at her expense and wanted to know directly from the First Lady how she thought a family could get the nourishment it needed on *less* than $27. The working mother did get a response, though not one she could have anticipated: The First Lady sent a White House recipe for crab-stuffed artichokes. Cost-per-serving: $20.

Her office later claimed there had been a mix-up in the mail room, but Nancy's "Let them eat stuffed artichokes" incident is a pretty fair representation of the attitude that Washington has had ever since the Reagan years, not only toward matters of poverty but also toward matters of deep concern to millions of middle-class people—especially those paid under $30,000 a year, which is roughly half of us. In our Land of Plenty, not only is this half of Americans caught in a wage squeeze, but they're also caught in a health-care squeeze (a fourth of them are without any coverage at all), a pension squeeze (six out of ten have no pension), and another squeeze that receives almost no publicity: housing. Since most politicians and the media live in upscale neighborhoods and have grown oblivious to "how the other half lives," it would likely surprise them to hear that schoolteachers, bank tellers, computer programmers, police officers, secretaries, travel agents, firefighters, hair stylists, latte-slingers at Starbucks, and others whom they brush by in their busy lives are unable to afford skyrocketing apartment rents, much less the purchase price of today's homes.

Indeed, like the wage squeeze, the housing squeeze is buried in a blizzard of blithesome statistics. "How can you say the middle class is hard hit, Hightower," asked an incredulous Pittsburgh caller to my radio talk show, "when the papers are full of stories about people everywhere buying new houses?" He was right about the news coverage: "Sales of new homes rose in November to a record," exulted a 1999 *New York Times* piece. "Low mortgage rates and consumer optimism pushed up sales of new single-family houses. . . . The housing market is on track to register a third consecutive yearly record," the *Times* marveled. But, as Yogi Berra once said, "Half the lies they tell me aren't true," and the full truth behind today's red-hot housing stats is that they hide more than they reveal.

It's true enough that construction abounds—just follow the sounds. From sea to shining sea concrete is being poured, power saws are buzzing, nail guns are going bam-bam-bam, and new homes are being raised like totems to the Gods of Prosperity. If you need a house, just reach out and grab one, since houses aplenty are being built. But this "grab one" attitude reminds me of a series of radio and television ads that Fort Worth oil-well magnate Eddie Chiles ran incessantly in the late seventies. Known as "Mad Eddie" for his right-wing diatribes against Jimmy Carter, his ads closed with this tag line, delivered in a hard Texas twang: "If yew don't own an awl well, git one!"

The problem with "gitting" either an oil well or a house is money. This is where the economic powers clobber the housing-hungry middle class coming and going—most folks have seen no pay hikes coming, even as they've seen housing prices going, going, going . . . right through the roof. For them, the construction boom is just a lot of noise.

Practically all of those power saws and nail guns we hear are at work on expansive and expensive homes for the bankers, lawyers, executives, media managers, and politicians. In Austin, the high-tech boom town where I live, construction is roaring. A recent article, for example, reports that sixty-two more homes are going up in the Costa Bella subdivision. Grab one, if you can—this is a gated subdivision in which the developers require that each house contain at least 5,500 square feet of living space and at least a three-car garage. My entire *block* in south Austin doesn't have that much square footage. Prices go as high as $5 million, though, in fairness, I should note that a mix of economic classes are welcome at Costa Bella; some homes there sell for as little as $750,000. Probably starter houses.

OK, your bankers, bosses, and big shots need housing, too, so we can't begrudge the industry for meeting this market demand. But where is the industry when it comes to the swelling demand for homes priced at $80,000 or under? I'm not talking here about public housing projects or federally subsidized housing (though as the number of the working poor has risen so dramatically in the nineties, and as Washington has whacked funding for housing programs, there's a surging need for this housing, too). Rather, I'm talking about the vaunted marketplace that we're told is so omniscient that it responds to all demand. Well, there's a tidal wave of demand that has built up for modest homes with mortgages that a family making $20–$25–$30,000 a year can afford without having to sell off their kids. Try to find such a house.

Sticking with the Austin example, the city council approved a measure last year to offer a mortgage discount to police officers, firefighters, and paramedics if they buy a home in the city. At present, the very people we entrust with our safety and lives, people who should be a living part of our community, mostly commute from outlying areas, chiefly because housing prices are through the roof. Rodolfo Estrada has been an APD patrol officer for five years. He lives in an apartment in the city but is looking to buy a home for his family. He earns about $39,000 a year, but he says, "I've been looking in the city of Austin, and I've also looked in Hays County [to the south of us]. I'd prefer to stay in the city, but it's so expensive." More than half of Austin's police officers live outside of the city they are sworn to protect, and about half of our firefighters are also out-of-towners.

The rule of thumb is that you can't spend more than 30 percent of your monthly pay on housing and still have enough to cover food, car, and other expenses. Most bankers, however, are even stricter, refusing to grant a mortgage that takes more than 25 percent of your paycheck. For someone making $30,000, this comes to $625 a month. You're going to go house shopping on that?

Forget a new house. Homebuilders today would get a hernia from laughing uncontrollably at you if you came around flashing that kind of money. Hey, they'd say between bursts of guffawing, we'll sell you one of these three-car garages for $625 a month. Of course, the square footage in some of the garages being built would do nicely for the modest-home market, but it's way more profitable for developers to serve the luxury clients, so that's where practically all of them have gone. In the small but growing city of Austin, there are some 350 developers putting up some ten thousand homes a year. Less than 5 percent of these houses, however, are priced below $100,000. Of the 350 developers, only a couple are even trying to build for the rising surge of Austin families who make under $30,000 a year, and they are faced with indifference and outright rejection from the financial community. One who is trying to respond to these families is Haythem Dawlett, a developer who says lenders had zero knowledge about this market and even less interest in serving it. Just to prove that there is a demand, Dawlett and his partners built three model houses with their own funds, then held an open house. They got forty-eight buyers in a single weekend. Those homes got built, but still the lenders and builders hold back, not because these homes aren't profitable, but because they are not mega-profitable like the high-end houses, so this gusher of a market goes begging.

So, you say, I don't have to have a new house, I'll just get a used one. Well, get in line fella. The kind of used home you've got in mind already has someone using it, and even if they're moving out there's a long line of buyers at the doorstep. Since the industry is no longer building this scale of house, the supply of them is so low that even the most modest old houses are being priced way beyond that six-and-a-quarter a month you've got in your pocket, especially if they're in a neighborhood being gentrified, as so many are now that more upscale buyers decide they want to live near downtown rather than out in the scenic hills, the lake region, or other primo spots of ultra-urbia.

Not that *every* old house is priced out of reach. If you're willing to go far enough out, you can find affordable housing around every city. Here in the Austin area, for example, Clyde Puckett will sell his house to you, and the price might be right. Drive about thirteen miles from Austin to the neighboring town of Manor, then go another seven and a half miles northeast from beautiful downtown Manor and there you'll find Puckett's place, just off Hog Eye Road. Local humor writer John Kelso, after hearing so many complaints that housing here has become prohibitively expensive, went looking for affordable and came across Clyde, who's thinking of selling because even Hog Eye Road is getting too crowded for him. He says there are nearby neighbors now, and their dogs make it impossible for him to let his chickens run loose in his yard anymore. Besides, he no longer feels entirely comfortable stepping out on his front porch to take a piss.

His house is what the real estate people might call a "fixer-upper." It's a trailer that he bought twenty-three years ago, plus a wooden structure adjacent to it that is presently filled with trash. "I was tearing it down," says Clyde of the wooden building, "but I ran out of steam." So it's still there, lending a bit of rustic charm and available for whatever creative whimsy the new owner might bring to it. He concedes that the main house—the trailer—could use a new floor, though he's kept it patched up pretty well, including having put a Neighborhood Crime Watch sign over "one of the bad spots." But, he notes proudly, "I don't have a rat or a snake. I got six cats, and they run a tight ship."

The Puckett Place sits on two acres that offer exciting landscaping opportunities. At the moment, the grounds are graced with an abundance of "yard art," including eight rusting vehicles, a pile of used tires, an oil drum, a supermarket basket, an old kitchen sink, and many other fine pieces. "If I didn't live around junk, I don't know what I'd do," Clyde says of his collectibles. Much of the junk is inoffensive, though, because it's invisible, covered with weeds that range up to fourteen feet high. "I'm a naturalist," says the keeper of this kingdom. "I think if the good Lord put it out there to grow, give it a chance." Writer Kelso, who took a tour of the place, says there is no pool or hot tub, but there's a sizable low patch near the road with standing water in it, which the realtors would describe as a "natural habitat." Clyde, being more down to earth, simply warns: "Don't fall in this pond, or a bullfrog will eat you."

What will it cost to make all this yours? Clyde says, "I imagine I could get $40,000 if I cleaned it up and mowed a little bit."

Alright, alright, you scream in frustration, the American dream of home ownership has been put out of my reach, so I'll simply have to settle for renting a place. Good luck. Affordable apartments are becoming a thing of the past, too. Again using Austin as a bellwether, rents have almost doubled here during the nineties and are now averaging nearly $900 a month for a small, two-bedroom apartment—well beyond the budgets of the middle-classers I'm talking about. Damion McKeon, an Austin firefighter earning $30,000 a year, says he can't touch an apartment here: "I would be pretty much scrimping by if I lived in Austin. The rent is astronomical here." Because there are so many people chasing so few apartments, even complexes that the experts refer to by the architectural expression "a dump" are bringing premium prices.

The good news is that apartment construction in Austin is up in the last couple of years. But these are not being built for working stiffs. Of the 4,312 apartment units built in 1998, only 5 percent were moderately priced. Indeed, a bitter irony for the construction crews building these apartments is that they're averaging maybe ten bucks an hour and have a hard time finding anything they can afford to live in. They sure won't live in these new complexes, which are mostly luxury nests for the affluent, including a new category of upscale rentals called "corporate accommodations," catering to those executives needing an in-town place.

Just a couple of blocks from Threadgill's World Headquarters, the great Southern-cooking Mecca from which we broadcast our daily radio program, is a downtown apartment complex named River Woods. It's nothing fancy, but its twelve brick buildings, nestled among a dozen graceful, old live oak trees is plenty pleasant. The cars parked here are mostly American with a lot of miles on them: Malibus, some Ford pickups, a low-slung Camaro, a Jeep, a meter-reader's truck, several vans, a '72 Lincoln Continental, a Mercury Cougar, and two dump trucks. There's no swimming pool, but there are barbecue grills on the balconies, children's toys on the patios, and one apartment with a couple of prized racing pigeons in a cage. River Woods is a place of two- and three-job working families, and they're paying $550 for a two-bedroom here. Located on South Congress Avenue within sight of the state capitol building, the complex is the kind that most cities need more of, yet this one is about to be bulldozed. Dallas mega-developer Trammel Crow has bought the property, and the Austin newspaper has reported excitedly that he is contributing to our downtown's revitalization by planning to raze River Woods and erect some 250 fabulous new luxury apartments going for $1,500 a month and up. Crow's new digs are to bear the appropriately toney name of Reserve on Congress. Current residents have already been told to take their Malibus, barbecue grills, and pigeons and kindly fly the coop, get out of the way, vamoose.

Also in downtown Austin is Sixth Street West, a low-cost apartment complex in a neighborhood that has long prided itself in its economic and racial diversity. But the boom at the top of the economic ladder is destroying the diversity. Ruth Granjeno, her husband, and her two boys, José and Erik, are residents of the complex, which has 129 units for folks of modest means, with apartments priced between $350 and $600 a month. She works as a janitor and is a housecleaner for five nearby families, plus she is vice president of the PTA for Matthews Elementary, the school her boys attend, only five blocks away. She has lived there fourteen years. "This location is safe," Ruth says. "I walk to work. I walk to the houses I clean. I know everyone." A grocery store, a washateria, a dry cleaner, a drugstore, and other services are right there in her neighborhood. It is what city living should be for families like hers.

But along comes Royce Gourley Jr. He owns ten apartment complexes in Austin, and in 1999 he added Sixth Street West to his fiefdom. This is a hot and happening area now, with antique shops, beaucoup boutiques, sidewalk cafés, espresso joints, and other wondrous improvements coming to the neighborhood. So many improvements that families like Ruth Granjeno's are viewed by developers as low-class cyesores who need to be sent packing. Last summer, Gourley tried to do just that—one month before school was to start, he started handing out thirty-day eviction notices to Ruth and about twenty of her neighbors. Think about that. Not only were these families being dumped out of their homes and forced to scramble furiously to find a place before school opened, but their children also were being booted out of Matthews Elementary by this developer, since no other affordable housing is available in the Matthews district. "I'm willing to pay $800 for a two-bedroom apartment," said Ruth, "but there aren't any." When asked by the *Austin American-Statesman*, Gourley said he didn't really even know how many families he was booting, nor would he say what his new, upscale rent structure would be, but, he snickered, "Obviously, I'm not spending money over there to keep the units leased at $350 a month."

He didn't snicker long, however, because a coalition of Matthews families and eight tenants, including the Granjenos, sued Gourley for racial discrimination. It seems the tenants he booted out all just happened to be Mexican-American. A judge issued a restraining order against ousting the families that were suing, and that brought Royce galloping to the settlement table. The Granjenos will have their rent raised substantially, but they get to stay: "When I thought we had to leave, I cried because I thought we'd lose the school and my friends. Now I'm very satisfied." It does pay to fight the bastards. About a third of the families, however, had already moved out or could not afford the jacked-up rents.

Where are the families of Sixth Street West and River Woods to go? Away. They'll end up like so many other families who find themselves in what the bureaucrats coolly term "inadequate" housing. Dora Johnson knows about such inadequacies. She and her two-year-old daughter live in a two-bedroom Austin apartment, but not alone. Four others are crammed in with them, none able to find apartments with rents they can afford on their own. That's six people trying to get along in two bedrooms, one bathroom, a kitchen, and a living room. The same local paper that hailed Trammel Crow's luxury project reports that it's no longer a matter of poor people being left out but of "working, middle-class citizens [whose] chance of finding an apartment or house that is affordable is more difficult than at any time in Austin's history." Nationally, some 40 percent of renters don't have the income to qualify for the average two-bedroom apartments in their area. What do they do?

- They do what Dora and her little girl are doing—they live with family, friends, co-workers, or strangers, cramming together in small spaces.
- They live in rundown places, often in dangerous areas of town, where the rents are lower (but still expensive—in Austin; $500 a month has become the low end for a one-bedroom apartment).
- They go to the outer edges of the city, which means they are in slurburbia, facing long commutes to their jobs— Courtney Gentry and her roommate, for example, came to Austin with $500 each to spend on rent, which they hoped would put them in the University of Texas area, near where they worked. "We couldn't find anything," she says, so they're in a complex out in northwest Austin, nowhere near the center of the city, commuting for forty-five minutes in rush hour, and still paying $980 for their apartment.
- Or, they lie about their income or find a manager who'll let them in even though the rent is substantially more than a third of their paycheck, which means they have less to spend on food, medicine, and other needs (70 percent of renters in the United States now pay more than a third of their monthly income on rent).

They make do . . . and stew. They also scorn a political system that doesn't respond to them, doesn't want them, doesn't seem to know them. In a song he titled "I Ain't Got No Home," Woody Guthrie wrote about an everyman of the depression era who is a direct ancestor to today's majority that's been rendered invisible in a culture of wealth and is being ignored by both political parties:

I mined in your mines, and I gathered-in your corn
I've been working, mister, since the day that I was born
And I worry all the time, like I never did before
Cause I ain't got no home in this world anymore.

Well now I just ramble 'round to see what I can see
This wide wicked world is sure a funny place to be
The gambling man is rich and the working man is poor
And I ain't got no home in this world anymore.©

How soon we forget our own history—or, rather, how quickly our real history is buried by the Powers That Be in the futile hope that if today's citizens don't know about it, we won't think to rebel in similar fashion. The economic disparities, social dislocations, and political alienations of the twenties and thirties produced a massive upheaval that had the cock-sure capitalism of the time grappling uncertainly with everything from native fascism to homegrown socialism. It was this grassroots rebellion against the Wall Street elites and their corrupted cronies in Washington that finally produced—after angry and bloody battles all across the countryside—the social contract and the middle-class framework of laws that are now being so cavalierly dismantled. Today's economic destruction is being wrought under cover of a media-hyped middle-class prosperity that simply does not exist. It's a suicidal social order that thinks it can push its majority to the edges. It's a stupid political system that has two political parties representing the 20 percent minority, and none standing up for the 80 percent majority. Hush, say those in charge, everything is golden. Let the people eat stuffed artichokes.

FIGHTING THE SIN OF WAGES

There's a comic strip I like entitled "Frank & Ernest"—two disheveled, often beleaguered, somewhat Chaplinesque fellows who live on the hardscrabble side of life yet are always mirthful about the absurdity of the system and of the situation in which they find themselves. Created by Bob Thaves, a recent strip showed a frazzled Frank at the end of the work-week with his desk still piled high with stacks of paperwork to get done, his wastebasket overflowing, his files a jumble, saying: "I think the only person who ever got his work done by Friday was Robinson Crusoe."

And, as you'll recall, Friday was not actually paid money.

There you have the tension in today's economy for most folks: *mucho* work, *poquito* money. Peek behind the facade of our national prosperity, and you'll see that it's propped up by the working poor who are working diligently in high-rise office buildings, in the celebrated service economy, in the industrial parks of our cities, and elsewhere—people who are there day in and day out doing all the basic chores that keep the system going, yet getting shorted every payday. "You know why they call it 'take-home pay'?" asked a caller to our radio show. "Because that's the only place you can go on it." READER ALERT: STUNNING STATISTIC DEAD AHEAD: Twenty-five percent of the jobs in today's celebrated economy pay a poverty wage! That's 32 million people.

There is very good news, however, for something is being done to lift these wages. Not by Washington (where both parties continue to tinker around with the minimum wage, doing their part to keep it as minimal as possible), but by a grass-roots movement of America's low-wage workers themselves. It's called the *Living Wage* Campaign, and it has spread from Baltimore, which enacted its ordinance in 1994, to twenty-eight other cities that have already put living wage standards on their books and to another forty where campaigns are under way. This is an amazing success story of people taking matters into their own hands, getting organized, and defeating the formidable power structure of city after city, yet you would not know from the arbiters of national news that it is even happening (no doubt they are too busy celebrating the roaring economy in which, as *Money Magazine* told us in a 1999 cover story, "Everyone Is Getting Rich").

These campaigns start from a basic principle of justice: Full-time work ought not leave you in wretched poverty. Yet talk with the people on the front lines of poverty—the churches and social workers—and they'll confirm that every city in America is experiencing a crush of working families living in homeless shelters and going to soup kitchens for meals. To fight paycheck impoverishment, the Living Wage movement has begun by targeting corporations that are given contracts and subsidies by local governments. Why should our tax dollars be paid to companies that return only poverty pay to our communities? Annually across the country, for example, billions of dollars worth of tax abatements and taxpayer-financed giveaways are handed out to corporations as lures to get them to build a store here or a factory there. The rationale for the handout is always that it will produce JOBS! But in case after case, the city gets suckered—many of the promised JOBS! are never created, and those that are pay too little for a family to make ends meet. Many billions more of taxpayer dollars are being given through contracts to corporations—build a public swimming pool, provide meals for the jailhouse, handle the city's waste disposal, manage the public parking lots, run the buses, process the payroll, landscape the parks, and all sorts of functions that the city (or county, school district, etc.) used to do but has since privatized. But privatization has meant privation for the people hired by the corporation to do the work.

Here's a radical thought: Our public funds should not depress the wages of our own citizens and be the cause of poverty, which saps the vitality of a city and costs taxpayers even more in social services to the deprived workers. This has been the compelling political message of the Living Wage movement, which has pushed through various initiatives and ordinances requiring that corporate contractors and recipients of corporate subsidies pay a wage that a family can live on, even if it is at a meager level. How much? Every local campaign has developed its own standard, with most using the poverty level for a family of four in their area, which usually puts the wage somewhere between seven and ten dollars an hour. As the movement has gained experience and strength, more of the ordinances also require health care benefits and some paid vacation time.

Los Angeles Times writer Nancy Cleeland wrote in February 1999, about that city's ordinance, putting a face to the technicalities of it: "Let the academics, politicians, and labor leaders debate the definition of a living wage. For airport janitor José Morales, it means two concrete things—a bed and a car." Working for a private company that has a contract to provide janitorial services at LA International Airport, Morales, thirty-six years old, was making $5.45 an hour, which doesn't stretch very far, certainly not in Los Angeles. Cleeland reports that, for housing, "he shared a converted garage with his sister, her husband, and the couple's two young sons. Too poor to buy furniture, they scavenged cardboard boxes from a nearby supermarket and spread them on the floor to make a communal bed." Mr. Morales had to get up at 4 A.M. each day because his only transportation was the city bus system, and it took two hours, including changing buses, to get from his garage to LAX. It was also a two-hour bus ride back to his garage. Twice he was mugged at his corner bus stop.

Now life has picked up a bit for him, thanks to the city's 1997 Living Wage law, which lifted his pay a buck-eighty an hour. It doesn't seem like much, $1.80. A pack of cigarettes costs more, a draft beer is more, a single copy of *Money Magazine* is more. But it's $3,600 a year for a full-time American worker like José Morales. Admittedly this is not as generous as the $4,600 that members of Congress gave themselves in a cost-of-living pay raise in 1999, on top of the $3,100 cost-of-living "adjustment" they received the year before ("I know there are members that have three or four kids," wailed House Speaker Dennis "The Menace" Hastert during the 1999 debate; "I am not crying crocodile tears, but they need to be able to have a life and provide for their families"). Meanwhile, back on earth, Cleeland writes that the $1.80 boost for Morales "moved him from a chronic state of crisis to a more manageable level of poverty [$7.25 is about $14,500 a year gross income]. He still counts pennies. He still scans the garbage he dumps for discarded treasures. He still considers a rare fast-food meal to be a dining-out experience."

Morales concedes that "The truth is, it's not a very livable wage. But it's a big change for the better." As an active union member, he will keep organizing and working with others to put more livability in people's paychecks, more fairness in the system. For now, however, the Living Wage victory at least provides what he calls a *salario digno*, for it has meant that he and his extended family could get out of the garage and into a two-bedroom home. It's only 800 square feet; it's not exactly in the 90210 zip code, and it's still mighty cramped with the five of them in there, but it's a real house. And it has a real bed in it— Morales' first purchase was to get the family off of that stack of cardboard. Slowly, they have since been able to add other furniture, including a small dining table. His second purchase was a '93 sedan—so, no more two-hour commute, no more 4 A.M. wake-up, no more bus stop muggings. Another big change was that the LA Living Wage law includes health insurance, "and for families," Mr. Morales says simply, "that means a lot."

In my work, I spend a big chunk of time flying around the country. In an airport a few years ago, I noticed for the first time a routine that I've since seen repeated several times in various airports. I saw a custodian making his rounds, gathering the trash that passengers leave strewn about the gate area when they board their plane. I watched him work his way down the concourse from one gate to another, and as he went, he would quickly make a pass along the banks of pay phones between the gates, checking the coin slots to see if anyone had left some change. Maybe it's a compulsion, I thought, or just an amusement (like some sort of custodian's Las Vegas). My assumption was that airport jobs, while not Fat City, were after all city positions and certainly wouldn't be so poorly paid that coin-slot change would count as income.

But that was before realizing just how extensive privatization has become in local governments. In Los Angeles, for example, most of the janitorial jobs—from the airport to the zoo—have been "outsourced," a bit of new economy jargon that means public tasks (and public money) have been farmed out to private interests. This has been sold to voters on the ideological assertion that corporations can run the public's business better than governments can, so just give us the contract and, by Jove, watch us save the taxpayers a bundle! Local politicians, eager to look like budget saviors (even as they take campaign contributions from the contractors), have been more than happy to go along. But the corporation always builds into its contract a juicy profit for itself, incredible salaries for its executives, an advertising budget, and other costs far beyond what a government agency has—so where does it get the "savings"? From José Morales and the janitors I've seen gleaning change from pay phones.

This hidden subsidy for privatization was the genesis of the Living Wage Campaign in LA, which David Reynolds of Wayne State University has described in an excellent and comprehensive guide he authored with ACORN, the grassroots organizing group, bearing the straightforward title "Living Wage Campaigns: An Activist's Guide to Building the Movement for Economic Justice." In the City of Angels, the campaign began in 1995 with an organizing effort at LAX by two unions (Hotel Employees Restaurant Employees, and Service Employees International). During the next several months, more than a hundred Los Angeles organizations joined the grassroots coalition to battle the wage ripoff—from homeless groups to small businesses, from taxpayer groups to churches, from political groups to retirees. It would be an arduous battle against a recalcitrant power structure that included Mayor Richard Riordan and the city's business establishment, which presented itself under the disingenuous name of The Coalition to Keep LA Working and snidely referred to the Living Wage proposal as the Job Destruction Ordinance. Their claim was that $7.25 an hour would force the privateers to eliminate the jobs rather than "suffer" the economic blow of paying a higher wage (though who exactly was then going to do the janitorial chores the company had contracted to perform was not addressed—perhaps some junior executives from headquarters). Of great worry also for the corporate crowd was that this ordinance would "only add to the perception that Los Angeles is not business friendly." Oh, great, better that the Morales family sleep on cardboard boxes stacked on a garage floor than that the city be seen as less than embracing to every rapacious contractor that wants to make a killing.

With the mayor in the pocket of the business establishment, the Living Wage advocates had to win not merely a majority of votes on the city council, but a veto-proof supermajority. Reynolds reports that they laid siege to the council, steadily barraging the members with letters, phone calls, faxes, e-mails, and visits. At Thanksgiving, 1996, more than a thousand plates arrived in council offices, each one hand-decorated with some illustration of the "challenge" of trying to feed a family on poverty wages. In the Christmas season, a hundred clergy led others to city hall, accompanied by an actor draped in chains and playing the part of Jacob Marley, decrying Mayor Scrooge's opposition to the living wage. In addition, a group of merry carolers went to city hall and nearby restaurants singing carols with lyrics suitably adjusted for the message of the campaign. At LAX itself, low-wage workers like Morales took the media on a tour to highlight their working conditions.

They also kept expanding their coalition—as any janitor knows, the more straws in your broom, the more dirt you can sweep out. To the suprise of the establishment some business leaders supported the coalition, ranging from companies like Bell Industries to retailers like All American Home Center to smaller shops like The Stationery Place. Executives from these firms pointed out that good wages are *pro* business, since they reduce turnover, increase morale, produce better-skilled employees, and improve productivity. They also noted a basic lesson of economics—your workers are your customers. As Henry Ford wrote in 1926, "An underpaid man is a customer reduced in purchasing power. He cannot buy. Business depression is caused by weakened purchasing power. Purchasing power is weakened by uncertainty or insufficiency of income. The cure of business depression is through purchasing power, and the source of purchasing power is wages." These business advocates also raised the point of fair competition—the public subsidy of low-wage contractors undercut those, like themselves, who pursued a high-road business strategy of good wages.

A big breakthrough for the Living Wage advocates came when Protestant, Catholic, and Jewish leaders were organized into Clergy and Laity United for Economic Justice—CLUE. Bringing a moral and theological dimension to the campaign, CLUE leaders prompted discussions of the wage issue in their own congregations, preached of the justice aspect from their pulpits, wrote op-ed pieces, made pilgrimages to city hall, and used their own political contacts to press the issue.

In January, 1997, council members were greeted by a flood of New Year's cards beseeching them to do the right thing. For the next three months, coalition delegations visited the council twice a day, three days a week. They kept reaching out, kept focused, kept pushing—and on March 18, they won a *unanimous* vote for a living wage of $7.25 an hour indexed yearly to inflation increases, with family health benefits, and twelve paid days off each year. Mayor Riordan vetoed it. The city council overrode his veto.

Versions of this success story have been repeated, so far, in:

Baltimore	**Chicago**	**Detroit**
Boston	**Cook County (IL)**	**Duluth**
Buffalo	**Dane County (WI)**	**Durham**
Cambridge	**Des Moines**	**Gary**

Hayword (CA)	Multnomah County	San Antonio
Hudson County (NJ)	(OR)	San Jose
Jersey City	New Haven	Santa Clara
Los Angeles County	New York City	Somerville (MA)
Madison	Oakland	St. Paul
Miami-Dade County	Pasadena	Tuscon
Minneapolis	Portland (OR)	Ypsilanti (MI)

Key players have been ACORN (which operates the National Living Wage Center); unions like AFSCME, HERE, and SEIU; an up-and-coming progressive political group called the New Party; the central labor councils in these cities, along with an umbrella labor group called Jobs With Justice; and local churches and interfaith groups like CLUE.

The Living Wage campaigns themselves are only a start, for the wages established still can be achingly low and apply only to the relatively few workers employed by government contractors. But they *are* a start, and an encouragingly strong one, too, delivering substantial benefits for regular folks too long ignored. The effort alone is enormously important, for it is getting thousands of people informed and involved, getting them into the streets, giving them confidence that their activism matters, developing battle-experienced grassroots leaders, and uniting a broad coalition for the long haul. The effort is also generating a phenomenal debate that Washington and Wall Street thought had been suppressed—a debate not only about the working poor, but also about questions of fairness and justice in a society that is being taught to value nothing but predator economics.

The very existence of such a movement—one that is now organized and linked from coast to coast, one that has the moral high road, and one that is actually *moving*—sends a chill through the nation's economic and political powers. It's like the hunter's nightmare, in which someone shouts: "Look out—the rabbit's got the gun!"

RETURN OF
THE ROBBER BARONS

During my political campaigning years, I came to a Zen-like understanding of Ernest Tubb's country-music classic, "There's miles and miles of Texas." Simply getting from here to there, crisscrossing the 262,000 square miles of this huge state, can be daunting to a statewide candidate. (I know that you Alaskans presently claim bragging rights on size, but no one's fooled by all that ice—a little more global warming and the ice will melt, leaving you guys standing on Rhode Island West.)

Of big help to me in my long-distance travels was Air Hightower—the private airplanes that a dozen or so of my supporters owned and would occasionally make available to me. These were not corporate jets with uniformed crews, luxury accommodations, and full meal service, like some of today's presidential candidates have at their disposal, but a collection of rather rudimentary single- and twin-engine prop planes (one literally was a crop duster) that were owned by farmers, lawyers, and other generous souls who volunteered to fly me around. Each of these owners would serve as a crew of one, combining the roles of pilot, navigator, mechanic, flight attendant, troubleshooter, chaplain, beer supplier, and freelance political adviser on our trips together.

Stuff happened. In a 1986 incident, two other politicos and I needed to fly from Austin to Lubbock for an evening political rally and get back the same night. Bob Armstrong, who had been a longtime Democratic officeholder and was then an Austin attorney, volunteered to ferry us out and back, a wearying seven-hundred-mile round-trip in a cramped plane. It was eleven or so by the time we returned to the Austin area, and we three passengers, having exercised on the home leg by doing a few twelve-ounce elbow bends, were slumped in our seats napping. Sitting in the front seat next to Bob, I was gradually brought out of my airborne snooze by the sensation of our plane circling again and again in a slow, droning loop around the hills on the city's west side. It seems that Bob's transponder had gone on the fritz. It could receive, but not send, signals, so he was unable to contact the tower to let them know we were approaching for our landing. We could even see the airport, but you can't come in to a public airport without permission, so Bob's theory was just to keep circling until they noticed and contacted us. They didn't.

After twenty minutes of not being noticed, Bob switched to Plan B. We flew to Executive Airpark, a small, private airport about ten miles north of Austin. It was closed for the night; but we landed anyway and taxied up to the double-wide mobile home that served as a terminal. There we executed a high-tech telecommunications maneuver that saved the day— or, in this case, the night. Bob and I hopped out of the plane, I gave him a quarter, and he used the pay phone outside the double-wide to ring up the air traffic controllers in the tower over at Greater Austin International to let them know we were ready to come in. Then we piled back in the plane, took off, got just high enough for the radar to find us, and were brought home at last.

If only there was a political party that would notice that America's majority is going around and around in circles somewhere out in the hills, within sight of the bright lights of prosperity, yet not being brought in. Instead, even the Democrats are zeroed in on the special needs and peculiar whims of the dominant business executives and investors who are rapidly and radically consolidating power within practically every economic sector, affecting the kind of jobs we get, our families' access to quality health care, the prices we pay, the purity of our food and water, the news we're fed, and much more. This reordering of America's (and the globe's) economic structure is being done with no public discussion about whether it's anything we want. Indeed, it's presented as the work of immutable market and technological forces, as though it's been ordained by the Economic Gods. This reminds me of a song by the Austin Lounge Lizards, titled "Jesus Loves Me, but He Can't Stand You"—apparently these economic gods love the executives and investors doing the consolidating, since their fortunes and power are greatly expanded, but they can't stand us, since ours are diminished. Don't worry your fuzzy little heads about it, we're told— watch TV, play golf, go to the mall—it's nothing but progress on its inevitable march into the new millennium. As farmers say, when you find something gooey and stinky on your boots, think bullshit.

There is nothing inevitable, much less beneficent, about the corporate consolidations, downsizings, wealth concentration, and other enormous changes rocking our economic and social order. They are the result of nothing more mystical than brute force and old-fashioned scheming among the power elites. The executives and investors plot with each other, conspire with politicians of both parties, and employ academics and media flaks—all to create the legal framework for their power grab, to implement it, and to devise the buzzwords of conventional wisdom to rationalize it ("global competitiveness" being the current cover-all).

These elites have plenty of precedents in American history for putting a mask of inevitability over the face of avarice. Go into a high school or college history class, and you'll find text-books that still glorify the nineteenth-century industrialists who "followed their destiny" to build great industrial empires: Jay Gould's railroads, John D. Rockefeller's oil refineries, J. P. Morgan's steel factories. But Gould's empire was built less on entrepreneurial genius than on bribes and fraud; Rockefeller was not a marketer but a ruthless monopolist who lied and cheated to build his $2 billion fortune; and Morgan's U.S. Steel Corporation *became* the steel industry not because of any natural superiority of product or business skill but, as the great historian Howard Zinn puts it, "by closing off competition and maintaining the price at $28 a ton; and by working 200,000 men twelve hours a day for wages that barely kept their families alive."

In his superb book, *A People's History of the United States,* Zinn added, "And so it went, in industry after industry—shrewd, efficient businessmen building empires, choking out competition, maintaining high prices, keeping wages low, using government subsidies." A hundred years after the reign of these Robber Barons, we're back to the future, for Zinn's description is just as apt for Bill Gates, Sanford Weill, Philip Knight, Ron Perelman, Hugh McColl, Michael Eisner, Henry Kravis, and their allied Robber Barons who reign at the dawn of 2000. No less self-centered and ruthless than the Goulds, Rockefellers, and Morgans, these men have engineered today's world of conglomeratization and monopolization, demanding tribute from the rest of us in the form of low wages, high prices, and tax subsidies, while amassing unfathomable personal riches and spinning golden cocoons to isolate themselves from the consequences of their actions.

MERGING, PURGING, AND SPLURGING

When I was about twelve, I decided I should read the Bible from cover to cover. I did fine with the early chapters, which are filled with familiar stories I learned in Sunday school.

Then I came upon Chronicles I and hit the wall of genealogy delineating the royal line of David. Page after page is devoted to such scintillating information as, "Caleb son of Hezron had children by his wife Azubah (and by Jerioth). These were her sons: Jesher, Shobab, and Ardon. When Azubah died, Caleb married Ephrath, who bore him Hur. Hur was the father of Uri, and Uri the father of Bezalel. Later, Hezron lay with the daughter of Makir, the father of Gilead, and she bore him Segrub. Segrub was the father of Jair, who controlled twenty-three towns in Gilead. . . ." And on and on it went. I finally waded through it, reading every "begat," "firstborn," and "bore"— understanding none of it.

It occurs to me that this is the way most people feel when they come upon the seemingly endless list of corporate mergers that are reported almost daily in the business pages of the newspapers. The largest ones might even make front-page news, though there's never any interpretation that would help a reader understand why this is happening and what it means to them: Exxon took over Mobil, and BP got Amoco. Travelers Group, which earlier had consumed Solomon Smith Barney, swallowed Citicorp, thus becoming the gargantuan Citigroup. NationsBank subjugated BankAmerica, not only gaining its assets, but also seizing its name, like some feudal baron might appropriate the coat of arms of a conquered foe. SBC Communications snared Ameritech, Bell Atlantic grabbed GTE, and AT&T picked off TCI. From Germany, Deutsche Bank reached into Boston and snatched Bankers Trust, while Daimler-Benz reached into Detroit and took away Chrysler.

The urge to merge—the urge of one corporate giant to devour another—has been insatiable in the nineties, completely remaking the economic landscape for all of us. The short list above includes but a few of 1998's large mergers among corporate baronies. The financial value of that year's consolidations totaled more than a trillion and a half buckaroos, which beat the record-setting year of '97, which beat the record-setting year of '96, which beat the record-setting year of '95, which . . . et cetera, all the way back to 1990. And '99 was expected to set yet another record. The corporate couplings have become so massive that the thesaurus can no longer keep up. "Big" became "giant," which became "huge," which became "gargantuan," which became "mega-mammoth," which will become some worse contortion of the language. When Price Waterhouse, one of the Big Four accounting firms (they were the Big Eight as recently as 1997), merged with another biggie, CoopersLybrand, the subsequent name was too long to get on a letterhead, so it was reduced (along with competition) to the still-cumbersome PricewaterhouseCoopers. My favorite indicator of how far beyond us these behemoths have gotten comes to me when Southwestern Bell, my local phone monopoly (now a *deregulated* monopoly), sends me its monthly bill. Southwestern, which was one of the seven "Baby Bells" created by the 1984 breakup of AT&T, controlled local service in its original territory of Texas, Oklahoma, Kansas, Missouri, and Arkansas until 1996. That year, it reached out and plucked another Baby Bell, Pacific Telesis, giving it control over California and Nevada phone customers, too. Then, in '98, it added a third Baby Bell, Ameritech, to its roster, giving it the customers in Illinois, Indiana, Ohio, Michigan, and Wisconsin. Don't look now, but Ma Bell, as AT&T was derisively referred to prior to the breakup, is being reincarnated as Southwestern Bell, which now defines itself on its bills with this charming slogan: "Your friendly neighborhood global communications company." Lily Tomlin at her satirical best could not top that.

Last year, a merger consultant told *The Wall Street Journal* that "the whole mentality of corporate America is M&A driven right now." M&A doesn't refer to kinky sex, not exactly, but to the kinky business phenomenon of mergers and acquisitions (it's so common that there's even a magazine called M&A, which some of your better stores keep in plastic wrappers on the top shelf with other XXX-rated material). "If you're not consolidating, you're not in the game," said the consultant.

Hmmm. Game. Did you know you were in a game?

Mergers are a game the barons play at great profit to themselves, yet millions of people who don't even know the game is being played, much less have a say in the rules, end up on the losing end—workers, customers, small businesses, communities, ordinary shareholders, and even the company itself.

WORKERS. Typically, news stories about corporate mergers make no mention of anything so downbeat as job cuts. Instead, there's usually a photo of two gloating CEOs, a statement about how out-of-this-world HUGE the deal is, a cute little anecdote about how the executive duo first came up with the idea of marrying their companies ("We were in the same foursome at the Rolls-Royce Golden Golf Getaway at Platinum Pines last year, and when we both birdied number 7, I said to Jack, 'This could be the start of something big,' and we looked at each other, and both of us knew then . . . "), plus the stories invariably contain a liberal sprinkling of voodoo incantations, such as "synergies," "market compatibilities," and "strategic dynamics," designed to appease skeptical Wall Street analysts about a marriage that otherwise looks about as well thought out as your average $25 quickie wedding in Las Vegas.

Actually, merger stories do include cryptic allusions to job cuts, but you have to know the jargon. Trying to figure out what corporate officials are saying is no easier than deciphering government gobbledygook, since plain English is passé and CorporateSpeak has invaded the language. Consider these gems culled by AP writer Eric Quinones:

> "Population Equivalents"—a term used by cellular phone companies to mean "people."
>
> "Mortality Experience"—coined by life insurance companies to denote "death" (an "adverse mortality experience" is

the industry's phrase for "more death claims than expected," though the deceased can be forgiven if they think that their own individual mortality experience is adverse).

"Social Expression Product"—the greeting card industry's generic jargon for "birthday card," "get-well card," etc.

So, wink-wink, when a merger is announced, those who know the game know you don't look for some straightforward statement like "jobs by the jillions are being whacked by these bloodsucking curs," but instead you must seek out certain tell-tale code words: "To build shareholder value, *operating efficiencies* have been identified"; "The merger will result in a *restructuring* of the firm"; and, "Executives intend to pare *structural redundancies* resulting from the acquisition."

Of course, *you* are the "redundancy," if you're one of the hundreds of thousands of employees who have gotten the boot in the past decade after hundreds of major corporations have merged. Unlike the full media treatment given to the merging, the subsequent purging gets little coverage—usually a one-paragraph notice back in the business pages, much like an obituary: "Citigroup to cut 10,400," "Wells Fargo to cut its workforce by 4,600," "America Online plans 1,000 layoffs," and "First Union to cut 5,850 jobs" are a few of the obits that ran last year, months after these companies had announced their mergers.

While no one is safe, the employees of the subjugated firm in a takeover feel especially vulnerable, and they often feel betrayed by their own top executives who helped orchestrate the merger. When British Petroleum acquired Amoco in 1998, for example, word soon spread through the corporate grapevine that six thousand employees would pay the price, and that most of these cuts would be made on the Amoco side. Sir John Browne, BP's steely-eyed, job-whacking CEO, didn't mince words: "We have to get through the harvesting of low-hanging fruit," he said as he eyed the Amoco personnel chart.

The Wall Street Journal reported that a bit of gallows humor quickly spread down the hallways of Amoco's Chicago headquarters: "What do you call the new CEO? Sir John. Our old CEO? Sur-render. Chicago management? Sur-plus." The good news is that Browne didn't slash six thousand employees. The bad news is that he slashed more than ten thousand.

John Challenger of the job-tracking employment firm of Challenger, Gray & Christmas reports that corporations fire at least one out of every nine employees after a merger. If each job loss were marked with a simple white cross in a field, as is done at many battlefield cemeteries, the sight would be staggering, just as the reality is staggering to the families who suffer the loss.

OTHERS. Beyond the immediate impact on jobs, mergers ripple throughout our society, and I don't mean the kind of gentle ripples you get when a pebble is tossed in a pond, but the kind of ripples you'd get by dropping a cement block in a punch bowl. Start with the obvious fact that the whole idea of these massive consolidations is to eliminate competition. Oddly enough, however, CEOs puff themselves up at press conferences and publicly assert that the new jumbo-combo company was created to "improve competitiveness." One wonders whether such vacuousness comes naturally to them or whether they have to practice it. You don't need to be a CEO to see that where there were two, there is now one, and this is not generally a competitive plus for the rest of us.

Take the oil industry, which has recently been rushing to reconstruct Rockefeller. Old John D. put together the Standard Oil Company by hook *and* crook in the 1870s, monopolizing the industry and generally operating in such a tyrannical fashion that the Supreme Court intervened in 1911 to bust his trust into thirty-four companies. Just as a salamander can grow another leg, though, these thirty-four legs have been trying to grow another salamander. The Standard Oil trust has steadily been coming back together in the past few years, especially the biggest parts of it.

- Standard Oil of Ohio (Sohio) and Standard Oil of Indiana (Amoco) have been taken over by British Petroleum, which also is taking over the old Standard Oil's Atlantic Refining Company (ARCO).
- Standard Oil of California (Chevron) has taken over Gulf, and now Chevron itself is in talks to be merged into Royal Dutch Shell, which already has absorbed Texaco.
- Standard Oil of New Jersey (Exxon), the largest U.S. oil company, took over Standard Oil of New York (Mobil), the second largest U.S. oil company.

The $80 billion merger of Exxon and Mobil in late '98 brought the two largest chunks of John D.'s empire back together, creating the world's largest corporation, surpassing General Motors. The two barons, Lee Raymond of Exxon and Lucio Noto of Mobil, had begun their flirtation only six months earlier at a meeting of the American Petroleum Institute (the industry's cozy club and lobbying arm), and Raymond spoke grandly at the news conference about his and Noto's selfless motivation in forging the new combine, saying it was simply a matter of wanting "to deliver more value to our shareholders, and our employees, and customers."

Customers and employees, however, saw it for what it was—two giants gaining more control over them. "Rockefeller's Revenge," one consumer group called it, noting that the combination meant that the refineries and stations of the two largest oil companies were no longer in competition on price and service. For employees, the Christmastime merger certainly was a lump of coal. At least nine thousand of them learned they would lose their positions in accounts payable, receiving, finance, information systems, and the other back-office divisions of the two companies. Nor has it been any blessing for hundreds of gasoline dealers who leased their stations from either Exxon or Mobil. The companies often had stations competing across the street from each other. But with the merger, one is gone—and so is the family that ran the place, along with the hired help they had. These are people who never heard of Mr. Raymond or Mr. Noto, but suddenly the impact of a meeting between two corporate autocrats at the American Petroleum Institute has rippled across the country and turned their little corner of the world upside down. Also, the small-business operators who leased from Mobil now find themselves in an Exxon corporate culture, where station rents are up to five times higher than what Mobil charged, and where leases are for three years instead of the ten-year term offered by Mobil. Meanwhile, down in Beaumont, Texas, some nine hundred workers at Mobil's largest refinery worry that the merger will shut it (and them) down. Exxon has two refineries of its own along this Gulf Coast crescent, so a third one might fit that category of "structural redundancies." Beaumont itself will take a body blow if this refinery is closed. From cafés to car dealers, bars to barbershops, hundreds of other people in the area depend on the good paychecks that those nine hundred union refinery workers earn.

Like marriages in the heyday of royalty, corporate mergers are not about love or natural affinities; they are pure and simple power arrangements, and the size and reach of them now overwhelm balances of power that such competing social forces as unions, consumers, environmentalists, farmers—even governments—had established since the Robber Baron days of infamy. Here is a sampler of what has been wrought by corporate fiat in just the last three or four years:

- *Health Care.* Met Life, Prudential, New York Life, Travelers, and John Hancock are among the major HMO competitors that were there a moment ago, but are now gone, gulped

down whole like a boa constrictor eats a pig by the likes of
Aetna, Cigna, and Unitedhealth Group. Not only are these
three already the dominant national players in what is now
referred to as the health-care *industry,* but they divide up
the national territory to give them near monopoly power in
city after city, which is where it counts, since most people
don't leave town to go to the doctor. Aetna, which is notorious for squeezing the care out of health care, has captured
40 percent of the Philadelphia market, nearly 60 percent in
several New Jersey cities, and a third in Atlanta, Orlando,
and San Antonio. As Consumers for Quality Care put it in a
letter to antitrust officials, "With greater market share in
key cities and states, Aetna [has] put itself in a position to
offer more patients less coverage for ever higher premiums." Two-thirds of the U.S. market is now in the hands of
the ten largest companies. Already, the consolidated HMO
industry is acting not in competition but in concert—in
1998, the biggest national firms decided virtually on the
same day to dump their Medicare service for rural seniors,
and in 1999 every one of them uniformly hiked premiums
for all of their patients.

- *Environment/Government.* British Petroleum's takeover of
ARCO is also a takeover of the Alaskan economy and environment. In the nineties, five other oil firms pulled out of
Alaska's North Slope, the largest oil field in North America,
turning over their leases to either BP or ARCO, which once
were fierce competitors. But now they are one, giving BP
monopoly control of the Alaskan pipeline, control of nearly
75 percent of the oil in Alaska, and ownership of 80 percent of Alaska's economic base. A state legislator notes
that his homeland has essentially become a colony of the
London-based conglomerate, which can now dictate the
price of oil leaving the state (a price that determines 75
percent of state government revenues), the terms for developing Alaska's untapped natural-gas fields, the wages and

employment conditions for oil workers, and the nature and
extent of environmental protection.

- *Food.* Monsanto has spent $8 billion to pluck such seed com-
panies as DeKalb and Asgrow from the competitive field,
and Du Pont has snapped up Pioneer Hi-Bred, the country's
largest seed company. These two biotech giants now control
half of the U.S. market for soybean seeds and more than
half of the corn seed market, America's first- and second-
largest crops. If you control the seed, you begin to control
the crops, the farmers, and food itself, and Monsanto and
Du Pont are using their duopoly to do all of that. (Monsanto,
for example, has genetically altered the DNA of its seeds so
the crops can absorb more of a particular pesticide the company makes.) Farmers are also squeezed by the merger-fed
growth of middleman monopolies—Cargill, the world's
largest privately held corporation and the world's number
one grain shipper, took over the shipping operations of Continental Grain, previously the third-largest shipper. Bottom
line for grain farmers is that typically they are paid a penny
or two a bushel less than they would get if the merger had
not happened—which adds up to a loss of more than $2,500
a year for the farmer. As the head of the National Farmers
Union puts it, "Mergers and acquisitions in agriculture are
occurring—and being approved—at breakneck speed with
little regard for the consequences to America's farmers."
Attention food shoppers: Do you buy your groceries from
Royal Ahold of the Netherlands? No, you say, I shop at the
Bi-Lo stores in the Carolinas, Georgia, and Tennessee; at
Edwards supermarkets in the New York region; at Tops in
upstate New York, Ohio, and Pennsylvania; at Giant in the
D.C. area; at Pathmark stores in Metropolitan New York and
Philadelphia; or at Stop & Shop in New England. All of
these, however, have been taken over by Royal Ahold, mak-
ing it the dominant food retailer on the eastern seaboard and
the fourth largest in the entire United States.

- *Air Travel.* Deregulation of the airlines, which was supposed to spur competition, instead shrank it, with majors
buying each other while also squeezing out or buying up
the regional and discount companies. Essentially, there are
only six major airlines—American, Continental, Delta,
Northwest, United, and USAir—and they cooperate, rather
than compete, on most routes, dividing up the turf through
their hub system. As Continental's CEO confided in a 1998
industry confab, "American kind of controls Dallas–Fort
Worth and Miami. We've got Newark, Houston, and Cleveland. Delta's got Atlanta. . . ." And so on. To eliminate the
inconvenience of any actual competition, the government
routinely grants immunity from antitrust laws for airlines
that want to "cooperate" (can you spell c-o-n-s-p-i-r-e?) on
prices and schedule. And indeed they do conspire—a rare
glimpse of their price collusion came in the mid-eighties
when court documents revealed a phone conversation
between Robert Crandall, then CEO of American Airlines,
and Howard Putnam, president of a now-defunct airline:
  CRANDALL: Yes, I have a suggestion for you. Raise your
     goddamn fares 20 percent. I'll raise mine the next
     morning.
  PUTNAM: Robert, we . . .
  CRANDALL: You'll make more money and I will too.
  PUTNAM: We can't talk about pricing.
  CRANDALL: Oh, bullshit, Howard. We can talk about any
     goddamn thing we want to talk about.
  Now proposals are afloat to combine the big six into the
big three (American–USAir, Delta–United, and Northwest–
Continental), giving this trio *98 percent* of the takeoff and
landing slots at all high-density airports in the United States.
To squeeze it all even tighter, the whole global market of
some two hundred airlines has already been consolidated
into four huge air-travel "alliances" (One World, Atlantic
Excellence, Star Alliance, and Wings) that stifle competition,

letting them set routes, schedules, and prices—all beyond
the reach of any one nation's regulators. *Condé Nast Traveler*
cites the chairman of TWA, which doesn't belong to any of
the four alliances, as saying that attempting to compete with
these airline "cartels" would be "like trying to compete with
Standard Oil before it was broken up."

- *Books.* The publishing industry, too, of which I'm a teensy
  footnote, is succumbing to the tidal wave of conglomeration
  and consolidation. By 1997, eight publishing octopi had
  their tentacles around most of the book world: *Bertelsmann*
  (Bantam, Doubleday, Dell, the Library Guild, etc.); *Viacom*
  (Simon & Schuster, Pocket Books, Scribner, etc.); *News Cor-*
  poration (HarperCollins—Me!); *Time Warner* (Warner
  Books, Little Brown, Time-Life Books, Book-of-the-Month
  Club, etc.); *Advance Publications* (Random House, Alfred
  Knopf, Crown, Ballantine, etc.); *Pearson* (Viking Penguin,
  Putnam, Dutton, Signet, etc.); *Hearst* (William Morrow,
  Avon, etc.); and *Holtzbrinck* (Farrar Straus, St. Martin's,
  Henry Holt, etc.). Three years later, Bertelsmann has
  grabbed Random House, News Corporation has taken
  William Morrow and Avon, and Time Warner is moving on
  Simon & Schuster. The few become fewer, and the choices
  for writers and readers shrink.
- *Garbage.* Even the humblest of industries is not beyond
  merger mania, and consolidation in the waste-disposal
  world is causing a real mess. As we enter the high-tech millennium, the low-tech world of garbage has fallen to two
  companies that own most of the landfills and waste collection terminals in the country—Waste Management Inc. and
  Allied Waste Industries. Built by a series of rapid mergers,
  these two now control more than half of America's residen-
  tial, municipal, and industrial solid-waste handling. As
  they have gained control of market after market, fees have
  steadily risen, often dramatically. Within weeks of consum-
  ing its largest competitor in 1999, for example, Waste Man-

agement jacked up its landfill fees by 40 percent. But this is not the only price of waste-disposal monopoly—it is much more profitable for these companies to dump everything in their landfills than to sort out materials for recycling, so the environmental advances that so many cities have made are endangered by the sudden grip that these private firms have gotten on our garbage. Neil Seldman of the Institute for Local Self-Reliance puts it bluntly: "They will use their size to control the bins and trucks and to discourage recycling wherever they can."

WHY IS THIS HAPPENING? Butch Hancock, one of the wonderful singer-songwriters who sprang forth in the 1970s from the unlikely musical soil of Lubbock, Texas, says that he was taught two big lessons growing up in this strait-laced farming town: "One is that God loves you and you're going to burn in hell. The other is that sex is the most awful, dirty thing on the face of the earth and you should save it for someone you love."

With this kind of logic in his background, perhaps Butch is the one to explain why the political system is so benign toward a handful of individuals who are causing so much damage to so many with their merger schemes. It would be one thing if the junior Rockefellers doing the scheming were generating real efficiencies, growth, and value for the companies and their shareholders, but the most embarrassing aspect of their deals is that mostly they don't work—not even in a business sense.

The corporate landscape is littered with the carcasses of mergers that collapsed of their own weight, the victims of executive excess. There's Quaker Oats, the solid purveyor of breakfast cereals and pancake mixes, reaching in 1994 for a snappier image by paying $1.7 billion to grab the cool beverage of the time, Snapple. Just three years later, the goof had proven to be so huge that Quaker unloaded Snapple for $300 million—nearly a billion and a half dollars less than it paid for its prized acquisition. Or, look at First Union, the sixth largest bank in the country, constructed not of granite and sound loans but of mergers, gobbling up such firms as CoreStates Financial and the Money Store, for which it paid too much, boasted too loudly, and managed too poorly. One financial analyst says of First Union, "For years I complained about the prices they paid for acquisitions, but I always said they ran a good bank. But now they're having serious problems running the basic bank—the wheels are coming off the cart."

A textbook case of merger malaise was the 1985 combination of RJ Reynolds with Nabisco, which then was taken over in 1988 by the swashbuckling, junk-bond wielding investment syndicate of Kohlberg Kravis Roberts. It was the largest deal ever at the time, and it was glorified on Wall Street and in the business media as a bold and sparkling model of what financial engineering could do. Yes, thousands of people would lose their jobs; yes, the company would be saddled with enormous interest payments on the $30 billion KKR borrowed to seize the prize; yes, whole chunks of the prize would have to be sold off to pay the bondholders; and yes, there were a few stuffy analysts who said the match was one made in hell, not in heaven—but, get out of the way, spoilsports, we're talking about geniuses. With money! The geniuses got away with corporate murder—KKR took billions in fees and profits when they sold out in 1991—but regular investors saw their RJR Nabisco stock fall by half, and, by 1999, the company was in such a mess that it split itself apart, leaving Nabisco an independent company again, but a much weaker one than when it was caught up in the grand experiment fourteen years earlier. The same analysts and media that gushed about the deal back then used terms like "a sad saga," "a notorious chapter," "financial ignominy," and "the Debacle" to describe it last year. Yet, KKR is still doing deals, and the investment bankers that made hundreds of millions in fees for putting the merger and subsequent takeover together collected even more millions for taking RJR Nabisco apart.

There's a country song entitled "If I Tell You I Love You, Consider Me Drunk." Wall Street expresses a drunken love for just about every merger that comes along by bidding up the stock price of the mergers. Then sobriety sets in. Academic studies abound to show that, after a year or so, most mergers turn ugly as it becomes apparent that they won't deliver promised efficiencies and corporate harmonies, so the stock prices fall and shareholders are stuck with a loser. The *New York Times* has covered several of these studies, reporting that "most mergers result in stocks that lag behind those of other companies in their industry [and] many mergers result in actual losses for their shareholders"; "most acquisitions fail, academics say, because the post-merger business cannot support the price paid to forge the combination"; and, "the most comprehensive study of conglomerate mergers . . . found that the profitability of acquired companies on average declined."

So who the hell is pushing these hellacious deals? The people sporting the big toothy grins at the press conferences when they're announced: the CEOs of the merging companies and the investment bankers who are paid multimillion-dollar fees to broker the deal. The Wall Street brokers get the least attention, so let's start with them, giving credit where it's due. All the major Wall Street firms have M&A divisions whose job is to encourage companies to merge. Like lobbyists in Washington, M&A agents are on the prowl wherever CEOs gather—whispering, presenting possibilities, advising, urging. There are massive fees to be made, and reputations, too. Being a top-ten M&A broker gets you prestige, bragging rights . . . and more lucrative deals, since CEOs looking to merge want someone who's been around the block a few times. There's even a formal ranking, called the League Tables, that list Wall Streeters by the dollar value of the mergers they pull off. Top of the list in the last year of League rankings was Goldman

Sachs, with 339 deals valued at nearly a trillion dollars. Merrill Lynch was second, followed by Morgan Stanley Dean Witter, Solomon Smith Barney, and Crédit Suisse First Boston (notice for amusement's sake that the last three are themselves products of mergers). The bankers' incentive to push for more consolidations is clear—in the Exxon/Mobil merger, for example, J. P. Morgan for Exxon and Goldman Sachs for Mobil split about $50 million for a few weeks' work.

Not that a lot of pushing is needed. CEOs, who tend to have egos about the size of a supernova, get a jollies-jolt from having their pictures splashed across the front pages of major dailies. The media splash lets them strut around the next Predators' Ball as the baddest merger men in the whole damn country.

Just as some people have to have the biggest, flashiest car on the block, executives develop one-upmanship rivalries. Some say that Edward Crutchfield Jr., CEO of the Charlotte-based First Union bank, put his empire at risk with too many ill-advised mergers because he was in a pecker-measuring contest with his crosstown rival Hugh McColl Jr., CEO of Charlotte-based NationsBank. McColl bought Boatman's bank of St. Louis; Crutchfield bought CoreStates Financial; McColl bought Barnett Banks of Florida; Crutchfield bought the Money Store; Crutchfield announced a thirty-story office tower to dominate the Charlotte skyline; McColl announced a forty-five-story skyscraper; Crutchfield then suggested he might erect a hundred-story edifice. Even ineptness seems to be a point of rivalry—just as First Union announced last May that it had suffered heavy financial losses and was toppling over into the ditch, NationsBank announced in the same month that it was staggering with the top-heavy load of its acquisitions, especially its merger with BankAmerica, which turns out to have had a number of land mines in its investment portfolio and to be burdened with out-of-date computer technology. (You would do more checking into the purchase of a $600 used pickup than some of these guys do into a $60 billion bank merger.) As one analyst said of First Union's buying binge: "This is a tale of ego run amok."

It is not simply ego, however, that fuels the executive urge to merge—it is visions of sugarplums dancing in their heads. This is where merging begets splurging. No child's Christmas fantasy can come near the reality of the payday that top executives arrange for themselves when cutting these deals. In November 1998, a double-trunk ad appeared in newspapers. Filling one page was a life-sized head shot of Jürgen Schrempp, CEO of Daimler-Benz, Germany's top auto company. On the opposite page was the well-groomed mug of Robert Eaton, CEO of Chrysler. Linking the two heads was a banner headline proclaiming "Vision Meets Vision." These two "visionaries" had just forged the DaimlerChrysler corporation through a $40 billion amalgamation operating under the new slogan "Expect the extraordinary."

The extraordinary thing in this transaction is that Chrysler's top brass literally turned themselves into gold, whether or not the merger proves to be successful for anyone else. Eaton is the most golden of them all—he got $3.7 million in cash right off the top, $70 million in stock grants, and $149 million worth of shares in the new DaimlerChrysler corporation. It was explained that this $223 million handout to Eaton was needed as incentive to keep him on the job for a couple of years to make sure the transition went smoothly. If he quits or is fired during this period, he would get another $24.4 million—plus, the company even pays the taxes on his golden parachute (and, since paying the taxes is considered compensation that itself is taxable, DaimlerChrysler also would pay Eaton's taxes on the taxes—not a lot is left to chance by these boys). One more sugarplum: The fifty-eight-year-old Eaton was awarded an extra $30,000 *a month* on his pension, bringing him to $1.7 million a year, every year, for the rest of his life. Making sure that none of you more cynical types misunderstood his motivation in selling America's number three car company to the Germans, the visionary Eaton felt compelled to state publicly that this merger was strictly about corporate efficiencies and shareholder value, "and obviously my own personal situation had no bearing whatsoever."

Generous to a fault, Eaton also took care of those below him. Not secretaries or line workers, you understand, but those in the suites adjacent to his: Robert Lutz, a Chrysler vice chairman, got a $62 million package from the merger; Gary Valade, Chrysler's chief financial officer, got $52 million; and Thomas Stallkamp, Chrysler's president, took $50 million.

Likewise, Lou Noto hit a big one. He's the Mobil CEO who peddled his company to Exxon in a deal bigger than the annual economic output of most of the world's countries. A spokesman told *The Wall Street Journal* that Noto pushed the sale solely because "it is in the best interests of the company" and that he "has never made decisions based purely on his own financial gain." Explain that to the nine-thousand-plus workers fired, who note that Noto's personal gain from the merger was about $16 million, including $7.8 million in severance, $2.1 million in "retention" pay, and $200,000 worth of "other" pay. Also, he gets $5.7 million to cover taxes on his package. In addition, don't forget the $33 million he gets in stock grants and the $12 million coming to him for his shares in Mobil. That's a total of about $66.6 million—clearly the work of the devil.

The quick-buck award goes to Robert Annunziata, who became CEO of Global Crossing Inc. last year, having been lured to the Bermuda-based telecommunications firm with a $10 million signing bonus, a $5 million low-interest loan to buy company stock, and a three-year employment contract at a million per. He didn't last. Within three *months*, Annunziata sold Global to the regional phone company U S West. He gets $135 million from the deal.

And so it goes—Sanford Weill and John Reed, the barons of Travelers and Citicorp taking $26 million each from their merger, which cost 10,400 workers their jobs; Richard Note-baert, who was paid $30 million when Southwestern Bell took over his Ameritech regional phone company, plus a special bonus of $2.5 million for "extra work" related to the merger, not counting $32 million in stock payments; Frank Newman, whose stewardship of Bankers Trust led to massive losses for the shareholders and layoffs for employees, getting $135 million in his sellout to Deutsche Bank; and William Esrey, the CEO of Sprint, who guided his company into the maw of MCI WorldCom, thereby enriching himself with a personal payout of nearly half a *billion* bucks, a record so far on the merger merry-go-round. "The corporate executive maximizes his own welfare first, the company's second," observes economist Walter Adams, "He doesn't ask himself what will the company look like ten years down the road if I negotiate this acquisition."

Lest I give the impression that merger mania produces absolutely no economic benefit outside of the executive suites, I hasten to point out a growth industry that has been spurred by all this M&A activity: sign making. With corporate names changing faster than some traffic lights, sign companies are busy covering the changes. Here in Austin, for example, the people who run the General Neon Sign Company were some of the few citizens who found a silver lining in the takeover of our First State Bank by faraway Norwest Bank. General Neon got the 1998 contract to bring down the blue-and-white signs at thirty-two First State branches, replacing them with the green-and-white emblems of Norwest. Barely a year later, General Neon is bidding to undo all the signage it just completed. Norwest has been acquired by Wells Fargo Bank, you see, and its colors are red and gold.

PIRATES. The poster boy for the merging and purging that is ripping so violently through our society could well be Gerry Cameron, a lesser light on the global corporate marquee, yet one whose actions pretty well sum up this sorry saga of greed.

Cameron was boss hog at U.S. Bancorp, based in Portland, Oregon, until May 1997, when it was announced that the bank was being absorbed by a grasping, national banking empire with the anonymous (and vaguely ominous) name of First Bank System Inc. Shortly after the takeover announcement, "The System's" CEO, John F. Grundhofer, uttered the words that sent a chill through the normally chill-hardy people of Portland: "By eliminating redundancies and increasing efficiency, we can improve service and offer a broader portfolio of products."

"Redundancies." Four thousand Oregonians were to be made redundant by the deal struck between Cameron and Grundhofer—one of the largest mass firings in the state's history. U.S. Bancorp's headquarters building in downtown Portland was to be emptied, with those functions being assumed by the new parent company in Minneapolis. U.S. Bancorp's credit-card processing center was to be shut down, too, with its functions moved to The System's own processing center in Fargo, North Dakota (rentals of the macabre movie *Fargo,* by the way, shot up dramatically in Portland video stores as word of the merger ripped through the city). Did Grundhofer say the firings were designed to "improve service"? Maybe he thought the people of Portland all rode into town on a turnip truck—in addition to four thousand fewer employees to serve the public, the merger plan included eliminating forty-four branch offices of the bank.

Gerry Cameron did prove to be a stand-up guy for one of U.S. Bancorp's employees, however: himself! The new, merged bank has Grundhofer as president and CEO, but a sly, smiling Cameron sitting next to him as chairman. It's not merely a title he gets—Gerry negotiated a sweetheart package that assures him the same $1.6 million annual salary and bonus he had been getting, a lump-sum payment of $12.4 million (sort of a gratuity for doing the deal), a grant of stock in the new company worth a good $8.6 million, and the payment of the taxes he owes on the entire generous package. Untold millions more were to come to him from profits he would gain by cashing in the stock he held in his old bank. Oh, one more lollipop: a cool million dollars a year for his retirement.

In a special touch of class, Cameron's $12.4 million gratuity was to be handed to him the same day those four thousand employees were to begin cleaning out their desks.

The workers and their families were not the only ones taking a hit for Cameron's merger maneuver. Other businesses in and around the U.S. Bancorp Tower were also rocked by the sudden blow: The janitorial and cleaning crews, for example, were faced with an uncertain period of empty floors and no work; Your Store, the coffee shop on the ground floor, had an immediate drop in business when Gerry's merger was announced, as did Grampy's, the sandwich shop across the street ("People are scared," Grampy's owner told the *Portland Oregonian*. "They don't know where they're going next"); higher up in the tower, the law firm and the accounting firm handling the bank's business were looking at their own job cuts; and business at Geranium Lake Flowers, which catered to bank employees, began declining as soon as the bad news hit, with one exception—it had a temporary uptick in orders for sympathy bouquets to be delivered to bank employees who were being fired.

When I hear about such voracious and reckless executives, so willing to enrich themselves at the expense of their co-workers, I find myself enraged and wanting to shout, "You bunch of pirates!" But then I realize that this is unfair. To pirates.

Not to romanticize the buccaneers of the high seas, but they practiced a form of floating democracy that was extraordinary compared to the way other businesses acted in those days . . . or in these days. Writer Bart Jones of AP has reported that pirates voted on such basic issues as whether to attack a particular ship and which direction to sail, and everyone on board got a fair share of the booty. Kenneth Kinkor, a historian who studies pirate records and their shipwrecks, says that the sharing of gains from pirate raids typically paid the captain two shares, the quartermaster one-and-a-half shares, and every crew member one share. By way of illustration, if $100,000 worth of loot was to be split among a ship with a hundred pirates, the captain would get about $2,000, some $1,500 would go to the quartermaster, and the other ninety-eight pirates would get about $1,000 each.

At the time, the captains of merchant ships were getting fifteen times more than the crew, and it was not uncommon for the sailors to get stiffed by the mercantile trading companies, ending up with nothing. Compare those captain-crew spreads to today's corporate captains, who routinely are taking 419 times what the typical "crew member" gets, and who have been regularly abandoning the crew in mergers and massive downsizings.

Pirate society was surprisingly civil in other ways, too. Who provided the first workers' compensation plan? None other than the notorious Captain Kidd, in 1695. It was common, says Kinkor, for pirates to be awarded a handsome disability payment by the captain and crew if they lost an arm or leg in battle, and widows sometimes got payments, too, when pirates were killed. There was even a remarkable level of racial equality—about a third of the pirates were black, mostly former slaves, and they were entitled to the same vote and the same share of the plunder as white crew members. Indeed, Kinkor found records of black pirates being chosen captains by crews that were mostly white. And, while these pillagers certainly could be vicious brutes, Jones reports that "pirates often treated prisoners decently to encourage other ships to surrender rather than fight to the death." (The black skull and crossbones of infamy was not raised as an attack flag but as a warning to surrender—an all-red flag was hoisted to say "here we come.") Jones also notes that "many pirate ships imposed rules such as no smoking below decks after sunset, lights out by eight, no women or boys aboard, and no gambling, which often led to fights."

Piracy, which lasted about fifty years over the late 1600s and early 1700s, was largely a rebellion against the enormous injustices and legalized thievery of the merchant shipping corporations and other respectable men of commerce, so it's not surprising that the maritime revolution offered an onboard social structure more humane than the autocratic and abusive one it was fleeing. Then, as today, the real pirates weren't the ones with eye patches and peg legs.

HAS ANYONE SEEN TEDDY? The massive mergers that are ongoing are the black holes of our economic universe, sucking money and power from everyone around them into the dark-star vortex of the corporate barons who are at the center. Industry after industry is succumbing to this downward swirl of competition that eliminates choice, raises prices, cuts jobs and wages, reduces the quality of service, stifles innovation, and permits tighter corporate control of the political system. The Establishment titillates us with the zing-pop-and-sizzle of computer technology that, we're assured, is breeding change faster than bunnies on Viagra, promising that this change is going to remake our economy and our drab little lives in ways we could not have imagined in the Olden Tymes of, say, 1998. But while they have us gazing numbly into the BillGatesian Future, they are busy grabbing, whacking, destroying, congloming, and conspiring to remake the global economy in their own private image—which is the image of Rockefeller, Gould, and Morgan. This awesome massing of power is by far the biggest and most threatening development to America's workers, small business, farmers, consumers—and to our democracy—in a century, yet there's not a peep about it from the political system. Neither party has merging and purging on their legislative agenda, nor is it on the 2000 election agenda.

There's a famous political cartoon of Teddy Roosevelt swinging his big club of antitrust, with assorted fat barons splayed at his feet, labeled Railroad Trust, Oil Trust, and so forth. While Roosevelt turned out to be more bluster than action in his trust-busting efforts (he took campaign funds from the very trust builders he was trying to bust, including $150,000 from J. P. Morgan in his 1904 presidential campaign, and he was a softy compared to the true populist challengers of corporate power, such as Wisconsin congressman "Battling Bob" La Follette), he nonetheless used the bully pulpit of his office to rally the public's seething anger at their imperious economic masters and to give the issue of unbridled corporate greed the national prominence it warranted. He did enough to cause steel magnate Henry Clay Frick to utter his famous complaint, "We bought the son of a bitch and then he didn't stay bought."

Modern-day barons have had no such problem with Bill Clinton, who has been perfectly content to stay on the porch and watch the big dogs run right over the middle class, offering not so much as a bark, much less a bite. Imagine Clinton calling Weill, McColl, Kravis, Perelman, Noto, Newman, Cameron, and the rest "the biggest criminals in the country," as Teddy once called Rockefeller and his fellow robbers. Why, that would be unthinkable, since these are people Clinton socializes with, golfs with, invites to formal White House dinners, sends on trade missions to Asia, consults with on both global and domestic economic policies, and, of course, raises money from. In a 1998 interview with *The Wall Street Journal,* Clinton simply shrugged his shoulders when asked about the furious rate of mergers sweeping the economic landscape, saying he thought it was "inevitable." What a giant. Thank God he's not in charge of the fire department.

Yes, there is the widely reported case against Microsoft's anticompetitive practices, pushed by the extraordinary Justice Department prosecutor David Boies to prove that there's at least one tooth left in the old watchdog. But Microsoft is a case of such egregious, arrogant, and stupid monopolistic abuse that even many in the computer industry wanted it brought, and it represents no awakening to the much more damaging and systemic corporate concentrations that are clobbering us in practically every industry. Indeed, Clinton has been squeamish and closed-mouthed about the Microsoft unpleasantness, seeming to wish it was not happening on his watch, and certainly not wanting it to prompt a larger political debate. The Clinton administration's antitrust policy is more wet noodle than big stick. It even has adopted two unique antitrust theories: One is that if merging companies can claim that internal corporate efficiencies will be gained, resulting in more profits for them, this private gain can be used to offset any social losses produced by the merger, such as jobs and consumer choice; the other theory is that "potential competition" can prevent merged giants from gouging consumers—a theory that conveniently allows Clinton's reluctant regulators to presume that other competitors will somehow arise from somewhere, sometime in the future, even though none are in sight.

Far from opposing the mating dances of corporate Goliaths, Washington actively encourages them. In 1995, for example, the Pentagon was so pleased that the giant weapons maker Lockheed was going to take over competitor Martin Marietta that it ponied up nearly a billion of our tax dollars to pay for the merger costs, including shelling out some $3 million in a bonus to Lockheed CEO Norman Augustine and $31 million more in bonuses to other top executives who engineered the merger—a combination that cost nineteen thousand workers their jobs. The government payouts to Augustine and the other executives were orchestrated by then-secretary of defense William Perry and his deputy John Deutch—both of whom had previously been highly compensated consultants to Martin Marietta and had a close personal relationship with Augustine.

(An interesting footnote to this government-induced merger is that one fellow who lost his job as a result of it went away with a big grin on his face: Lamar Alexander—the hapless candidate for the Republican presidential nomination! He had been a well-paid ex-board member. The merged company wanted a smaller board, so it paid Lamar $236,000 for agreeing *not* to serve on the new Lockheed Martin board.)

Washington also lent a helping hand in the 1997 creation of Citigroup, which for the first time since the depression brought a major bank (Citibank) together with a major insurance company (Travelers) and a major brokerage house (Solomon Smith Barney). This convergence of financial enterprises under one roof was hailed by Wall Street as "the future"—a conglomeration that could sell insurance to its banking customers, sell stocks to its insurance customers, and sell banking services to its stock customers. Unfortunately, the massive Citigroup merger was illegal at the time, specifically outlawed by provisions of the Bank Holding Company Act of 1956 and the Glass-Steagall Act of 1933. Bankers, stock speculators, and insurers have been kept apart because periodically one or the other of these three financial branches will step into deep doo-doo and slide toward the abyss of complete collapse. The concept is the same as on a kindergarten playground—you don't tie three kids together, because if one falls, they all go down. If, say, an insurance company is collapsing, it could raid the assets of its bank and brokerage to try to save itself, thus pulling down all three. Better to keep them apart. Yet, there were Citibank, Travelers, and Solomon—joining together.

How could they do this? Because they're By God CITI-GROUP, and the politicians and regulators looked the other way. Ralph Nader reports that Sanford Weill and John Reed, the co-CEOs of Citigroup, met with Federal Reserve chairman Alan Greenspan ten days prior to the announcement of their merger for a secret tête-à-tête to prevent any rude public questioning of their deal by impertinent regulators. Loopholes were found—not loopholes that actually fit this huge merger, but like a rhinoceros squeezing into panty hose, Citigroup was nonetheless squeezed through the available loopholes. Besides, said the winking politicians of both parties, we're planning to "modernize" those fussy old laws so the Citigroup deal will become perfectly legal after the fact. Three years later, however, the laws still have not been modernized, yet there stands Citigroup.

Imagine you trying this. Let's say you get caught smoking marijuana—a mood-altering product that many expect to be legalized someday. Do you think the country's drug prosecutors would stand by, letting you keep taking tokes by invoking the Weill-Reed defense of "it's gonna be legalized someday, man"? It's more likely that drug czar Barry McCaffrey would kiss Willie Nelson full on the lips at one of Willie's Fourth of July picnics than for that to happen.

The difference between you and the Citigroup executives can be quantified: $2,291,780. That's how much they've funneled into Republican and Democratic coffers in the last two years alone. You can add $17,003,000 to the tally also—that's how much they spent on lobbying fees since '97. (Ironically, one result of the Citigroup merger was a few pink slips for lobbyists. Citibank had twelve Washington lobbyists before the merger, plus having at least two outside lobbying firms on contract, while Travelers and Solomon Smith Barney had two lobbyists and three firms on contract. Now the combined company has a couple fewer lobbyists, but, with its size, an even more powerful impact on legislation and regulation.)

If you're hoping that, perchance, Al Gore, Bill Bradley, George W. Bush, or John McCain will take on Citigroup, don't. They've all taken campaign contributions from its executives or PACs. Overall, those who are doing the merging, purging, and splurging have put hundreds of thousands of dollars into Election 2000, which is why neither party will be mentioning merging, purging, and splurging—the biggest structural change taking place in our economy.

CEOs WITHOUT A CLUE

A bumper sticker asserts: "It's lonely at the top, but you do eat better."

We should only know. We peasants are rarely allowed even a peek over the walls into the compounds of privilege where America's corporate royalty lives and plays. But I have my sources, so I can offer the following unbelievable-but-true glimpse into the lifestyle and mind-set of those at the very top. To protect the person who brought this on-the-scene report to me, I've made up names—call him Bob, and call his firm the GlobalGigantica Fund.

GGF is a major Wall Street investment outfit that annually curries a bit of tax-deductible favor with its corporate clients by laying on a lavish three-day golf outing and pig-fest. It's held at someplace like Faraway Shorthills-on-Hudson, one of the posh resorts where demanding executives get the pampering (an old hometown buddy of mine calls it "poodling") that they've come to consider their due. The 1999 GlobalGigantica affair drew an air show's worth of $35–$50 million Gulfstream executive jets to the resort's private landing strip, and each CEO from various brand-name baronies of our country would disembark like a proper potentate, step into a waiting stretch-chariot, and be whisked to his spacious cabaña, there to be afforded all the amenities that money can command.

Nothing surprising so far in our narrative—this is about the level of gross indulgence you might imagine them getting. But now is when Bob enters the picture and the wretched excess gets weird. Along with several other bright young executives on the rise in the GGF hierarchy, Bob was given the honor of spending time prior to the golf-o-rama weekend tending to a myriad of details, making certain that absolutely nothing unpleasant would intrude into the consciousness of the VIP guests. Among Bob's duties was product-advance. This involves obtaining a list of all products manufactured or marketed by the company of each of the visiting CEOs. The appropriate brand names are then meticulously placed in the various suites of the executives—you don't want the head of Procter & Gamble, say, to open his bathroom medicine cabinet and suffer the indignity of finding Colgate toothpaste rather than his firm's Crest brand, do you? You certainly do not. Nor should the top man at Philip Morris, maker of Miller beer, be sickened by the sight of a Michelob in his cabaña's fridge. And you can imagine how traumatic it would be for the CEO of WestPoint Stevens textiles to freshen up when he arrives by splashing water on his face, then towel off before realizing, too tragically late, that he has a Fieldcrest towel in his hands.

Creating the perfect in-room product ambiance was the easy part for Bob. What about the resort's kitchen, the pro shop, the bars? Each one was its own field of land mines ready to destroy a CEO's fragile state of mind. The maker of Tylenol needs to be on the tee thinking "left arm straight, head down, smooth follow-through," not murmuring darkly, "Bayer aspirin, these goddamn goofballs at GGF are taunting me with Bayer goddamn aspirin in the gift shop."

From golf balls to cigarettes, from cereal to wine, the right brands had to be front and center, and the wrong brands had to disappear from the entire resort. How to make this happen? Al Capone once instructed: "You can get much further with a kind word and a gun than you can with a kind word alone." No, Bob didn't use a gun. That's not (usually) the corporate way. He did the job the old-fashioned way: with a kind word . . . and corporate cash. He was furnished a large sum of dollars by GlobalGigantica to spread bribes liberally among the kitchen manager, the golf pro, the bartenders, the director of procurement, and other key personnel to, as Bob expressed it, "cleanse the commercial landscape."

It would be one thing if Bob's story was about one wild and wacky weekend—a special splurge for very self-important people—but he and others can confirm that such white-glove treatment is no longer exceptional, that it is a fair reflection of the deference now accorded the executives who, despite our democratic pretensions, have emerged atop America's economic, social, and political structure. When it comes to making decisions that matter, it's not public officials who are the arbiters but these CEOs and their financiers. Let's admit it, we have a royalty! It's not an inherited royalty—à la the queens and other poobahs of the world—but it's nonetheless authoritarian and antidemocratic, being self-selected from inside maybe a thousand private firms by self-perpetuating boards of directors. Top executives are like sultans, each one living a protected and pampered life while exercising practically unchecked power over people and communities. At the same time, each one is collecting millions of dollars every year in pay and perks—part of the tribute that comes to them as a result of their global raids on workers, consumers, the environment, their competitors, and our government treasuries. They rule the world, yet they are not in the world. Their positions and their fortunes isolate them from the rest of us and from ever having to come face-to-face with the consequences of what they do to us by corporate fiat.

MILLIONAIRES, SCHMILLIONAIRES. I'm talking here about power wealth, not mere millionaires. Four million Americans have attained millionaire status, but this does not put most of them in the neighborhoods of the power elites (I mean, one Silicon Valley zip code—94062, Woodside, California—is reported to have 250,000 millionaires tucked into it. How common. Silicon trash, I say). Instead, I'm talking about the top partners at Goldman Sachs and other Wall Street brokerages who're knocking down $25–$50 million a year each; I'm talking about annual paychecks of more than $50 million being hauled home by the likes of Charles Heimbold at Bristol-Myers Squibb, Sanford Weill at Citigroup, M. Douglas Ivester at Coca-Cola, Reuben Mark at Colgate-Palmolive, and

Jack Welch at General Electric; I'm talking about head Mouseketeer Michael Eisner at Disney taking $287,000 in 1998—*an hour* (total pay of $575,292,100); I'm talking about the $625 million it took in 1999 to rank number four hundred on the *Forbes* magazine list of the four hundred richest Americans; I'm talking about the 268 Americans who are *billionaires;* I'm talking about J. Paul Getty, who said, "If you can count your money, you don't have a billion dollars."

By the way, how much is a billion bucks? Think of it in terms of time:

- A billion *seconds* ago, it was 1969.
- A billion *minutes* ago, Jesus was walking in Galilee.
- A billion *hours* ago, no one walked upright on earth.

How far away from terra firma does such income and wealth put you? Ask John K. Castle: "One of the things about my lifestyle is that I don't want to know what anything costs. Once you're well-to-do," he told *The Wall Street Journal,* "price doesn't really make any difference."

In the 1980s, Castle was president and CEO of Donaldson, Lufkin & Jenrette Inc., the Wall Street investment bank that financed many of the corporate takeover schemes back then that resulted in thousands of people losing their jobs. Lost jobs were just collateral damage, though—the *Journal* reports that Castle kept the original drawing of a *New Yorker* cartoon on his wall that declared: "Money is life's report card." Give John an A+, for he has amassed a personal fortune that is circumspectly described as "well in excess of $100 million." He now spends wads of money on adventurous travel, thoroughbred horses, and houses, among other fancies. In 1995, he bought his fourth house—the thirteen-thousand-square-foot Florida oceanfront home in Palm Beach, Florida, that had belonged to the Kennedy family and had served as JFK's winter White House. The *Journal* says that Castle now delights in letting visiting CEOs plop down on the assassinated president's personal bed and in occasionally sending out letters written on stationery printed with his name and the words "Winter White House."

What is it about houses? There seems to be a wealth gene that involuntarily causes the recipients (of the gene and of the wealth) to pursue a "mine is bigger than yours" building program. Anyone who has traveled to Newport, Rhode Island, and cruised by the "summer cottages" built by the Vanderbilts, Astors, Kings, Oelrichs and other Robber Barons of a century ago have seen this historic gene in action—the "cottages" are massive, ornate, and, some would say, grotesque mansions—examples of taste being trumped by wealth, in spades.

Some things never change. Today, a favored expression of edifice-erectile envy by your modern barons is the infamous "teardown"—spend millions to buy a place, knock the old mansion down, then spend millions more to construct something bigger and/or elaborately ugly in its place. Steven Wallace is exemplary here. He sold his Pacific Brokerage Services to Mellon Bank in 1997, then got the edifice-erectile itch and bought Jimmy Stewart's old 6,300-square-foot Italian-style villa in Beverly Hills for $5.6 million. A couple of months later, Jimmy's house was gone, nothing left but a hole in the ground. Rosemary Clooney, who lives just up the street, was out of town when Wallace's hired bulldozers did the destructive deed, but she says she was saddened by the loss of her old movie friend's 1928 house: "If only we'd known," she said to the *New York Times,* "we'd have taken a brick or something." No time for sentimentality, though, for Mr. Wallace said Stewart's house had cracks in it and "was just a dump. How he could have lived there I don't know." No problem—Jimmy's dead, the house is gone, and Wallace has built a new 12,800-square-foot structure with a three-car garage. It's "kind of an Italian villa," he says, noting that it's new but built to look old. Plus, he hired Jimmy Stewart's maid as his own. Ah, tradition.

A man's home might be his castle, but even castles have problems. The difference between the wealthy and us is that they don't have to deal with these problems personally—they hire people to do that. Barry Gesser, a Wall Street hedge-fund manager (don't ask) found the house he wanted in the posh town of Bedford, New York, but he wanted it renovated and decorated so it would be loaded with personality and cause visitors to go "wow." Problem was, he apparently isn't loaded with personality himself: "We Wall Streeters want the best," Barry told the *New York Times*. "We want to buy the right stuff, but we don't necessarily know what it is. I figured if anyone knows what the right stuff is, they do," he said of the two pricey Manhattan decorators he hired to "do" his new ten-bedroom manse, which came with a pool house, stables, tennis courts, and not one three-car garage but two. His personality outfitters assembled a team of 170 people who saw to every detail—the monogramming of mint julep cups for Gesser, choosing the right clothes hangers, stocking his paneled library with books they selected for him, bringing in peacocks to strut about the terraced lawns, registering him as a member of the local historical society, and buying picture frames and knickknacks to add the homey touch. The only thing they asked of Barry was for personal photos to go in the frames. The house was done, the guests were arriving for the Fourth of July housewarming party he was throwing—and still he had not furnished the photos. So, the *Times* reports, one of the decorators put various snapshots of his Chihuahua, Pancho, into the frames. About a year later, Barry bought a multi-million-dollar town house on Manhattan's Upper East Side, and he asked the same decorators to "do" it for him. They met to discuss arrangements with Gesser at the Bedford house and noticed that Pancho was still there in the picture frames, providing loads of personality.

Now here's a problem all homeowners can identify with: a leaky roof. Aaron Spelling, the television mogul, however, doesn't simply have a roof over his Holmby Hills manor in Los Angeles. He has a "roof system." He and his wife, Candy, bought and bulldozed Bing Crosby's estate to build their 56,500-square-foot "house," which is approximately the size of the U.S. Capitol. Just the roof cost $5 million. And it leaks. So the Spellings' lawyers are suing everyone in sight. This is not Aaron's only complaint about the craftsmanship on a home that includes a bowling alley, a personal doll museum, and a gift-wrapping room. He previously protested that the bowling balls provided for them were too heavy.

The award for "Whiniest Executive with a Huge House," however, goes to my fellow Austinite, Michael Dell. He's the namesake of Dell Computer Corporation, and his personal fortune is a few hundred million above $16 billion. He and his wife, Susan, had an earthmoving firm scrape off the top of one of Austin's scenic hills west of town so they could have a relatively flat surface of sixty acres on which to build a sprawling, thirty-three-thousand-square-foot edifice. The thing is three stories of concrete-granite-limestone-and-steel construction, with eight full bathrooms, thirteen half-baths, a conference room, a kitchen big enough to hold Paul Prudhomme *and* Emeril Lagasse, an exercise room, an indoor pool, an outdoor pool, cabañas, a three-story spiral staircase, separate quarters for domestic help, and a five-level terraced lawn. I've not been inside, but I can report that the outside looks like a combination conference center and a strip shopping mall, though without the charm. As the Yiddish proverb puts it: "If you want to know what God thinks of money, look at the people he gives it to."

The ugliest part, however, was not the house, but Dell's little tax tantrum. The billionaire computer tycoon built the place to show his billions as ostentatiously as possible, but then he tried to weasel out of paying his full and fair share of local property taxes, which fund everything from our schools to the county roads going out and up to his Xanadu. Of course, the Dells have their children in private schools, but it has always struck me as curious that computer barons like him (Bill Gates is another who has tried to duck the tax bill on his Taj Mahal outside Seattle) moan so loudly about the American education system's failure to turn out enough graduates with the skills to fill the cubicles in their high-techie empires, yet they are the first to unleash the sharp-fanged hounds from their legal and lobbying departments to avoid paying their share of the cost. If hypocrites could fly, they'd be jumbo jets.

The Dells' house is the most expensive in Texas, and I'm counting Ross Perot's! Michael and Susan didn't skimp on architects, landscaping, interior decorators, furnishing, or anything else to build their palace—they only got cost conscious when their tax bill arrived. The initial estimate by the county tax appraiser was that the thing on the hill was worth about $22 million, which would mean (based on the flat-tax rate that everyone in Austin pays) that the Dells owed some $600,000 in school, county, and city property taxes. For you and me, that's a lot of money, but for this thirty-three-year-old who paid himself $1.4 *billion* in 1998 (the largest one-year paycheck ever recorded for a CEO, according to compensation expert Graef Crystal) and who sits on a burgeoning net worth of $16 billion, it was pocket change (the equivalent of 42 cents for a family whose net worth is $30,000—the national median).

But he squawked like a little red rooster, siccing his lawyers, accountants, appraisers, and other hirelings on the local appraisal board, asserting that his showcase estate was really worth only around $6 million. Since there are no houses locally or even in the state to compare his "very unique property" to, the county had to hire Vickie Gill from California, who is an acclaimed expert known as "the appraiser of the rich and famous." (She had assessed Aaron Spellings' leaky-roof temple, O.J.'s Brentwood estate, and Donnie Trump's Palm Beach digs, among others, and she once appraised the chateau of an executive whose self-esteem and extravagance were such that he had a beveled glass skylight installed in the shower to create the illusion of a crown on the owner's head when the sun beamed in.) With the Dells, though, Ms. Gill really had her work cut out, since it took a year of negotiations by Dell's nitpicking and stalling legal team before she was allowed to step on the property. Even then, she and a videographer were given only three hours to scamper through the place, as opposed to the twenty-four hours it normally takes to do such a large job. Still, with the videos, she was able to make her calculations and present her expert opinion: $15 million. No way, wailed Dell, and his lawyers resumed snapping and snarling at everyone who was vexing their deep-pocketed client. At long last and at great expense to us taxpayers, the opera ended last year when the county's own hard-pressed appraiser agreed to come down to $12 million. Since Dell is also entitled to a $2.4 million "homestead exemption" on his billionaire's bungalow, he actually ended up with a taxable value of $9.6 million.

This was not Michael Dell's first petulant brush with the real world. In 1993, he stamped his little feet and demanded that the city of Austin provide more than $100 million worth of tax breaks and other special benefits to his company or he would move his sales, service, and support operations elsewhere. He was acting like a spoiled brat, and, to their credit, the local council members didn't surrender to his highway robbery. This put him in such a snit that he moved just across the county line to the town of Round Rock, where he got everything but the rock for which the place is named: $50 million to construct buildings, twenty years of property tax abatements, waiver of city permit fees, and a kickback of half of the sales taxes the company would owe the town. His public petulance and demand for tribute was such an embarrassment that Lee Walker, the former president of Dell Computer Corporation, felt compelled to express his disgust in an op-ed piece: "Our community has nurtured and supported Dell from its infancy, and we deserve better than to be regarded as just another cost center to be managed. We need corporations that are committed to staying in Austin and that regard paying their full burden to the common good as a necessary and desirable responsibility. We need corporations that deeply believe that paying one penny less for our schools, police, and fire protection is a false saving. We need corporations that will lead us by example, not tell us through their actions that might makes right."

THE MONEY POWER. Mark Twain once observed: "Make enough money and the whole world will conspire to call you a gentleman." America's corporate barons—no less than the Robber Barons of a century ago, and no less than the royal barons of the Middle Ages who lived in splendor off the labor of serfs—are obsequiously referred to and deferred to in gentlemanly terms by politicians of both political parties, the media (which is its own barony), the leaders of academia hustling for spare corporate change, the clergy with its always needy building fund, civic and charitable organizations seeking favor, and practically every other part of the social order— save the people themselves.

There's a local gentleman's club (i.e., a titty bar with airs) called the Show Palace. It regularly runs a newspaper ad that highlights its "Gourmet Kitchen," its limousine service to and fro, and, demurely, its "Exotic Entertainers." Occasionally, though, the ad will blow the club's sophisticated cover by including a special promo for such upcoming events as: "Wed. May 5th OIL WRESTLING MANIA!!!" In similar fashion, the country's establishment institutions can conspire to call corporate and financial CEOs "gentlemen," but polls and experience show that ordinary people see these barons for what they are—aristocratic authoritarians who routinely run roughshod over anyone who gets in their way.

This is not to say that, personally, CEOs are all a bunch of heartless bastards, but they have willingly clambered atop a corporate system that flatly rejects any suggestion that its executives have any responsibility whatsoever to anyone except major corporate shareholders—an elite group that includes the CEOs. The system unapologetically insists that the sole goal of those at the top is to increase the price of stocks, no matter who else gets hurt. Hearts be damned. The operating corporate ethic is that maybe might doesn't make right, but if you're mighty enough you sure as hell can beat right to a pulp, and make a pretty penny for yourself while you're doing it. I'm sure that most of these CEOs (I know a few) are sweet to their families, love puppies, and have a gentle inner child within them—but that's not who goes to the office.

Not only are these people enriching themselves with absurd levels of loot by being as ruthless as they wanna be or gotta be, but they also operate in a rarefied atmosphere that seals them from having to be aware of, much less accountable for, the havoc they wreak on others. Corporate headquarters is like a castle of old—there's a moat of carefully crafted laws that encircles the HQ, separating the top executive's actions from any legal responsibility for the consequences; there's always a gaggle of staff and servants saying "yessir" and ready to hop to every need of the chief, including handling personal chores like buying gifts for the children's birthdays and anything that requires standing in line—CEOs don't do lines; there's a hand-selected coterie of counselors called the board of directors that gathers ceremonially from time to time to authorize whatever plunder the CEO has in mind; there are palace guards everywhere, both electronic and human, to keep the masses from getting close and to fend off any aggression (in these times of global unrest and downsizing, the Pinkertons and other agents are increasingly being hired by such firms as AT&T, General Motors, The Limited, and UPS to provide "executive protection," which can top $1,000 a day in expenses); there are the golden chariots, including the dark-tinted chauffeured limousines and the fully appointed company jets and helicopters, which let the executive go anywhere without hassle, either zipping through or flying over neighborhoods and communities where depression, impoverishment, anger, or other unpleasantness reside; and there are skilled attendants in the royal court to powder and puff the image of the CEO whenever a decision goes awry and creates a public fuss—it was only after Microsoft's bullying business practices landed the company in a widely publicized antitrust trial, for example, that Bill Gates suddenly started appearing in fuzzy, self-deprecating, regular-Joe ads about his golf game and that he just as suddenly became both a celebrity philanthropist and a million-dollar contributor to Washington politicians.

Isolated by their phenomenal wealth and power, the barons issue decrees from on high that enhance their own wealth and power, without ever having to see the fallout. From the seventy-fifth floor of a Manhattan skyscraper comes some edict like "The executive committee approves the FC–7.g site for the new repository for manufacturing parings and production remnants." Translation: An unsuspecting, poor neighborhood in East St. Louis is about to get a cancer-causing toxic-waste dump as a neighbor. From the corporate campus of a *Fortune* 500 firm comes an obscure notice to shareholders that "the board of directors has authorized a fourth-quarter charge of $800 million against earnings." Translation: 4,100 employees will receive pink slips in December—Happy Holidays. Of course, the CEO, the executive committee, and the board of directors will never go to East St. Louis and will never see the faces or the families of the 4,100 terminated people, nor will those people ever get to confront the ones who did this to them or discover how much money the CEO reaped personally from the decision.

Last year, Burlington Industries announced it was closing its textile plants in Mooresville, Forest City, Oxford, Cramerton, and Statesville, North Carolina, as well as plants in Bishopville, South Carolina, and Hillsville, Virginia. In one blow—BAM!—2,900 jobs were gone. These seven are tiny towns, with populations like 2,008 (Hillsville), 7,475 (Forest City) and 3,560 (Bishopville). To lose a plant employing some four hundred people at maybe $9–10 an hour is like a nuclear bomb going off in the very heart of these small communities. Whole families will have to pick up and move, the others will be lucky to get $6-an-hour jobs, the corner grocery will close, the church collections will drop. Did Burlington's executive committee decide it didn't need this amount of manufacturing capacity? No, it decided it didn't need it in the U.S. of A.— while shutting these seven plants, Burlington was spending $300 million to build seven low-wage plants in Mexico, all of which arc to makc clothing for sale in the United States. A Wall Street analyst was delighted with the executive decision, commenting that the job slashing here at home should put Burlington "in good shape." Tell that to the good people of Mooresville, Forest City, Oxford, Cramerton, Statesville, Bishopville, and Hillsville. Meanwhile, Burlington's CEO, George W. Henderson III, was paid more than $3 million last year, plus being given stock options in Burlington worth at least $1.6 million. No matter how the employees, the communities, or even the company fare, George truly is "in good shape."

Being CEO means never having to say I'm sorry, even when you screw up. Jerry McMorris is a multimillionaire trucking magnate in Denver, as well as part owner and chairman of the Colorado Rockies baseball team. One of his trucking companies, NationsWay Transport Service Inc., was a successful regional firm with some 6,500 employees until Jerry began making what some say were strategic business mistakes around 1993, about the time he got involved in the Rockies. For the past few years, while McMorris became a peer of Denver's downtown establishment, NationsWay drivers and other workers have been suffering through a series of downsizings, delayed payment of wages, deteriorating working conditions, and a continuing squabble with the CEO over money he owed their pension plan. The final blade fell on May 20, 1999, when the remaining three thousand workers were issued letters coldly stating: "Employment is terminated today." McMorris had filed for bankruptcy protection that day, owing the pension fund $4 million.

"The guy just let everybody down. He let things go," said Mike Martin, a driver who'd been with NationsWay for four-teen years. "He'd never admit it, but in the last six years, he's made some damn poor management decisions," twelve-year veteran Rick Smidt told the *Denver Post*. "Jerry McMorris does not know the people he has hurt," said Bob Vigil, who had driven for the company for twenty-two years. Even company supervisors were stunned: "I have no plans at the moment. I didn't anticipate this, and I'm totally unprepared for the future," one said.

For Jerry, however, things were not nearly so bleak. "I have not personally guaranteed anything or cross-collateralized any-thing," he told a press conference, explaining that he and his legal team had taken care to build corporate firewalls between NationsWay and his personal fortune, as well as between the failed company and his other businesses. So he screws up, costs thousands of people their jobs (and maybe their pen-sions), yet he's off the hook, still holding two other trucking companies, ranches and farms covering fifty-three thousand acres, and the baseball team. "I plan on being here at the Rockies full-time as early as next week," McMorris told the media when he announced the demise of NationsWay.

It is certainly true that such aloofness, arrogance, and abuse by the economic elites is not new in the relatively brief trial of American democracy. "The money power preys upon the nation," said a weary Abraham Lincoln, who had experi-enced the likes of J. P. Morgan, a banker's son who bought five thousand defective rifles for $3.50 each from a U.S. Army arsenal, resold them to a Union general in the field for $22 each, and skipped away to the bank with his profit while the rifles exploded in the hands of soldiers who fired them. (Historian Howard Zinn notes that Morgan himself had bought his way out of military service in the Civil War by paying $300 for a substitute, as had such other Robber Barons-to-be as John D. Rockefeller, Andrew Carnegie, and James Mellon—indeed, Mellon's father wrote a letter to him stating the elitist case frankly: "A man may be a patriot without risking his own life or sacrificing his health. There are plenty of lives less valuable.") Lincoln added that the money power "is more despotic than monarchy, more insolent than aristocracy, more selfish than bureaucracy. It denounces, as public enemies, all who question its methods or throw light upon its abuses."

The difference between Lincoln's day and ours is that, back then, there were national politicians willing to question the money powers rather than suck up to them.

WHEN TOO MUCH IS NOT ENOUGH

Ted Turner—the media mogul, sports owner, philanthropist, and famous husband—was being interviewed in 1998 by the *New York Times* about his underwriting of the Goodwill Games. This quadrennial event, which is sort of an Olympics for the world's professional track-and-field stars, had bled a $100-million river of red ink in the dozen years Turner had been financing it, and the *Times* reporter wanted to know if this loss bothered him. In answer, Turner jumped up from his chair, darted over to his computer, and checked the price on the sixty million shares of Time Warner stock he owns. "Ha!" he exclaimed, turning back to the reporter, eyes twinkling. On that one day, he made $120 million on his stock.

This is impossible to fathom for most of us. Let's say you work from the time you're twenty years old until retiring at sixty-five and that you made $30,000 in each of those years, which is what the typical American earns. In your lifetime of work, then, you would bring in roughly $1.3 million—about a hundred times less than Ted landed in *one day* without lifting a finger.

How to spend such money? Of course, you can't. If you had a billion dollars, and spent $100,000 a day, every single day of the year, it would take you twenty-eight years to deplete your fund. Ted has $8 billion. Still, those with power wealth do buy things, just like the rest of us, sort of:

UNDIES. Eddie Arcaro, the champion jockey who hung out with a lot of rich people and made some bucks himself, has observed that "once a guy starts wearing silk pajamas, it's hard to get up early." Well, who says you've got to get up—you're rich! But no matter how rich you are, there are certain basics you've got to have, like underwear. Silk is nice, but would it be enough? No. For the truly rich, mere silk is as plebeian as popping into Kmart to pick up a couple of packets of Jockey undies on sale. For your undergarments, you want something much more distinctive, like the $3 million bra offered by Victoria's Secret. This extraspecial Miracle bra has been available the past couple of years during the holiday season, and the miracle is that "some" have been sold (such sales info is one of Victoria's secrets, we're told). Apparently, the attraction is that this item of intimate luxury is somehow or other bedecked with rubies and diamonds set in platinum. If you have to ask how to wash the thing, you can't afford it.

CARRYOUT. Sheesh, you can't eat at Lespinasse or some other four-star restaurant *every* night, and sometimes you get tired of the concoctions of your home chef—what you really want is a yummy pizza or Chinese carryout from your favorite joint. If you've felt this way before, then you know why Steve Wynn, the billionaire baron of gambling casinos, has been known to send his Gulfstream jet from his Sun Valley chateau back to Las Vegas to pick up some Chinese food for him. The thousand-mile round-trip sets Steve back more than $5,000. But when you get the hungries, you can't let a few bucks get in the way. Know what I mean?

PETS. What kind of human being would you be to pamper yourself, yet let your pooch live like a common dog? It just won't do, so you buy the Gucci. The same purveyor of luxury apparel that sells $300 loafers also makes the ultimate in pillowed comfort for the privileged canine: a doggie bed that's twenty-four by sixteen inches, made of Lucite with a stainless-steel frame. The bed and mattress go for $1,490. Well, it *is* a Gucci. But you won't want to stop there. Gucci also offers a matching set of stainless-steel food and water bowls with their own Plexiglas tray that attaches right onto the bed frame—$1,100 for the set, not including Perrier water. To complete the package, go ahead and get the rabbit-fur pillow for only $395. The total tab to bed down Fido in Gucci style: $2,985.

SPORTS. The thing is not merely to engage in a suitable sport (yachting, polo, golfing, horse racing, mountain climbing, competitive ballooning), but to make a power statement with your sport of choice. Any fool with enough money and the proper corporate ties, for example, can join an exclusive golf club, but Wayne Huizenga raised the bar a notch for his fellow billionaire golfing buddies. The CEO of AutoNation bought his own country club in exclusive Palm City, Florida, registering him and his wife, Marti, as the sole members. It's a two-thousand-acre spread with an eighteen-hole golf course, a fifty-five-thousand-square-foot clubhouse, three helicopter pads, two guest houses, and sixty-eight yacht slips. Still, nothing says wealth like polo, and Mickey Tarnopol not only plays, he also bought Team Revlon, a pro polo team that operates out of the tony Hamptons on far-out Long Island. Tarnopol, the vice chairman of the Wall Street investment house Bear Stearns, foots the bill of some $2 million a year for fielding the professional team, and he also insists on playing, even though he rates only a "1" on the sports skill-rating scale of 0 (truly bad) to 10 (excellent). "It's in my blood," Tarnopol told *The Wall Street Journal*. At least he hasn't tried to own the very name "polo." Leave that to Ralph Lauren, the billionaire marketer of upscale clothing and other stuff bearing the Polo logo, which features a little polo man and horse. Lauren himself doesn't have any involvement with the sport, but nonetheless his stable of corporate lawyers have gone after *POLO,* the official magazine of the U.S. Polo Association. They claim that the magazine is violating Polo Ralph Lauren Inc.'s. trademark on the word. The editors fired back with their own lawyers and this riposte: "Who is the interloper here? Ours is the game of polo, but his seems to be monopoly. Get a grip, Mr. Lauren, not a stranglehold. If you decided to call yourself Football Ralph Lauren, does that mean you can keep others from using the word football? Let's get real. Just because Mr. Lauren chose to change his name from Ralph Lifshitz does not mean that we are willing and able to give up ours." The case still is in the hands of lawyers, which is the main thing wealthy CEOs spend their money on.

BATHROOMS. Ask your regular working family living with their kids in tight quarters what they'd most like to have, and chances are they'll snap back with "another bathroom." The same with your corporate clites, though it's not the number of bathrooms that concerns them (they have at least a couple per person), but the self-indulgent opulence therein. And please don't call theirs a bathroom. It's a "clean suite," according to *New York Times* "House & Home" reporters. You can have your modernistic, white-tiled, two-room bathing sanctuary, featuring a spacious sitting room with daybed and chair in one part and, in the other part, an elegant cleaning complex with silver-plated appointments, a two-sink "prep station," and a shower large enough to wash your SUV. Or, if you love the luxury of a good tub soak, go for the Romanesque bath suite, including a tub ensconced within a two-step limestone-and-mosaic platform and surrounded by walnut bookcases holding volumes conveniently enveloped in plastic for your watery reading pleasure.

AIR TRAVEL. Not first class, chum, but *your* class. CEOs don't stand in line (even though first-class ticket holders now get to board before children, people with infants, and people with disabilities) and they don't wait on someone else's schedule—they have their own planes. Nathan Myhrvold, the billionaire CTO (chief technology officer) at Microsoft, loved the high-flying world of corporate jets so much that he bought his own jet, then penned an almost orgasmic article in *Vanity Fair* about how everyone should buy one. Titled "My First Gulfstream," Myhrvold tells us how he paid $10 million for a used Gulfstream III, then had it custom redesigned: Italian faucets for the lavatory; $25,000 for a hand-woven carpet by the top carpet weaver in the world; halogen reading lights for $15,000; two flat-screen TV sets costing $36,000; $100,000 for a digital telephone and $20,000 more for a fax machine adapter; $80,000 for a sound-absorbing floor pad. Nathan gushed about the work done by Lee, his interior designer: "In the end, every stitch of fabric in the plane was custom-woven. The plates in the galley were custom-designed and painted in Austria to match the stripe Lee did for the exterior. Much of the leather was custom-dyed, and Lee traveled to the sawmill to select the logs that would be turned into veneer." Total tab for the interior re-do was $2 million. Then there's operational costs—half a million a year to hire the crew and mechanic, rent a hangar, pay insurance, etc., and that's without flying anywhere! At $2,500 an hour to put the Gulfstream III in the air, Myhrvold's travel is an extravagance, but he points out that "in bulk, jet fuel . . . is actually cheaper than Diet Coke." He says it costs him $1.5 million a year in fuel and operating costs, but it's worth it: "A trip across the country is now no

more daunting than hopping in the car for a drive. I can
attend an event in Santa Barbara, a party in Chicago, and a
meeting in Manhattan in as many days without breaking a
sweat. It's no longer a big deal to pop down the coast to have
dinner with somebody.... My view of geography has been
fundamentally transformed."

TOYS. It's your boy's tenth birthday. How about getting him
that toy car you saw advertised? Not the one that scoots
around on command of a handheld radio transmitter. That's
fun, but he can't get in it and ride it, like he can with the
Range Rover for kids. I'm talking about the real thing—a
quarter-sized Range Rover that'll do 20 mph. It has a five-
horsepower gasoline motor, leather upholstery, and an AM-FM
radio. At $18,500, it costs more than a Ford Taurus.

VACATIONS. The rich are not merely different than you
and me, they're weird. You would assume that they vacation
at posh hideaway resorts where they are pampered with every
luxury, and they certainly do go to such places. But they also
go to such places as the Meridian Club in the Caribbean. *The
Wall Street Journal* reports that the club is on a private island
and caters to the hoity-toity set. Yet, its rooms have no television or radio, no telephone, no air-conditioning, and not much
of anything. It's "almost like a motel room," says one guest
who returns to the Meridian Club every year. Yes, but you can
get a Motel Six for under $50 a night—the Meridian charges
$675 a night! You can get room service, says a club
spokesman, "but it's just a waiter with a tray. There's no silver
dome." Such places are called "downscale deluxe" by the
upscale hospitality trade, and they've become very trendy.
Nonamenities in these less-is-more resorts include no golf, no
tennis, no drinks at poolside, no fax, no e-mail, no newspaper,
no bedtime chocolates, and, if there is a TV, *no remote control.*
Primitive. One guest at an upstate New York resort paid

$1,200 for a weekend stay and got a room she described as being decorated in the Bates Motel motif right out of *Psycho*.

SOUP. Proving that "excess" now must be redefined when dealing with the consumption patterns of those at the top, Lespinasse, one of New York City's swankiest restaurants, began about a year ago to charge $35, not for an entrée, but for a bowl of soup. "Thirty-five dollars?" responded another upscale restaurateur when queried about it by the *New York Times*. "You sure that's for one person? Maybe it's for six." No, it's one bowl for one person, literally moving luxury spending from soup to nuts.

"America now has the strongest economy in the history of the United States," beamed Al Gore last June when he launched his presidential drive. Bill Bradley, George Bush, John McCain, and the rest of the Election 2000 menagerie pretty much concede the point, as though it was true. Like the media, politicians swallow whole the monthly statistics about consumer spending reaching ever higher heights, never questioning what's inside the numbers, like a $5,000 Chinese carryout and a $3 million bra, and never publicly engaging the reality that most people's "unbridled consumption" is a struggle to meet the basics—food, rent, utilities, clothing, and transportation—and that a growing portion of their spending is being put on already strained credit. Nor do the political and media sparklies ask the obvious questions of how an economy can be strong when it is destroying the mass-production jobs of the middle class and pretending that selling foreign-made $3,000 dog beds and $18,500 toy Range Rovers is a positive contribution to our gross domestic product. And certainly don't expect candidates of either party to challenge the fact that we ordinary taxpayers are subsidizing the multiple homes of the corporate barons (with their clean suites), their corporate jets fueled by Diet Cola, and their power lunches (that start with $35 bowls of soup).

GLOBALIZATION
IS GLOBALONEY

"Alice in Wonderland" almost killed me.

I was but a small boy when my mother took my brother Jerry and me to the Rialto theater to see the animated film of this great story, and I was quite taken by the many fantastical scenes, such as the fading Cheshire Cat with nothing left but the grin, and the regal blue caterpillar that smoked from the long flexible tube of a hookah, blowing smoke rings and saying to Alice in theatrically elongated phrasing: "Whoooo are yoooou?" I thought that caterpillar was hilarious, and I was still mimicking the "Whooo are yoooou?" routine when, after the movie and supper, Jerry and I were dispatched to take our bath and get ready for bed.

I was first in the tub, and, to my delight, I spotted my daddy's electric razor cord. He kept it plugged into a socket on the light fixture above the sink, letting it dangle off to the side by the tub. It was handy for him, and I never thought a thing about it until that silly night, when it dawned on me how much it resembled the smoking tube of the caterpillar's water pipe. I quickly had it in my hand, lying back and taking drags on it like the caterpillar did, and saying "Whoooo are yoooou?" Next thing I know my "smoking tube" had latched hold of my tongue like a rattlesnake locking on a horse's leg. It was shooting electricity through my scrawny body, and I was screaming, thrashing about, ducking my head under water a time or two (which was real helpful), going every which way at once trying to get loose, but it stayed stuck. Luckily, I ricocheted off the wall at the back end of the tub and shot straight out onto the bathroom floor, knocking poor, horrified Jerry down and cracking his head on the toilet. With this, the cord popped loose from my electrified tongue and swung back to its usual place, innocently dangling there as though nothing had happened.

There's another Alice-in-Wonderland adventure taking place today, and it is delivering a bigger shock to the hard-working people of the world than that razor cord did to me. "Globalization" is the moniker attached to it by its political, corporate, and financial architects, and, Oh, Golly, what a fantabulous concept or process or thing or whatever it is! Remember the late-night television ad touting Veg-O-Matic that could slice, dice, chop, peel, grate, puree, drive you to work, and pretty much do anything you needed done? Well, it was as nothing compared to the widely advertised glories of globalization, which we're told again and again promise prosperity to all, has "democratizing action" built right in, cleans whiter than white, contains no saturated fat, has a thirty-two-valve V8 with a maximum torque of 290 ft./lbs., and is more thrilling than a trip to Disney World.

For some, even the term globalization is inadequate to express the fullness of the blessings they believe to be inherent in this economic/technological/cultural phenomenon. Author Daniel Yergin, who seems caught up in the fever of the phenomenon, wrote in *Newsweek* last year of his "gnawing dissatisfaction with the word" and of his struggle to conceive something more apt. He explained that he was "trying to convey something else, something larger than business and economics, though encompassing both: something pointed more towards the new century. Not a process, but the results of a process—a place, a condition, the situation that comes afterwards." Uh-huh. Whatever that means, he says he suddenly found the word he was seeking: globality. Rhymes with banality. "Globality popped into my head in the middle of the night," Yergin explained excitedly. Probably the work of that gorgonzola-and-sardine sandwich he had before retiring for the evening. "But what," Yergin finally asks, "is globality?" He answers breathlessly: "It is the 24-hour interconnected, hyperactive world, in which sleep deprivation becomes endemic as one pounds out e-mails in time that should belong to deep sleep and alpha waves. It is the world symbolized by Amazon.com, which sold its first book less than four years ago and now has 6.2 million customers. It is a world where governments, as the finance minister of one of the world's leading economies put it, have less leverage over their own economies. And where companies really do operate on a global basis—increasingly, as Hewlett Packard CEO Lewis Platt put it, in 'a 7-day, 24-hour work week where things are changing very rapidly.'" Whew. He should save some of that breath for breathing.

Of course, *globality* is not in the dictionary. There is *glob, globalize, globate, globigerina ooze, globoid,* and *globuliferous.* But Bill Gates likes Yergin's confection so much he wants it for Microsoft's computerized dictionary. Now *that's* globality—manufacture a word one day, and Bill Gates has it on your spell check the next. Is this a great globe we live on, or what?

THE HOLY HYPE. With all due respect to Mr. Yergin, I'll stick for now with the old-fashioned "globalization" (which itself was coined only about a decade ago). However, to imbue the term with the awe that its devotees expect it to hold for us heathens who are the objects of their missionary zeal, it should always be written and pronounced as though God was speaking, as in "GLOBALIZATION!" Why not, since it is offered as a new utopian theocracy, with FREE TRADE as its inviolate precept? Reduced to its core, the holy dogma of globalization is as simple-minded as Ronald Reagan's old Laf-

fer-curve concept of trickle-down economics, only writ worldwide: Just get the world's governments the hell out of the way
so the Great Stallions of Global Commerce can be unleashed,
then, By Gipper, through their strength and cunning, these
beasts will naturally generate wealth here, there, and everywhere—wealth that will ripple and trickle, eventually lifting
all boats by their bootstraps, just as Adam Smith predicted
when he wrote the Horatio Alger series, starring Mickey
Rooney and Dolly Parton. Sillier yet are the actual elements of
the globalization agenda, which include these basic demands:

- Throw open the borders of all nations so that any corporation can control the market in any country for everything
  from auto sales to grocery shopping, from air travel to
  banking.
- Rewrite the rules of investments so that any corporation or
  speculator group can own the factories, farms, mines,
  banks, hospitals, and other essential resources of any and
  all countries.
- Delink trade and investment policies from any principled
  concerns over such matters as human rights, working conditions, impoverishment, ecological destruction, and totalitarian repression, having faith that "free trade" (the
  unrestrained movement of corporate power and money)
  must come first, and all else will follow.
- Do not allow any national, regional, state, or local government to impose any restrictions on any corporation's exercise of free trade, specifically including any attempt by
  governments to protect their workers, farmers, or environment from the ravages of free traders.
- Establish supreme tribunals through NAFTA, the World
  Trade Organization, and other supranational trade entities
  to protect the rights of corporations and speculators against
  infringements by individuals, groups, or governments.

You don't have to be the sharpest knife in the drawer to realize that this is insane. A reader could be excused for thinking, "This time, Hightower, you most certainly are pulling my leg, for no people would freely submit to such a preposterous grab for power, allowing the narrowest and minchiest segment of world society (corporate CEOs and global speculators) to reign supreme over all other interests." Indeed, we did not freely submit to this new global sovereignty, for it never has been submitted to us—either as a demand from a conquering force or as a proposition for democratic debate and vote. Yet, there it is. In the pages to come are stories about how much of the dogma of globalization is already in place and having the most absurd consequences.

Meanwhile come the media, academic, and political apologists for this stealth coup, rationalizing it as both a secular blessing and the preordained march of history. Thomas Friedman, for example, the *New York Times* columnist who can't seem to stop his tail from wagging with delight whenever he gets within butt-sniffing distance of a member of the global elite, hails globalization as a "golden straightjacket" that prevents governments from interfering with business schemes, thus, he says, allowing people in even the most impoverished lands to park a Lexus in their garages. Never mind that most families in those lands make the equivalent of maybe $350 a year and *live* in places smaller than it would take to park a Lexus, Friedman constantly pounds out columns and books extolling what he calls the "globalution" of consumerism made possible by the "Electronic Herd" of speculators roaming the world and dumping cash on low-wage, high-return investments in any country with a welcome mat for unbridled greed.

In 1999, Friedman's *Times* colleague, Paul Lewis, brought the dialectic of history to the rationalization process, citing assorted academicians who maintain that global corporate rule is the next big step in the natural order of things: "Once nation-states exercised absolute sovereignty over a clearly defined territory, 'bundling together,'" he wrote, noting that "no higher authority existed than the ruler of such a state, be it a king or a parliament. But no longer. Today, nation-states are being 'unbundled.'" With great enthusiasm, Lewis cited multinational corporations, global markets, and cyberspace as the great "unbundlers," adding that "increasingly nation-states are surrendering sovereignty by joining together in international organizations."

Oh? When did *you* vote to surrender your country's sovereignty to the WTO or any other international organization? Did either Bill Clinton or George Bush put this proposition to you in the '92 election? Did Clinton or Dole discuss it with you in '96? Have you heard Al Gore or George W. Bush put it on the Election 2000 agenda? In this past decade of surrendering sovereignty, did your member of Congress ever come talk to you about undoing what Jefferson-Adams-Washington-Madison-and-the-boys put together two-hundred-odd years ago?

Lewis even lifts the march of globalization to the religious level, stating that while Christianity was the unifying belief for the Crusaders of the Middle Ages, "Free markets seem to be now," asserting that, "Free markets are an almost universally accepted ideology." Gosh, Paul, you might want to check that with the masses of folks in Thailand, Indonesia, Malaysia, South Korea, Russia, Mexico, Brazil, and other nations where turbocharged free-market speculators sucked the lifeblood out of their economies, then unleashed the autocrats of the IMF to impose draconian economic rules that put the burden of recovery on the backs of the very people who were left impoverished, while the speculators were bailed out with billions from the world's taxpayers. He might also want to check with some folks here at home, where six out of ten people say that the free-trade policies of the last decade have been bad for America—an opinion not based on trade theory but on the attention-riveting experience of losing hundreds of thousands of jobs, factories, whole industries, and even communities to the new Global Crusaders who are in holy pursuit of ever cheaper labor. God save any and all who are in their path.

Averting his eyes from such collateral damage, Lewis presses on, referring approvingly to the present period, in which the musty old concept of national sovereignty is being dumped on the ash heap of history. He calls the new century "neomedievalist," which he explains is a throwback to the Middle Ages "when the boundaries of kingdoms were often vague and subject to the fortunes of war and dynastic marriages." In today's delightfully retro medievalism, the "kingdoms" are corporate; the "wars" pit CEOs and shareholders against the world's workers, farmers, environment, and governments; the "boundaries" are whatever the various Star Chambers established by the WTO and NAFTA say they are; and the "dynastic marriages" are the global mergers consolidating corporate power into even fewer hands.

THE WIZARDS OF WASHINGTON

American humorist Don Marquis said, "An idea isn't responsible for the people who believe in it." So we mustn't blame poor little globalization for being puffed up so grandiosely by extollers like Friedman and Lewis when it's really not much of an idea at all—it's more of a rationalization, giving pseudo-intellectual and political cover to money and power as they stomp their way around the world. And the notion that "globalization" and "free trade" comprise an overarching belief system for the reordering of the world, après the nation-state, gives new depth to the term shallow. These two vacuous concepts embody no framework for a civil society—no Bill of Rights, no social contract, no ethos of fairness and justice, no religious and/or moral conscience, no nothing beyond the schoolyard bully saying, "Gimme your lunch money, you Twinkie, or I'm gonna pulp your face into guacamole."

Yet the dynastic duo of globalization and free trade is being religiously pushed from the highest pulpits of the land, as though they were inscribed on the stone tablets that Moses brought down from the mountain. From the bully pulpit of the Clinton presidency (and from Bush's before him) has come a steady stream of hosannas for the process and for the manna he says is being showered on us from Free Trade Heaven. Clinton has been some combination of Elmer Gantry, the Music Man, and the Flimflam Man in trying to sell the concept. So desperate has he been to legitimize his shameless fronting for Wall Street's global designs that he began a 1999 formal foreign policy address "with a little history," quoting from a previous president who was similarly enraptured by the glitter of world trade. It was William McKinley! A Democratic president has to be mighty hungry for political company to dig up the bones of Ol' Bill McKinley, a notorious Republican whore of the Robber Barons, a rank imperialist, and a man described by Teddy Roosevelt as having "no more backbone than a chocolate éclair."

Clinton has done a great deal more than talk, however—the candidate of '92 who railed against George Bush's corporate vision of "a New World Order" and against Bush's coddling of "the Butchers of Beijing," quickly hired on in '93 as Wall Street's coddler-in-chief and the general contractor for building the vision: He teamed up with congressional Republicans to ram NAFTA and the WTO into law and to gain privileged trade status for those same Butchers of Beijing; he has signed off on more than 270 separate trade deals; he has engineered multibillion-dollar bailouts of speculators whose global gambles went sour in Asia, Latin America, and Russia; he has used hundreds of millions of our tax dollars to underwrite the movement of U.S. factories and technology out of country; he has tried repeatedly (and, so far, unsuccessfully) to extend

NAFTA to Africa, the Caribbean, and all of South America, even failing in a shabby attempt in the spring of 1999 to slip the Caribbean-NAFTA provision into the relief bill for the people of Central America who had been devastated by the horrendous Hurricane Mitch; and he has dispatched cabinet members to join planeloads of corporate executives on trade missions throughout Asia so they could cut deals that would ship still more of America's manufacturing jobs into low-wage hellholes there.

All of this has been done without the approval of the American people, who consistently have opposed these "free trade" schemes for being the Wall Street scams they are. Occasionally, Clinton will try to gain public support by putting a little PR gloss on his overall globalization scam, but these staged events never seem to get beyond their hokeyness to connect with ordinary folks, and sometimes the hype backfires on the hypers. In September of '98, he put the national spotlight on a policy-wonk forum convened by the New York University School of Law, ponderously titled "Strengthening Democracy in the Global Economy: An Opening Dialogue." The dialogue, rather pathetically, was between the globalization establishment and the globalization establishment—Bill *and* Hillary were there, England's Clinton clone Tony Blair was perkily present, Wall Street execs were prominently arrayed, media barons were there both to cover the confab *and* to participate, supportive professors were invited to puff their pipes and puff up the academic aura of the proceedings, and some three hundred other members of the palace court were allowed inside. Not present were the people who actually are fighting for democracy in the antidemocratic global economy that this crowd has done so much to build. Nonetheless, the show went on, with some thirty television cameras and all the right newspapers covering it as though something real were happening.

Luckily, the iconoclastic Lewis Lapham, editor of *Harper's* magazine, wandered into this gathering of soft-headed and soft-handed establishmentarians and was there when the one discordant note of the day was hit. It went unreported, except later in Lapham's own column. Until the "incident," Lewis wrote, the proceedings were going according to script. He observed that the panelists were expert at the decorous, somnolent mouthing of all the approved conventional wisdoms of the moment, including the self-reassuring line that the recent untidiness in Asia, where the work of the global schemers in this very room had come spectacularly unglued, was not their fault or the fault of the scheme itself. No, no, no—it was the crude implementation of the scheme by Asia's own governmental leaders and bankers, don't you see—the problem was too much Cronyism, a lack of computerized data for sufficient market oversight, a problem with transparency, and so on . . . and on, and on. Lapham likened the tone of the dialogue to "the murmur of contented bees."

But then Laura Tyson spoke up unexpectedly and out of turn. The former head of Clinton's Council of Economic Advisors, she has now retreated to the security of academia, where she apparently has reclaimed her own voice. As Lapham describes the unusual moment, she "interrupted the discussion to observe that the heavy capital flows that had drowned the Asian economies didn't come from Asia. They came from Europe and the United States, from fully developed industrial countries well equipped with sufficient data and the instruments of democratic oversight. What we are talking about here, she said, is greed . . . stupidity, cowardice, and greed . . . about investors in London and Paris and New York seizing the prey of easy profits and then, when the luck went bad, seeking to transfer their markers to a government . . . about privatizing the gains, socializing the losses."

Wow! Wonder why that outburst didn't make the nightly news? Could it be because General Electric (which owns NBC), Westinghouse (which owns CBS), Disney (which owns ABC), NewsCorporation (which owns Fox), and Time Warner (which owns CNN) are all heavily into globalization schemes of their own and don't need any public questioning of the underlying correctness of the concept that their news networks have pushed as an absolute truth—especially criticism from an insider? Some questions answer themselves. Not only did the only newsworthy comment of the day fail to get a single second of airtime, it also failed to get a single response at this so-called dialogue. Lewis Lapham completes the story: "The distinguished company didn't pursue Ms. Tyson's line of argument. A gentleman associated with Goldman Sachs coughed discreetly into his microphone, Hillary Clinton smiled at a television camera, two media hierarchs adjusted their tics, and the murmuring resumed."

Last year, Clinton made one more try to sell globalization to the heathen masses. With his effort to win congressional approval for China's entry into the World Trade Organization coming a cropper, the President decided to go to the countryside. Well, he wasn't about to go out there *personally*, but he did dispatch Commerce Secretary William Daley to carry the message of globalization's glories into the hinterlands. The pitiable secretary was teamed up with CEOs from such job-killing outfits as Boeing, AT&T, Merck, and Tenneco to launch a "National Trade Education Tour," which would travel by luxury motor coach on five different jaunts in and around Boston, Chicago, Louisville, the Carolinas, and Los Angeles, stopping at factories, schools, and cafés to talk with the "common folks of America" about joining in a "national consensus" for Clinton's trade policy. It was as absurd as a pack of coyotes going out to invite a flock of lambs to join them for supper.

The tour turned into a PR disaster, which could have been predicted, given the message and the corporate contingent he was hauling around. On all five trips, feisty groups of local protesters, led by the Citizens Trade Campaign, dogged Daley's deluxe bus in a yellow van with a huge sign warning: "Free Trade Fat Cats On Board." The receptions inside the scheduled events, which were supposed to be orchestrated for positive media coverage, were not much warmer. At Al Mac's Diner in Fall River, Massachusetts, the secretary and his traveling troupe of CEOs were cornered by clothing and textile workers from local mills, asking more hard questions than the big shots could answer. Also, in an example of sadistic scheduling, Daley and group found themselves in Racine, Wisconsin, for a tour of the Case tractor plant. The plan was to highlight happy workers making tractors for export in the global economy. However, it turns out that Case had recently been bought by New Holland, a Dutch equipment maker, which in turn is owned by Fiat, the Italian auto giant. The Case factory workers' sentiments about globalization were a lot less bullish than the official entourage had hoped for, since the new foreign owners were talking of streamlining and out-sourcing work—code words for downsizing. Would jobs be lost at this plant, the Case president was asked during Daley's stop. "There's always that possibility," he replied.

If the gods on high have ordained corporations and their financiers to assume global sovereignty, why does this sovereign need so many legislative fixes, subsidies, PR campaigns, and other heavy lifting from its earthly adherents to get to the throne? Maybe it's not such a natural and inevitable ascendancy after all, contrary to what the dogmatists tell us. Clinton Democrats are hardly alone in trying to engineer the "inevitability" of globalization—the congressional Republican leadership has been equally engaged in the heaving and ho-ing. One rarely gets to pull back the Wizard's curtain for a peek at the real force propelling the march of globalization, but the curtain did part slightly in the spring of 1998, thanks to an internal tussle between the House GOP leadership and corporate lobbyists. This little reported contretemps came in the waning days of the Age of Newt, when Newt Gingrich still was House speaker. He had fallen into a snit because he felt big-business lobbyists were slighting him and his party on campaign donations (lobbyists were giving much more to the GOP than to the Dems, but not *enough* more to satisfy the Napoleon of Marietta). Gingrich, whose daily output of ego could inflate the Goodyear blimp, was good at snits. His tactic in this case was not subtle—he halted any movement of the globalist's congressional agenda, which included getting Congress to put $18 billion more of your and my money into the IMF for more bailouts of their failed speculations around the world, plus getting approval of a special legislative procedure called "fast track" that would allow more trade scams like NAFTA to be railroaded into law.

It didn't take long for the speaker's ploy to work. "The Business Round Table had a meeting with Newt yesterday," one of his top lieutenants told *Roll Call*, a Capitol Hill newspaper, "and he told them that fast track and the IMF would all be taken care of." Likewise, Myron Brilliant (I promise I do not make these names up) of the U.S. Chamber of Commerce and also head of the "Ad Hoc Coalition for IMF Replenishment" (neither do I make up the preposterous names of their groups) said after the meeting with Newt that he was "cautiously optimistic" that the IMF money would move. To seal the deal, Newt cleverly announced it publicly a couple of days later at a Republican congressional fund-raising dinner packed with corporate executives and lobbyists. "There was a huge roar in the room when he mentioned fast track," said an attendee, adding that "members who didn't favor fast track were surrounded by members of the business community who support them and were cheering and looking at them." It turned out to be the biggest fund-raiser the congressional Republicans had ever had. And Mr. Brilliant did get his $18 billion in bailout funds. Thus are sovereigns hoisted to their thrones—not by gods, but by the most mundane collusion of money and politics.

Particularly insidious and insulting to the larger public is the way that the corporate executives, their lobbyists, their politicians, and their other apologists frame the issue of globalization as one that pits those with the daring and compassion to be engaged in an interconnected world against the rest of us who are mouth-breathing, knuckle-dragging, xenophobic, isolationist cretins who would rather drink the blood of foreigners than have "foreign relations" with them. Bill Clinton is especially given to this rhetorical thrust and parry, picturing himself as Sir William of the Global Village with lance drawn against the infidel hordes of stony isolationism. In San Francisco last year before a selected audience, Sir William speaketh: "Some of the folks outside who were protesting when I drove up were saying by their signs that they believe globalization is inherently bad and there's no way in the wide world to put a human face on the global economy."

Horsedooties. I know some of the people and groups that were protesting outside (which is where ordinary folks have been relegated by this administration) against the sheer elitism and human destructiveness of his brand of globalism—a brand that has the money powers of our country making backroom financial and business arrangements with the totalitarian thugs who rule China, the forty families of Mexico, the corporate oligarchy of South Korea, and the thieving entrepreneurial mafia of Russia, among others. He wants us to salute that? I know Medea Benjamin at Global Exchange, Charlie Kernagan at the National Labor Committee, Harry Wu at Laogai Research Foundation, Randall Robertson at TransAfrica, and so many other true American internationalists who know more and care more about the "human face" of the global economy than an aloof, pampered, cynical, and glib Bill Clinton can ever imagine. What an ass! These are people on the front lines where his globalism is not a market theory but a brutish reality. They are working directly with the human faces trapped in the global sweatshops of Nike, Disney, the Gap, and so many other brand names, while Clinton hobnobs in luxury with the global rulers and corporatists who literally are smashing those faces he uses so freely as rhetorical props. *This,* not Monica Lewinsky's face, is why I find Clinton such a despicable president and such a pitiful excuse for a Democrat.

In *The Wizard of Oz,* when Dorothy, the Lion, the Tin Man, and the Scarecrow learn that the Wizard is just a little man who has been bamboozling everyone, Dorothy angrily says to him: "I think you are a very bad man." Shamefaced, he replies, "Oh, no, I am really a very good man, but I will admit that I am a very bad Wizard." Clinton certainly is a very bad Wizard, but he's not at all a good man, either.

PERCOLATE UP, NOT TRICKLE DOWN. We progressive critics of free-trade follies damn sure won't take a backseat to any Washington official or Wall Street CEO over who cares more about being engaged with the peoples of the world. Let me say it as plainly and proudly as I can: *I am an internationalist!* There, I feel better. All true progressives are. Our internationalism, however, is tied not to the dictatorial thugs and moneyed elites but to the people themselves. I believe it is un-American for our government to support Wall Street's endless pursuit of the cheapest wage possible—rather, America should be a global force for the same democratic values we espouse at home: economic fairness, social justice, and equal opportunity for all. Specifically, American policy should be to raise standards the world over for workers, farmers, Momma Earth, and all others being overrun by the forces of greed. Clinton himself keeps lecturing us that we are all one people on this great globe and that our interests are totally interlocked. Absolutely true. But here's what separates bullshit from bingo: The chief global interest of people everywhere is to keep the greedheads of globaloney from stealing our labor, stifling our middle-class aspirations, and subverting our sovereignty as free peoples. On these counts, Clinton and pals are bullshit.

I bring some internationalist bona fides to this table, for I have personally been involved in building trade relationships, though mine have been developed through a much different approach than that of Wall Street and Washington. As commissioner of agriculture in the 1980s, one of my goals was to help Texas farmers and small food processors break through the middleman marketing blockades that separate them from consumers in Texas, as well as from consumers across the country and around the world. It's not generally known (for it's not much reported by the media), but food producers mostly are kept a far distance from us consumers by a corporatized, conglomerated, and increasingly anticompetitive structure of shippers, traders, processors, packers, and wholesalers. Only a few companies dominate each of these middle sectors—three grain shippers (ADM, Cargill, and Continental), for example, control 80 percent of all the grain shipped in the world, and two of them are merging. This monopolistic structure puts both farmers and consumers at its mercy, which is not terribly tender, so farmers are paid barely a breakeven price for their crops (and that's in the *good* years), while food prices keep going up for us. Farmers today get only 20 cents of the food dollar that you and I spend, a nickel less than just a decade ago.

Small food businesses face a similar middleman structure that separates their amazing new peach salsa, their phenomenal corn cake mix, their mouthwatering crawfish étouffé, their superb merlot-grenache wine, and all their other innovative delectables from the supermarket shelves. Some prisons have fewer walls, razor wire barriers, and armed guards than food wholesalers and retailers use to keep upstart food makers off the shelves.

Susan DeMarco, who is brighter and filled with more spark than a bolt of lightning, agreed to be our assistant commissioner for marketing at the ag department and to figure out how to get these family farmers and homegrown processing businesses as directly as possible to consumers at all levels— local, statewide, nationally, and internationally. Every step closer would narrow the middleman gap and put more money in the pockets of the producers. She quickly assembled a unique and talented staff that combined grassroots organizers, experienced marketers, and creative promoters to go forth and do what had to be done. (The Bible teaches that Jacob died leaning on his staff, and I was equally vulnerable, but I had a happier outcome, for the staff I leaned on saved my political butt with the great work it did.) Within a short time, good things were happening:

- Small farmers were being organized into co-ops and were selling top-quality produce directly to Kroger, Safeway, and other supermarkets. (I literally rode into Houston sitting atop a truckload of watermelons, delivering the first of many loads to Kroger from a co-op of black farmers around Hempstead.)

- Wheat farmers were organized into an association to build their own flour mill in the tiny Panhandle town of Dawn, gaining not only a premium-priced, locally controlled market for their grain but also the value-added profit from the packaged flour they made—just one of some three hundred locally owned processing facilities we helped folks develop across Texas during our eight years in office.

- More than a hundred farmers markets were eventually organized in both big cities and small towns, helping even large farmers get an additional source of cash income by selling directly to consumers in these wildly popular and festive markets.

- A "Taste of Texas" program was launched by DeMarco and team, which not only gave small processors an identifying logo that was a marketing plus inside the state, but the program also held annual food shows around the country, allowing hundreds of our small companies a chance to connect with brokers who could put their products on the shelves in New York City, Boston, Chicago, San Francisco, and other places where we put on our high-stepping, good-tasting extravaganzas; the shows featured the companies' wonderful foods prepared on the spot by such renowned Texas chefs as Dean Fearing, Robert del Grande, and Stephen Pyles, as well as Texas beer and wine, such rollicking Texas musicians as Cajun rocker Marcia Ball and the outlandish Geezinslaw Brothers (I told the assembled brokers at our show in Tampa that if they did not agree to enough deals with our food companies we would *leave* the Geezinslaws in their city), and authentic Texas armadillo races (Hey, it was show business)—all of which made a good party . . . and produced millions of dollars in sales for grassroots businesses. (In some cities, we persuaded super-market buyers to create a section for various Texas food-stuffs on their ethnic aisles, so there would be Asian, Middle Eastern . . . and Texan.)

This is the direct opposite of the Reagan-Bush-Clinton trickle-down approach to economic development—it's *percolate up,* putting the tools of growth directly in the hands of grassroots people rather than in the already powerful hands of those at the top. DeMarco put the exact same principles and skills to work in pursuing the international marketplace. Why should farmers sell their grain, cotton, meats, and other commodities at cheap prices to a handful of giant exporting corporations when they could get a better price by selling directly to the foreign buyers? Same with the small food processors, who could bypass the international brokers and go directly to buyers around the world—*if* there was an alternative system to connect them to the buyers. As my friend Fred Harris, the great populist crusader and former U.S. senator from Oklahoma, has noted: "The 'free' in 'free enterprise' is not an adjective, it's a verb." At the Texas Department of Agriculture we took that thought to heart, deciding that our agency could help to free the incredible enterprise of Texas farmers and small business people from the monopolistic lock that a handful of international grain traders, cotton shippers, meatpackers, and processors had on the food export market.

While the Clintonites now serve the global plunderers, we decided back in the eighties to try serving the grassroots enterprises. There is nothing terribly complicated about the concept: Find the people who want to buy what we have to sell, connect them up, then get out of the way. With a sparse budget and a small but aggressive staff, DeMarco's international marketing division went to work to implement the concept: Regional specialists were hired for Asia, the Middle East, Africa, Latin America, and Europe—"specialist" meant they were from the region, spoke one or more of the languages there, and knew something about the market and knew some of the buyers; the department computerized a list of thousands of Texas producers with products for export, distributing this directory to buyers worldwide; the staff pioneered a computerized trade lead network that could instantly link a buyer's order in, say, Taiwan with the Texans who had that particular product for sale, giving our producers a jump on making an offer; we hosted a regular stream of foreign buyers, offering translators, transportation to farms and food companies, and other services; trade seminars were held throughout the state, informing our food producers about the export possibilities and teaching them how to do it; and we sponsored Texas trade shows in foreign cities, taking our products and producers directly to the buyers.

It worked. A mom-and-pop honey operation in Beaumont found itself making sales in Saudi Arabia, independent operators on the Texas Gulf Coast began shipping frozen crab to Japan, cooperatives on the High Plains were making deals to send their high-protein wheat to German millers, a black family in southeast Texas went from the brink of bankruptcy to making a profit by exporting rice to Mexico, an El Paso maker of Tex-Mex specialties got its products on the shelves of super-markets in England and Germany—just a few examples of the millions of dollars a year that were generated in new exports of commodities direct from Texas producers, bypassing the corporate-controlled export channels that siphon off all the profits from the actual producers.

Bill Clinton is not alone in believing in global trade deals, either. We established two important ones during my tenure—M-TEC, the Mexico-Texas Exchange Commission, which I signed with Eduardo Pesquerira, the Mexican secretary of agriculture in 1985, and TIE, the Texas Israel Exchange, which I signed in 1986 with Abraham Katz Oz, the Israeli deputy-minister of agriculture and a member of the Knesset, the Israeli parliament. But, unlike the Wall Street/Washington globalists, our approach to trade agreements was not to have the elites of our country cut the deal with the elites of their countries and pretend that somehow, someday, everybody is going to benefit. The one rule of thumb that really counts in any negotiation is this: If you're not at the table, you won't be part of the deal. For the NAFTA and WTO negotiations, there were no farmers, workers, environmentalists, human rights advocates, or other popular interests at the table. Only the corporate and financial elites are the ones eating high on the NAFTA and WTO hog, while the rest of us can't even get a bag of pork rinds out of the deal. As Huey Long used to say in his campaigns, which rallied the sharecroppers and other poor folks in Louisiana, "If you want some ham, by God, you've got to go into the smokehouse," since that's where the ham is. When I ran for ag commish in 1982, I was dubbed "Whole Hog" Hightower because I cited that Huey Long proposition in all of my tub-thumping speeches across the state and promised that, if elected, we were going to "kick open the door of the smokehouse and bring the people inside."

Having been elected, that's what we did. In both M-TEC and TIE, the role of us government muckety-mucks was simply to be a catalyst for bringing plain old dirt farmers, small processors, grocers, and other folks from the state of Texas together with their counterparts in Mexico and Israel. Ours was the Big Table approach to international deal making, essentially constructing a "table" that anyone could come to if they wanted to deal. With M-TEC, for example, the Mexican and Texan ag departments sponsored annual meetings at border cities where buyers and sellers of foodstuffs from both sides could gather and break into sessions dealing with their particular commodity or interest. There were also sessions on transportation, financing, bureaucratic problems, and anything else the participants wanted to add.

One final tale of my internationalist adventures came as the result of a dust-up between the United States and the European Union over hormone-free beef, in which I found myself siding with the Europeans (and common sense) against the Bush administration, which was fronting for America's corporate cattle feeders and beef packers. The EU was (and still is) rejecting U.S. beef that contained antibiotics and sex hormones, wanting an additive-free product. The additives are present because of the industrialized factory methods employed by today's huge feedlot operators—the hormones cause the cattle to add weight in an unnatural hurry, and the antibiotics are necessary because the animals are so jammed up against each other and unable to move about in these meat factories that disease is constant. At the behest of the feeders and packers, the Bushies worked themselves into a high outrage, barking that the EU was a bunch of sissies for worrying about a few hormones and antibiotics in their steaks and that their health concerns were just an anti–free trade ruse to keep our tender beef out of their markets. The Bush administration shouted across the Atlantic at our European customers: "Eat our hormones and shut up!" "No," said the EU, and there we were about to tumble into a truly dumb trade war over beef additives.

"Ahem," I said from Texas. "If the Europeans sincerely are not attempting to ban our beef exports, but only want to avoid the additives, then why not sell the customers what they want?" I pointed out that the farmers and ranchers of Texas have beaucoup cattle roaming the range without one iota of hormones or antibiotics in them, and that we had many small feedlot operators and meatpackers who would be delighted to sell and ship additive-free beef to them. Oh, what a hullabaloo came my way—you would have thought I had pissed on the Oval Office rug! President Bush himself whined about my "interference," and the U.S. Secretary of Agriculture fumed darkly that I was consorting with the enemy and possibly violating the Logan Act of 1800, which can get a citizen thrown in the federal pokey for engaging in unauthorized diplomacy with a foreign government. "If offering to sell Texas beef violates the Logan Act," I retorted, "then haul me to the dungeon, for I am guilty!" They looked like the fools they were and had to back off, and we did sell shipments of hormone-free beef to European buyers.

The real issue of globalization is not whether one believes in connecting to an interdependent world (of course we must), but whether that connection is going to be of, by, and for the few . . . or the many. True internationalization can and should build new channels around the present corporate blockages, giving workers, environmentalists, farmers, consumers, and others power and opportunities outside the grip of the global financial elites. But Ol' Bill just keeps plodding ahead like a mule with blinders, doing what he learned to do in Arkansas, which is to pull the load for the Tysons and other moneyed powers. It's as absurd as it is antidemocratic (and anti-Democratic)— these guys already have power; they don't need a president's help! Yet, he keeps pursuing a perverse policy of globalism (tightly embraced by the Republican hierarchy as well, but you would expect that) based on the elites getting an even tighter grip on the reins.

A few months ago, an event took place that indicates just how selfishly the governmental and financial elites guard their exclusionary control of their globalization process. On June 24, 1999, President Clinton, German chancellor Gerhard Schröder, and other Mr. Bigs sat down behind closed doors in Bonn for the semiannual U.S.-EU Trade Summit. They weren't alone, however, in mapping their latest schemes. Sitting with them were members of the TransAtlantic Business Dialogue, a group of corporate executives organized in 1995 at the request of the government leaders, specifically to work with them in framing public policies. The TABD group has been inside every summit since.

Finally recognizing that this formal relationship with the corporate interests put a bit of stink on them, the U.S. and European leaders agreed in 1998 that a TransAtlantic *Consumer* Dialogue and TransAtlantic *Environment* Dialogue should also be set up, loudly proclaiming that the trade agenda "should be shaped and driven . . . with the full participation of people from all walks of life." Clinton himself spoke in June of '99 about getting more openness and balance into the process. (Why do I have a sense of being suckered every time Clinton talks of inclusiveness, like Charlie Brown being enticed once more by Lucy to trust her to hold the football for him to kick, only to have her yank it away at the last moment as poor Charlie Brown kicks mightily at nothing but air and— kersplat!—falls on his back?) Sure enough, the TACD and TAED were formed, but just days before the June 24 trade policy discussions were to convene in Bonn, their requests to attend and participate were summarily rejected. They could form a group, but it couldn't sit at the table! Yet, as always, the corporate "Dialogue" group was invited to take its usual seat adjacent to the governmental leaders. Public Citizen president Joan Claybrook, who had agreed to join the TACD, even though she was wary that it would turn out to be "diversionary busy work," said of this rebuff, "It's hard to imagine what could be more hypocritical than President Clinton calling for a more open, balanced trade policy one week and the next week locking out consumer and environmental representatives from a trade summit where he will meet with industry."

Years ago, whenever company came to visit my parents, we kiddos would not get to eat at the dining table with them but would be put out on the back porch at a folding card table and eat only after the big people had gotten their fill of the fried chicken, fresh green beans, yams, pie, and whatever else was being served. That's where I learned to appreciate chicken necks, and if even the neck was gone, we'd get a baloney sandwich. Today, the larger public is being treated like children by the governmental and corporate big shots—we're told to sit out on the back porch while they sit at the policy table and decide who gets what from the global economy. They promise that "everyone" will eventually get a seven-course dinner, but ours turns out to be a six-pack and that baloney sandwich.

Election 2000 offers more of the same, especially from the front runners. George W. Bush's policy advisers represent a rehash of his daddy's "New World Order" wizards. Al Gore's advisers are an extension of Clinton's same old same old. Both have been to the inner sanctums of the global corporate leaders where they've given the secret handshake, pledged their fealty to GLOBALIZATION!, promised to push for even more of it, then accepted millions in campaign funds to seal the deal. Both are already on record for the full platter of globalization goodies currently being requested by the corporate leaders—extension of NAFTA everywhere, putting in the rules of the World Trade Organization new protections for global investors, membership for China in the WTO, continued subsidies for foreign factory-building by U.S. firms, etc. etc. etc. Far from questioning any of this, these two will engage in a one-upmanship contest, trying to outdo each other on who can pledge the most to their corporate benefactors.

One measure of just how short a leash they're on was taken in May of 1999 when young Shrub momentarily got ever so slightly off script and seemed to be criticizing the global agenda in China. It was a scream to watch him almost bodily yank himself back in line! The matter at hand was the issuance of the "Cox Report," the voluminous congressional denunciation of the Clinton administration for allowing China to steal our nuclear secrets and for letting some high-tech firms give away our missile technology to the Chinese. Bush, who was getting roundly ridiculed at the time for being ignorant, evasive, or both on foreign policy issues, had been prepped by his staff so he could show his smarts and demonstrate his decisiveness on this one. Like an alley cat pouncing on a small rodent, he leapt as soon as the Cox Report was released, declaring to the assembled media; "Today's report . . . shines a glaring light on the current administration's failed policies toward China."

Spontaneously and simultaneously, shrieks of horror emanated from within America's executive suites as CEOs from Wall Street to the Silicon Valley bolted upright at this bit of unintended heresy and shouted in unison at Bush: "Good-God-A-Mighty, Junior, those are *our* policies toward China you're talking about! Are you dumber than a sack of sand or have you simply gone insane?!" A chastened Shrub was very quickly issuing clarifications to explain that oh, my, no, not in any way did I mean to even hint that there should be any kind of *economic* sanctions against the Chinese, and most certainly these thieving thugs deserve full membership in the WTO PDQ, and let me reiterate my long-standing position that we must never let a country's cultural quirkiness (slave labor, forced abortions, totalitarian repression, and so forth) get in the way of our companies' being able to manufacture their products there, and everyone knows that free trade is about freedom, and, besides, I was only talking about that spy thing, certainly not about global trade policies, and it's really upsetting to me that the media misconstrued my words, and you can bet I won't be using those words again.

So much for the chance that any profiles in courage will emerge from our millennial presidential election. As far as the top contenders are concerned, there will be no debate on this issue of such profound importance to people worldwide, and the absurdities of trickle-down globalization will continue to pile up.

TOM DELAY DOES SAIPAN

Every time I see Tom DeLay, I can't help thinking: a hundred thousand sperm and *you* were the fastest?

This most unctuous member of Congress comes to you from the Houston area, where he previously was a bug exterminator servicing the finer homes in the ritzy River Oaks section. Now he is the number-three-ranking Republican in the House (the majority whip), though it's widely conceded that he is the real power behind the paper throne of Speaker Dennis Hastert, who is even more widely conceded to be an affable nincompoop who pretty much does what Tom says. A lot of people on Capitol Hill do what Tom says, which seems amazing at first because he says so many wacko things that one assumes he must have done way too much fumigating without wearing a mask in his earlier profession. For example, DeLay told a Hispanic Republican organization last year that he related well to U.S. Hispanics because, as a boy, he and his mother were flying from Venezuela to the USA, with a brief stopover in commie Cuba. While there, Tom vividly remembers, he and his mom had to walk from the plane to the terminal past "these really smelly, ugly soldiers." Apparently this single sniff of Castro's rebel (and decidedly Hispanic) soldiers has stuck with DeLay all these years, for in his talk to the Hispanic Republicans he set his jaw firmly, dropped to his sincerest tone of voice, and delivered the punchline to this tale of a boy's brush with Latin communism: "The fight for freedom in Cuba is sort of personal for me."

If coherence were money, Tom couldn't make change for a nickel, but this has never been a burden in Washington, where a position of real power can magically turn ugly men handsome, and make idiots seem suddenly sagacious. DeLay has that kind of power, including the power to create or kill legislation. Checking around, I've found that his various actions and habits have made him a man of many nicknames on the Hill: "The Exterminator," for obvious reasons (though the unkind reduce this to the less flattering "Bug Man"); "The Hammer," which is derived from the Mafia-like whammy he puts on corporate lobbyists when he feels they are not paying enough in campaign contributions to the GOP for the legislative favors they are getting; "Tom the Strange," again for obvious reasons; and, most interestingly, "The Man from Saipan."

To understand this last one, you have to look some 8,500 miles west of Washington to the Northern Mariana Islands—a balmy and beautiful place that has become an unlikely but important outpost in the new global economy. Unlikely because this fourteen-island archipelago in the Pacific is tiny, quite remote, and has little population and no industrial resources. The islands have only seventy thousand residents, most of whom live on Saipan, the largest island—thirteen miles long and six miles across at its widest point. The economy seems naturally geared to the tourists who come here, mostly from Japan. They come for the warm clime (the sun shines *every* day, and daytime temperatures rarely go above eighty degrees or below seventy) and to enjoy the lolling pace, glorious beaches, lazy palms, luxury resorts, snorkeling, championship golf courses, and other pleasures. If Americans know of the islands at all, it's because Saipan was the scene of a ferocious, monthlong battle against the Japanese during World War II. How many of us are even aware that Saipan and the other islands are now formally a part of the United States, having become a U.S. commonwealth in 1976?

WELCOME TO THE USA. There are a few Americans, however, who know all about Saipan, though they would just as soon keep their knowledge under wraps. This group includes such prominent citizens as Tommy Hilfiger, Ralph Lauren, Donna Karan, J. Crew, Lord & Taylor, Brooks Brothers, Banana Republic, Nordstrom, and other brand-name marketers of upscale clothing, as well as such mass marketers of cheaper lines as the Gap, JCPenney, Sears, and Wal-Mart. These clothiers import a billion dollars' worth of garments from Saipan to the U.S. mainland every year. The reason they would rather you not know about this is because they are getting their boatloads of goods by participating in a pernicious, tightly organized Saipan sweatshop system that ruthlessly exploits thousands of the world's poorest, most desperate workers who are brought to the island as indentured servants.

The system works according to the natural law of greed: (1) The brand-name clothing companies, practicing the most basic tenet of globalization, have long been abandoning their U.S. factories and scouring the globe for the cheapest manufacturing labor they can find; (2) knowing this, entrepreneurs from China, Taiwan, and South Korea smelled a chance to make a bundle and began building huge sewing factories on the island of Saipan in the 1980s, getting contracts with the companies by promising to produce clothing *very* cheaply; (3) to fill the sewing benches of these factories, the owners hire "recruiters" who travel the backroads of China, Bangladesh, the Philippines, Thailand, Sri Lanka, and other impoverished lands in Asia to entice the uneducated (mostly girls and very young women), desperate to make life better for themselves and their families, to become "guest workers" in beautiful Saipan, USA, promising wages as high as $1,000 a month, which is a fortune to people whose incomes average $250–$350 a year;

and, (4) the "guest workers" sign an indenture (a work contract) that commits them to up to three years on the job, they
pay a fee of $2,000 to $7,000 to the recruiters (usually borrow-
ing from their extended families or from usurious money
lenders) for having brought this amazing opportunity to them,
then they pack up and leave their loved ones for a great and
prosperous adventure in what many are told is "America."

More than forty thousand of these foreign "guest workers"
are in Saipan, which makes them more than half the population of the islands. When they disembark to begin their American adventure, they quickly discover it is going to be a
nightmare of peonage:

- Passports are seized, which makes each of them a "global
  prisoner," unable to go back home or anywhere else without getting their passports back, which they do only if they
  complete their contracted term and cause no trouble.
- Many must sign what are called "shadow contracts" waiv-
  ing basic human rights—including freedom of speech, the
  right to practice their own religion, the right to date or
  marry, the right to seek a raise, or the right to look for
  another job.
- They spend their days sitting on hard benches and sewing
  at a grueling pace for twelve to sixteen hours a day, often
  seven days a week, technically being paid $3 an hour, but
  many hours of "off-the-clock" work without pay is
  expected, and there are weeks when some workers are
  denied any pay because a supervisor arbitrarily rules that
  they were not "efficient."
- They are screamed at, groped, harassed, and beaten by factory supervisors—Robert Collier of the *San Francisco
  Chronicle,* who traveled to Saipan last year and interviewed
  workers away from their factories, reports on one woman
  from northern China: "She was forced to work long hours
  of unpaid overtime to meet production quotas. Her supervi-

sor yelled constantly and beat the workers 'whenever he felt like it,' she said. He also forced her and others to 'lend' him money that was never repaid."

- The factories literally are sweatshops, usually having no air-conditioning, no fans, poor ventilation, air that is filthy with cotton and synthetic fibers, heat so intense that workers faint, and no water available to the workers, plus such dangerous conditions as fire exits chained shut and safety shields (to protect workers' hands) removed from the sewing machines to speed up production.

- Factory housing compounds are more a prison than a home, with the barracks being locked down at night, surrounded by inward-pointing wire fences that are topped with razor wire and watched constantly by company guards who prevent workers from leaving without permission, which not only controls their movements but also prevents them from being visible to tourists and the local residents.

- Living conditions are abominable—as Collier described one place he saw on his trip, "In the company dormitory where 120 workers lived, eight to a room, conditions were primitive: Food was unsanitary and there were a total of three working toilets and five showers." Each worker is charged about $100 a month for the bug-infested food, and another $100 for their crowded rooms, which usually come with bare concrete floors and a bed made of plywood and a thin pallet.

Why do they stay, you ask? Aside from that nasty little passport problem, they or their families have gone deeply into debt to get them here, so they are stuck in a grotesque catch-22, having to stay until they earn enough to repay what they had borrowed to pay the recruiters who sent them on their American adventure. Some become so desperate that they attempt to sell one of their kidneys or other organs to pay off the debt.

But wait a minute, this is the USA, right? It's a territory like Puerto Rico and Guam, which have to comply with U.S. labor and immigration laws—so why not Saipan? Two words: "loophole" and "screw-you." First, the loophole. Under the "Covenant" that made the Northern Marianas a U.S. commonwealth in 1976, the islands were allowed a ten-year exemption from our minimum-wage and immigration laws—sort of a "breather" period during which they could attract some business investments, with the understanding that Congress would then bring them up to snuff with everyone else. By 1986, however, the Saipan sweatshop operators were already moving in, and lobbyists for them and the clothing companies were able to stall any congressional action. There was no great push in Congress to do it anyway, since few members had ever heard of this place and shipments of apparel from there were small. This ho-hum attitude allowed the operators time to build their exploitative system through an unregulated flow of immigrants and a subminimum wage.

Second is the screw-you factor. Even the federal and local laws that do apply are routinely ignored by the factory owners and unenforced by the authorities. Violations of federal safety and health standards, for example, are rampant in the island's garment industry, and the abuse of the immigrant workers has been so extreme that both the Reagan and Bush administrations were compelled to complain to the commonwealth's governor—yet nothing changes. The scandalous Saipan system has thumbed its nose at the feds, saying in essence that "we're-8,500-miles-away-and-we-know-that-you-don't-have-the-gumption-to-go-against-us-and-the-clothing-companies-so-screw-you." As for the extremely minimal local laws, Rep. George Miller (who has been to Saipan, issued two landmark reports on labor and human rights abuses there, has sponsored legislation to stop the abuses, and generally has been a steadfast champion for reform) politely refers to enforcement as "episodic at best."

As for the Gap, Ralph Lauren, Donna Karan, Tommy Hilfiger and the other labels that profit from the exploitation, they claim to know nothing, *absolutely nothing*, about what goes on, and if anything does go on please understand that they find such goings on to be *absolutely deplorable*, not to mention being against their "corporate code of conduct," which is *absolutely firm* on the matter of opposing such gross exploitation, but you've got to understand that some of these foreign factory owners can be *absolutely unscrupulous*, so what's a company to do?

Hold it right there, You-Who-Speak-With-Forked-Tongue. Even P. T. Barnum couldn't sell that line to a roomful of suckers. What do you mean you don't know what goes on in the factories? You regularly send your quality-control inspectors inside, and your buyers routinely are in the Saipan garment district to review production quality and discuss orders with the owners and managers. As for putting a "code of conduct" poster on the factory wall, that's about as effective as putting a "Please do not use profanity" poster at the entrance to a Marilyn Manson concert.

Carmencita Abad says such corporate innocence is an insulting sham, and she should know. She left her home in the Philippines in 1992 to come to a Saipan factory, where she spent more than six years in a factory making clothes for companies like the Gap. Now she's a plaintiff in a historic class-action suit against eighteen of those companies, alleging a racketeering conspiracy among them to profit from the use and abuse of indentured labor: "This abuse occurs while U.S. retailers watch," she says. "I have seen many times the Gap inspector come into the factory, look at the garment and fabric, then turn and walk out the door. In my factory, the Gap code of conduct is posted over the water fountain. But the code is written in English, a language the ... workers can't speak or read. Some U.S. retailers have offices on the island where their fabric inspectors work. Where are the people inspectors?"

Some companies go further than plastering codes of conduct around, claiming that they only contract with Saipan factories that have "good working conditions." But a human-rights watchdog group called Global Survival Network, which sends its own investigators into labor-trafficking areas like the Northern Marianas, looked into one such claim by a U.S. brand-name apparel firm and found its garments being made in at least two substandard factories "where workers endure appalling working conditions." The investigator also checked the barracks of workers making clothes for this firm and found less-than-charming accommodations, including one where "fourteen women shared a single room with one toilet."

Why do these corporations play such games, pretending that nothing is amiss here, and even if there is it's not of their doing? Because they desperately want the Saipan Sweatshop System to continue, since it's a bonanza for their bottom lines. Here they not only get the indentured labor savings in the making of their shirts, blouses, pants, and whatnot, but remember, Saipan is the USA. They can ship these items straight to a store near you without paying a penny in tariff or having to worry about any quotas! It's as though the clothes were made in Massachusetts rather than the Marianas—open up the ports and let the goods roll in, duty free! With a billion dollars a year *wholesale* arriving on our docks from Saipan, the brand-name companies save $200 million they otherwise would owe in tariffs.

There's another Saipan subsidy built in, too. All other U.S. territories and commonwealths must ship their products to the United States on U.S. ships rather than on the notorious cheap-labor boats flying certain foreign flags. Once again, however, the Northern Mariana Islands were given a temporary exemption when they gained commonwealth status—another loophole that Congress has not gotten around to plugging. So the apparel marketers get another special financial break by shipping from Saipan USA to mainland USA aboard foreign ships.

Let's tally the apparel subsidies available solely from this tiny island. One: You get your goods made dirt cheap for you by practically enslaved labor. Two: You can transport the goods at rock-bottom price some 5,500 miles to our West Coast ports on substandard ships using crews that themselves are wage slaves. Three: You get to unload without even nodding to Mr. Customs—Welcome to America, land of the free! And, just to put a pretty bow on the package, your whole load gets to have a "Made in the USA" label attached to it! After all, Saipan is America, too—even if its sweatshop system is decidedly un-American.

Factoid: In the 1990s, while Saipan's sweatshops were swelling with some forty thousand "guest workers" from the most impoverished regions of Asia, some sixty-six thousand mainland Americans lost their jobs making the very products now made in Saipan.

TOM, DICK, JACK, AND WILLIE. This brings us full circle to "The Man from Saipan." In a refreshing respite from the dreary Washington winter, Rep. Tom DeLay journeyed to the sun-splashed commonwealth of the Northern Mariana Islands in January 1998 for a week of "fact-finding." To help him search for facts, he brought his wife, Christine, his daughter, Dani, his chief of staff, his general counsel, and his PR man. Tom and team looked diligently for facts on the beaches, in their luxury resort, on the golf courses, in the CNMI governor's office, and in the executive offices of the owners of Saipan's garment factories. I'm sure he would have loved to have cocktails with Carmencita Abad, but the whip is a mighty busy guy, and you just can't see everybody.

His fact-finding mission was one of dozens that members of Congress (mostly Republicans) and their staffs have taken to the islands, usually in the prime fact-finding months of December, January, and February—all paid for by the government of the Northern Marianas. The price of these trips does not have to be publicly itemized or disclosed by the CNMI nor by the congressional offices, because the islands are considered to be the USA, so a congressional trip there is treated no differently from, say, a trip to Maryland. However, *Roll Call* newspaper estimates the total travel tab at more than half a million bucks for a dozen lawmakers and about ninety staffers. Every GOP leadership office has had staff members hosted on the islands as part of what Jack Abramoff describes as "an aggressive campaign to educate members." Abramoff is chief lobbyist for the Washington firm of Preston Gates Ellis, and *Roll Call* reports that he has hauled in more than $5 million in fees from the Northern Marianas' government for being its point man in the Nation's Capital. The upshot of his work is to preserve the status quo for Saipan's sweatshop system—no change in the wage and immigration loopholes, no change in the shipping loophole, no change in the island's free-tariff and quota status, and no change in the Made-in-the-USA privilege. Jack is a good choice for the government (which is nothing but a front for the powerful sweatshop owners, who account for a fourth of the commonwealth's total operating budget and are the backroom puppeteers of local politics), because Jack is connected.

He's especially tight with Tom. Abramoff and his wife, Pam, have given $20,000 to DeLay's assorted political committees. Also, to help coordinate business between the lobbyist and the lawmaker, DeLay's former top assistant has moved to Abramoff's lobbying firm, where he, too, lobbies to keep the sweatshop system intact.

Enter Dick Armey, the House majority leader. Five of his top aides have done the Saipan run, and he also has been the beneficiary of funding largesse from Abramoff. In turn, Dick has joined Tom in helping Jack and his faraway clients prevent any intrusion into the "Saipan way" of doing business. In June 1997, the two powerful lawmakers wrote to Froilan Tenorio, then the commonwealth's governor, to assure him and the island's garment moguls that they would be like two snarling Dobermans guarding against any Washington attempt to mess with their arrangement. As reported by the Global Survival Network, Dick and Tom wrote: "It has come to our attention that President Clinton recently advised you by letter of his belief that certain federal immigration, naturalization, and minimum wage laws should be applied to the Commonwealth. We are surprised by the President's position. . . . We want our fellow Americans living in the Commonwealth to rest assured that any legislation that would negatively alter the Covenant or in any other way harm the economic, social or political well-being of the CNMI is counter to the principles of the Republican Party, and this congress has no intention of voting such legislation. We commend you on the achievements you have made in the causes of freedom and encourage you to continue on your path to bring prosperity, liberty, and justice to the Commonwealth of the Northern Mariana Islands."

You can imagine, then, that when DeLay and his entourage arrived in Saipan for their January '98 visit, they were met with hallelujahs and cries of jubilation. DeLay was feted at a special New Year's party that was jointly hosted by Governor Tenorio and Mr. Willie Tan, a Hong Kong tycoon whose Tan Holdings Corporation is the biggest garment maker on the island (and one accused of stomping on more labor laws than the Pinkertons).

Tan and Tom were already buds, since Mr. Tan maintains his own lobbyist in Washington and had visited the whip before. Being in Tan's own domain and getting such an effusive reception, an ebullient DeLay overflowed with praise for their sweatshop system. In a speech first reported by *Salon,* the on-line magazine, DeLay said, "When [Willie Tan] came to my office at the Capitol, he told me about the conservative policies that the CNMI have implemented. . . . When I played golf with [Tan's Washington lobbyist] and the Speaker in Houston, they told me about the attempts of the Clinton Administration to kill prosperity on the islands. And when one of my closest and dearest friends, Jack Abramoff, your most able representative in Washington, DC, invited me to the islands, I wanted to see firsthand the free market success in the CNMI and the progress and reform you have made. Even though I have only been here for 24 hours, I have witnessed the economic success of the CNMI, and I have witnessed the friendship and good will of its people." Building to a crescendo, DeLay once again lambasted Democrats, promised to be resolute in his defense of the island's system, and closed with this: "Stand firm. Resist evil. Remember that all truth and blessings emanate from our creator. God bless you and the people of the Northern Marianas."

Goodness. Rhetoric like that should be bottled. Then put on a rocket and shot so deeply into darkest space that it'll never come back to harm anyone again!

Steven Galster, the director of Global Survival Network, conducted an undercover investigation that produced an unusually candid snapshot of how money power and political power collude. Posing as a garment buyer from New York, he arranged a meeting in Saipan with Willie Tan to discuss doing business together, but first he told Tan that he needed to know whether buyers like him could count on the sweatshop system continuing. Here are excerpts from their discussion, which Galster videotaped with a hidden camera:

GALSTER: I'm hearing about issues with wages and federal regulation. . . . What do you forecast in terms of Congress? Is that going to change?

TAN: I have a real good friend of Tom DeLay, the majority whip. And Tom tell me, say, Willie, as long as we are in power, they can't even see the light at the end of the tunnel, they don't even see the light. . . . Now, it look like George Bush son will become the next president. . . . Quite possibly. If we are Republican, we have no more problem again. . . .

GALSTER: So you think as long as the Republicans are in control there won't be a problem?

TAN: We have no problem. . . .

GALSTER: Yeah, well . . .

TAN: I'll be in DC next Friday. . . . I go to visit Tom, you know, some of my friends who are always helping me, they looking at schedule me to visit him.

GALSTER: That's another important thing for us to know, that political backing and stability . . .

TAN: Don't worry. . . . Because Tom DeLay will never let it go.

GALSTER: You're sure?

TAN: Sure. You know what Tom told me? He said, Willie . . . as majority whip, I make the schedule of the Congress. And I'm not going to put it on the schedule. They got to go through all committee before it come to me. Even if it come to me, I'm not going to schedule it. . . . So Tom told me, forget it, Willie, not a chance.

GALSTER: And you're sure his loyalties aren't going to change?

TAN: We very close friend.

Mr. Tan went on to offer a testimonial to DeLay's friendship and power, referring to the effort by George Miller to move his reform bill, called the "US-CNMI Human Dignity Act," which is graced with more than eighty cosponsors. Miller has been turning up the heat on Don Young, the Republican chairman of the committee that has jurisdiction over U.S. territories, demanding that the committee at least hold a hearing on his bill. He's not asking that Young approve of the bill, but that he just have a simple public airing of the Saipan situation. Willie Tan told Galster that his friend DeLay showed real leadership on this dangerous threat to debate a public policy issue:

TAN: And you know what he did, he call those guys. He call up the guy who is in charge of the committee, his name is Don Young from Alaska.

GALSTER: Yeah, I know who he is.

TAN: And he said, Don, nothing wrong with CNMI. He say, you gotta go there. . . . Tom explain to them. So, Don Young backed off.

Don also took Tom's advice to "go there." In February of '99, Chairman Young also took the winter trip to the Northern Marianas, declaring as he started, like some Marco Polo going west, "For too long, the people and issues of the U.S.-affiliated islands in the South Pacific have either been ignored or given little attention. This oversight trip will provide important insight into a number of the vital issues that will be addressed by [my] committee this session." Like DeLay before him, Young holed up in a luxury resort and met with the governor and the executives, never quite finding time to conduct unannounced inspections of the factories or barracks where the "guest workers" are so discreetly tucked away. He did meet for fifteen minutes with some Bangladeshis who were conveniently made available to tell him they had zero complaints about the Saipan system. An hourlong meeting with less controlled workers had been set up, but Young walked out as this session started. Perhaps he had a tee time he couldn't miss.

Whatever, when Young got back to Washington, he reneged on his Marco Polo speech, not only refusing to hold any hearings on Representative Miller's bill or address "the vital issues" of the islands but also sending a three-page letter to GOP senator Spencer Abraham of Michigan, who is sponsor of his own Saipan reform bill. The essence of Young's message: I've been over there . . . no problem . . . stay out of it. So far, everyone in the GOP has, and the system rolls on.

Meanwhile, "The Man from Saipan" has come away from all of this with a global lesson for us. He says that we should import the Saipan system to our shores! Do away with the minimum wage, Tom urges, let corporations here at home send recruiters into Mexico to find impoverished people who, he believes, would gladly sign an indenture for the chance to come to the USA, and have these "guest workers" labor in our factories, building a "free market success," Saipan style. Stand firm. Resist evil.

There is a ray of light in this dark story, however, for the companies involved in the Saipan scam are not all standing as firm as Tom would like. Under pressure from consumers, four retailers broke ranks last August and settled the claims against them brought by Carmencita Abad and others in the class-action racketeering lawsuit. J. Crew, Cutter & Buck, Gymboree, and Nordstrom have agreed to set up a $1.25 million fund to finance an independent monitoring program of their contractors in the Northern Marianas. Verité, a highly-regarded human rights group based in Massachusetts, will monitor compliance with strict new employment standards that include elimination of "recruitment" fees, payment of overtime, obeying U.S. labor laws, providing safe food and water, and guaranteeing basic civil rights. Verité will establish an ombudsman's office on Saipan to oversee the conduct of contractors, and it is authorized by the four retailers to make unannounced visits to the factories and dormitories, to investigate worker complaints, and to terminate contracts with factory owners who continue the abuse.

The Gap and others, sadly, have remained arrogantly recalcitrant, but as more and more Americans learn of the Saipan stain, these brands will have to come clean, too. When fighting for justice, think of the common mushroom—it seems so soft, so momentary, even fragile, yet it has the power and perseverance when growing to push through three inches of asphalt to get to where it wants to be. Now think of Tom DeLay's head. Three inches of asphalt. We can do it.

FREE TRADE GOES BANANAS

Alferd Packer had a bad winter back in 1873–74, but not as bad as the five other men who had joined him on a gold-digging expedition. Leaving their homes in Hinsdale County, Colorado, the prospectors set out to seek their fortunes in the Uncompahgre Mountains but got trapped by a blizzard and were forced to endure two months of bitter winter without adequate supplies. Finally, Packer made his way out, arriving at an army post to tell of cold so terrible and hunger so prolonged that only he had survived. The army officer in charge, however, noted that Packer seemed uncommonly healthy for a starving man. Even well fed. Alferd quickly found himself arrested on suspicion of murder and—gulp!—cannibalism. He never confessed, but back in Hinsdale County, Judge M. B. Gerry found him guilty and, when sentencing him, added a political dimension to Packer's repugnant deed: "There was only sevin Dimmycrats in Hinsdale and you, you voracious, man-eatin' sonuvabitch, you et five of 'em. I sentence you to hang until you are dead, dead, dead!"

Absurdist "free-trade" policies have become the Alferd Packer of the Dimmycrats 126 years later. In an act of stunning betrayal, national Democratic leaders have embraced the cannibals, advancing a policy of unbridled corporate globalism that is devouring the majority constituencies of the party, including working families, family farmers, and environmentalists. As a result, the expansion and protection of profits for global executives and speculators have been given primacy above everyone else and every other value and goal in the world—including the shared value of democracy itself. Oh, sure, Washington and Wall Street alike *talk* about how free-trade and democracy go hand in hand, but most often you'll find them gladly *walking* hand in hand with even the most vicious of the world's despots, providing capital, political support, and legitimacy for their ruthless snuffing out of the faintest spark of democracy in their homelands. The major media outlets join the cheering for trade *über alles*—a 1998 *New York Times* piece, attempting to provide cover for the embarrassing fact that globalism and despotism seem to be such frequent buddies, bore the title: "Finding Reasons for Optimism About Authoritarian Regimes." I can hardly wait for the follow-up: "Thinking Positively About Child Labor."

The American government has a long history of being on the wrong side of democratic struggles, so today's two-party collusion with corporate profiteers to stomp on democracy's flickering flame around the world is not surprising, though it continues to be appalling. What is surprising—and what I think the American people are going to find appalling to the point of rebellion—is this little known fact: *Our own democracy is being subverted.* The corporate powers and their politicians have quietly been putting new governing structures and rules in place that effectively cancel democratic autonomy in the USA and elsewhere. This subversion has been going on without the knowledge of "We the People," much less with our participation and consent.

These global governing structures and rules are so undemocratic that they are autocratic. They put the world's corporate interests above our national interest and supersede your local, state, and national authority to make your own rules on everything from environmental policy to wages. The new structures and rules exist solely to protect corporate and investor interests, and whenever one of your laws is in conflict with theirs—theirs prevails. It is every bit as awful as it sounds—nothing less than the undermining of the people's right to self-government. Believe it or not, Washington has already agreed to this, and more of it is to come. The corporate assault on our sovereignty has been officially sanctioned by a little-known provision buried deep inside the North American Free Trade Agreement, which was rammed through Congress by hook and crook in 1993, and by the WTO (World Trade Organization), which was okayed by a special lame-duck session of Congress in December of 1994. The passage of both of these massive and momentous bills was accomplished on a rush-rush basis, with the razzmatazz of the media, the lobbyists, and the two-party PR machine going full-tilt, promising *Jobs *Growth *Prosperity *Democracy *Ice Cream *Hugs *Free Beer, and *A Partridge in a Pear Tree for everyone. Alas, few members of Congress ever read either of the bills, much less comprehended them, and many would be as aghast as you are to learn what they hath wrought. From the Caribbean to Massachusetts, Canada to Mississippi, people of the world are being rudely awakened to the fact that someone, somewhere, has subjected them to the selfish rule of an awesomely powerful global regime.

BANANAS. In the fall of 1995, the most amazing exchange took place between Bill Clinton and comedian Paula Poundstone—amazing because it was hilarious, totally unexpected, unintentionally embarrassing, and, of all things, broadcast live on television. The show was at Ford's Theatre, where Lincoln had been assassinated, and the occasion was a gala benefit that drew a live audience of Washington big shots and major political donors. Clinton was in the front row, and Poundstone was onstage doing an impromptu bit in which she was asking the President how it was determined whether someone got to sit with him or was relegated to the back row:

POUNDSTONE: What determines who gets which seat? Do you do the whole seating chart? (Laughter) Do you know who that is behind your head . . . ? Who is that?
GALA HOSTESS SEATED NEXT TO CLINTON: Carl Lindner.
POUNDSTONE: Carl Lindner. I'm sorry, I'm not familiar. Alright, what made you give him that seat? (Laughter) Alright now, tell us who it is.
HOSTESS: A whole lot of money! (Laughter)
POUNDSTONE: A whole lot of money! (Applause and laughter) Carl, I'm sure it was much deeper than that, sir. It was money and love, little buddy, don't you worry. (Laughter) What's Carl's role in the community? Carl, why do you

have so much money? (Laughter) Is that rude to ask? (Applause) Sir, what do you do for a living? I should know, but since I don't, would you tell me? Mr. President, do you know who Carl Lindner is? (Laughter)

CLINTON: (Nods yes)

POUNDSTONE: Would you mind telling me?

CLINTON: It's a secret.

POUNDSTONE: It's a secret!! (Laughter)

CLINTON: He's in bananas, sort of like you are.

POUNDSTONE: He's in bananas! Is that true, sir? He's what? He's the Chiquita banana guy! Gee, sir, without the fruit on your head, sir, I didn't recognize you. (Laughter and applause) Is that true? Why does the President know the banana guy?

Bang! Lincoln was not the only president who got shot in Ford's Theatre! Unbeknownst to her, Poundstone's joking question was right on target, and Clinton was dying on the inside even as he laughed outwardly. Why *does* he know the banana guy? Because Clinton and this right-wing Republican businessman from Cincinnati have been engaged in a long-running globalist power play against Europe. Clinton and Lindner are unlikely political partners in a deadly serious effort to force the European people to buy more of Carl's bananas, which he produces on plantations in Central America, rather than them buying their bananas from small farmers in the Caribbean. Say what? I know this is hard to believe. In fact, it is so bone-deep stupid that even I can't believe it as I write it, yet there it is in all of its majesty: The President of the United States of America has been taking his time (lots of time) and the time of his cabinet and staff (lots and lots of time), using the full authority, power, and prestige of the U.S. government to tell the sovereign nations of Europe which bananas they can allow inside their own borders. This is how ridiculous U.S. policy, U.S. politics, and the whole globalization process have become, turning the world's most powerful nation into a shabby huckster for one particular banana baron.

How did it come to this? Let's start with the European Union, whose 15 member nations buy about $5 billion a year worth of bananas from all around the world. In 1993, the EU decided in its wisdom that it would set aside a small part of these imports for its banana-producing former colonies, especially the tiny Caribbean nations of the Windward Islands, including Saint Vincent, Saint Lucia, and the Grenadines. These countries are largely populated by descendants of Africans who were enslaved and taken there by the Europeans, so part of the EU's Caribbean banana policy reflects this history and a sense of obligation to be economically involved with them. In other words, guilt. On the other hand, many Europeans simply prefer the Caribbean fruit, which is slightly smaller than others, but tastier. Whatever their reasons, it strikes me that Europeans ought to be able to decide for themselves where they'll buy bananas. But then, I'm old-fashioned like that.

Enter "Crazy Carl," the Cincinnati Chiquita man. Lindner, a corporate buyout artist who has amassed an $830 million personal fortune through ownership of various businesses, made a hostile raid on United Brands Inc. in 1984, grabbing it and its premier brand, Chiquita bananas. This takeover literally makes him the globe's Top Banana, giving him control of 26 percent of the world's market (the Big Three—Chiquita, Dole, and Del Monte control two-thirds of all banana sales on earth). He's the biggest banana peddler in Europe, too, but the bigger the hog, the hoggier he gets, and Lindner wanted it all.

The Wall Street Journal reports that Lindner is fond of handing out cards proclaiming: "Only in America! Gee, am I lucky!" His homilies on America's free-enterprise mystique aside, Lindner doesn't count on luck or free enterprise for his fortune; he counts on pure political pull with his friends in high government places. When the EU announced its 1993 plan to award *less than 10 percent* of its market to the tiny Caribbean nations, Lindner didn't say, in true Adam Smith fashion, I'll become more efficient and earn more of the 90 percent-plus of the market not designated for former colonies. No, instead he went running to Washington, demanding that our government do something to squeeze out these small competitors.

He has plenty of swat in our Nation's Capital, since he and his company have stuffed more than $5 million into the campaign coffers of both parties this decade, the bulk of it to Republicans. Being such a longtime GOP fat cat, Carl naturally turned first to his retainers in that party. Former Senate majority leader Bob Dole was an early stalwart for Mr. Banana, having taken more than $150,000 in contributions from him since the Chiquita purchase, and having taken many rides on Lindner's fleet of corporate jets when he was running for the Republican presidential nomination in 1996. It had been puzzling to Capitol observers when, from somewhere out of right field, Dole up and announced in 1995 that his "top priority" in the congressional session was going to be getting a grip on the banana issue. Whoa, Bob, get a grip on yourself, thought many. But Dole was not alone among GOP leaders standing tall on this crucial matter of such concern to every American—Newt Gingrich, Trent Lott, and others joined Lindner's banana bunch, introducing legislation, holding up executive-branch appointments, writing official letters, making speeches, and generally beseeching and screeching, demanding that Europe get those little Caribbean Davids off the back of their favorite Cincinnati Goliath. But Europe didn't budge.

Then, a new sledgehammer fell into Lindner's hands. Congress approved U.S. membership in the World Trade Organization in the fall of 1994, and this obscure entity soon opened for business in Geneva, giving Lindner and his ilk just the tool they had been wanting for busting up the sovereignty of nations. Under the corporate-skewed rules of the WTO, any governmental action deemed to interfere in any way with a global corporation's sacred right to make and sell stuff wherever it wants, even when this does damage to others, is illegal. Deemed by whom? By a special international tribunal of global trade bureaucrats, whose sole criterion for judging a case is whether the governmental action gets in the way of a corporation's profit making, regardless of whether the government was doing something right for the larger community—like protecting the environment, preventing worker exploitation, promoting the growth of small business ... or providing a market lifeline for former colonies.

These WTO tribunals are Star Chambers. They meet in secret (usually in Geneva), they are presided over by "judges" who come from the corporate trade world and are in no way democratically chosen, they do not have to publish the reasons for their decisions, and there is no appeal of their rulings.

In short, they are an autocratic world court with a built-in corporate bias. "Purrrrfect," thought Lindner, "tailor-made for the likes of me." Carl's only problem was that he couldn't take his Chiquita case directly to the WTO—only governments can bring the cases, which in this case meant the White House. Hence, Republican Lindner's sudden fascination with Democrat Clinton, and vice versa. Necessity is also the mother of corruption.

The banana guy quickly moved onto Clinton's A-list—he had coffee in the White House, became one of the infamous "Lincoln Bedroom 938," and was one of Clinton's ten biggest contributors for his '96 reelection campaign. All the while, Lindner was pushing the administration to file a formal restraint-of-trade case against the EU on behalf of Chiquita. As *Time* magazine's Michael Weisskoff has reported, Lindner had been all over Mickey Kantor, a longtime Clinton confidant who was the U.S. trade representative. Weisskoff notes that "though hundreds of companies ask Washington to investigate unfair trade practices, the [trade rep] accepts only about fourteen cases a year. Even fewer are taken to Geneva for resolution by the World Trade Organization. And only rarely do such cases make the cut when hardly any U.S. jobs are at stake; Chiquita employs most of its 45,000 workers in Honduras and Guatemala. And yet Kantor took the case."

Despite the fact that the U.S. produces no bananas for export and had no national interest at stake, Kantor decided on April 11, 1996, to go to bat for Chiquita, filing a formal case with the WTO. *The very next day,* April 12, Lindner and his top executives began funneling more than $500,000 to Democratic Party committees in about two dozen states that were key battlegrounds for that year's presidential election. Lindner had been instructed by the Clinton campaign to send the money directly to these states, which have far looser public disclosure requirements than does the Democratic National Committee. Concerned citizen that he is, Lindner continued to shove money at the Democrats while his case moved through the WTO process, contributing $260,000 in 1998 (though he also continued to favor the GOP, putting $660,000 into its coffers in '98).

The WTO being what it is, Lindner won his case, which speaks volumes about the insanity of this organization's rules and the double insanity of our agreeing to let such a narrow interest reign supreme. It certainly was true that the Europeans were giving a small preference to bananas from one region of the world, but ... "NO BUTS ABOUT IT, BUCKO, THAT'S ALL WE HAVE TO KNOW," shouted the WTO tribunal, bringing down the hammer and declaring Chiquita the winner.

Some victory. Families in Europe will no longer get the product they prefer, and they can anticipate steadily rising banana prices as Chiquita locks up more of their market. In addition, when some guy named Lindner from some place called Cincinnati can go to something called the WTO and take away their right to decide which bananas they'll eat, Europeans have to admit that they no longer are a self-governing people.

But their dismay can't begin to compare to that of the islanders, who feel blindsided by their huge neighbor to the north, with whom they have been very friendly over the years. "Everyone is cursing the United States," Moses Eugene of Saint Lucia told the Associated Press shortly after the WTO ruling for Lindner. "When someone from down the street wants to buy your stuff and your neighbor interferes, it's not right." The entire economies of these Caribbean nations face devastation, for bananas are to them what cars are to Detroit. More than half of their export earnings come from sales of bananas, and nearly 20 percent of their total economic output is tied to the fruit. Well, you might ask, why don't they just switch to another crop? Because, one, why should they be forced to do that? And, two, they can't, at least not satisfactorily.

No other crop is nearly as suitable to these islands as bananas. The hilly terrain prohibits having fields for row cropping, but the banana plant can cling to a hillside and produce an enormous amount of fruit in a small space, plus the plants are naturally resilient, capable of withstanding the frequent battering of hurricanes that would destroy other crops. Also, bananas are ideal for the islands' small-farm economy and culture, since a family can make a living on the average farm of less than four acres—some twenty-four thousand independent farm families produce the fruit here. Contrast that to Lindner's massive banana plantations in Central America, where he and a handful of other barons own the land, while the people are reduced to propertyless laborers who are paid poorly and exposed to a toxic soup of chemicals in the fields, in their homes, and in their water. Chiquita alone has thirty-eight thousand banana workers on its plantations, and the company is aggressively antiunion, holding down its production costs by forcing powerless working families and the environment to pay the price. Yet, in the wondrous world of globalization, the Chiquita way gets rewarded and the Caribbean way gets punished.

In an article for *AlterNet,* David Morris tells us about Winston Graham, a banana farmer from the Windward Islands, who says, "We are told that the world has changed, that because of the WTO there must be a free market in bananas. But the market should not be so free that it can destroy people's lives."

FUNERALS, GASOLINE, TEA PARTIES, AND BLUE GOLD

It's common today for editorialists to call for gentility in political campaigns and to bemoan any personal criticism of an opponent, even if the so-and-so has the brain of a tapeworm and the ethics of an HMO executive. The result is to cleanse politics of its rhetorical spiciness, of the hot sauce and garlic that can give campaigns both pungency and truthfulness. I'm not defending the cowardly, negative attack ads on television, where candidates hire professional savagers to distort and lie about their opponents, but I'm referring to the insistence that candidates themselves must be oblique in referring to one another's political and personal failings. The result is a Bland-a-thon, a Bore-off, and a needless sanitizing of America's rambunctious and rowdy political tradition. I much prefer both the color and clarity of a good verbal shot, such as this one that Sam Houston fired at David Burnet in the 1842 campaign for president of the Republic of Texas: "You prate about the faults of other men, while the blot of foul, unmitigated treason rests upon you—you political wrangler and canting hypocrite, whom the waters of Jordan could never cleanse from your political and moral leprosy."

Even if the bland Al Gore or the beige Shrub Bush actually gave enough of a damn about some issue to work themselves into a genuine froth, their scripters and scrubbers would nix it instantly, instead arranging a carefully staged media event at which the candidate would be allowed to read a precisely worded statement that had been vetted through their top contributors and run through a focus group. You won't hear it from their lips, but one issue that cries out for the Sam Houston touch is the blot of foul, unmitigated treason that rests upon those members of Congress and those within the Clinton administration who knowingly saddled us with provisions in NAFTA and the World Trade Organizations that strip us of our democratic right to self-government. (I have to use the adverb "knowingly" because, sadly, most lawmakers who voted for these two sovereignty-busters had not read or understood the legislation they were voting on—if malfeasance won't get you, ignorance will.)

Knowing that our leaders have lied to us again and again, including in contemptible ways that sank us into wars costing the lives of tens of thousands of trusting young people sent to do their patriotic duty, I should not be shocked and amazed that they would so crassly sell out our very sovereignty at the request of their corporate contributors. But I am. More and more Americans are being shocked, too, as they discover, case by case, what has been done to them.

FUNERALS. Michael S. Allred of Jackson, Mississippi, was more than shocked to learn about the arcane and obscure "investor rights" provisions that lurk in Chapter 11 of NAFTA—he was dismayed, discombobulated, disheartened, flabbergasted, flummoxed . . . and ultimately furious. "It is a Gotcha that I certainly never thought was in there," he said in an interview on my *Chat & Chew* radio show.

Mike Allred is not a fellow who is easily stunned by anything in politics, nor is he a knee-jerk anticorporate lefty. He is a Goldwater Republican and an attorney who makes his living by representing businesses. When I say he's a Republican, I don't mean he has a casual affiliation with the party—he has been state chair of the Mississippi Young Republicans, a field rep for the state party, chair of Young Mississippians for Nixon, and general counsel of the state party for more than twenty years, and he remains today a legal adviser to the Republican National Committee. He counts Sen. Trent Lott, Sen. Thad Cochran, and former RNC chairman Haley Barbour as good personal friends. "You don't get any more true-blue Republican than me," he's pleased to say. But what, Allred wonders now, could Trent, Thad, and Haley have been smoking when they teamed with President Clinton to shove NAFTA through the Congress, Chapter 11 and all?

He became entangled in Chapter 11 after Jeremiah O'Keefe, a Biloxi, Mississippi, funeral parlor owner, asked him to handle his case against the Loewen Group, a massive funeral home conglomerate based in Canada. The business of burying people (or of providing "bereavement services," as the industry prefers to put it) has long been in the hands of local families like O'Keefe's. But, before you could say "ashes to ashes," a few very large corporate operators have swept into markets all across the country and locked them up, either by buying out the locals or muscling them aside. O'Keefe claimed that Loewen was muscling him, using various unlawful anti-competitive maneuvers in a strategy designed to drive him out of business, monopolize the market in the Biloxi area, then jack up the price on funeral services for the local people.

In 1995, a Mississippi jury not only agreed with Allred's arguments that Loewen was doing all of the above, but the jury was outraged by the conglomerate's unscrupulous behavior. "If there ever was an indefensible case," said juror Robert Bruce, "I believe this was it." O'Keefe was awarded $100 million in damages by the jurors, and they assessed another $160 million against Loewen in punitive damages, which are meant both as punishment and deterrent (just as jail time is for people), trying to prevent the corporation from doing it again. Loewen's lawyers, however, got the judge to force the jury to reconsider the punishment level, figuring that a new round of arguments in the courtroom would convince them that $160 million was too much. Arguments were held, the jury withdrew for deliberations—and this time they came back with $400 million in punitive damages.

Loewen next tried a couple of legal end runs to avoid the judgment, but they were unsuccessful, so it finally agreed in 1996 not to appeal the decision in return for a settlement that paid Mr. O'Keefe $175 million. And that would have been that. Except for NAFTA.

One can imagine some Loewen lawyer reading through NAFTA one night (yes, corporate lawyers often pass their time like this, hoping to come upon some morsel of legal avoidance, much like a hog rooting for acorns) and stumbling on Chapter 11. "Holy Saint Shyster," you can hear the lawyer shriek with delight! What this thing does is to give corporations like Loewen rights that you and I don't have, and rights that no corporation has ever had until this infamous trade agreement between Canada, the USA, and Mexico was passed into law. I'm going to be merciful here and skip the legalese, but what it comes down to is that, in 1998, Loewen suddenly sued the U.S. government for money, claiming that the Mississippi court system *expropriated* the assets of its investors and harmed their *future* profits. Was the company guilty, was it a thug, was it a complete asshole in its business dealings? Not an issue, assert the Loewen lawyers—the workings of Mississippi's legal procedures took money from us in violation of our international investor rights under NAFTA.

This is getting Kafkaesque. Bear in mind that these are the same legal procedures that U.S. citizens and corporations abide by in Mississippi, and that Mississippi, as Allred says, "follows the federal rules of civil procedure, so if there's anything wrong with our procedures they're wrong with every court in America." In other words, NAFTA has bestowed a legal right on foreign corporations that allows them to avoid the punishment our state courts impose on them when they do wrong, allowing them to demand that our national government pay for any fines and financial losses the corporation incurred as a result of the guilty verdict. In this case, Loewen is demanding $725 million from us taxpayers! (This might be a good time for you to pause, look up from your reading, take a deep breath, shake your head a time or two, and maybe pinch yourself, just so you know that what you just read is, indeed, what you just read.) What Loewen is claiming is so breathtakingly absurd that it needs restating: A foreign corporation can come to your state, attempt to monopolize your market illegally, get caught and convicted, agree to a cash settlement— then, citing NAFTA, claim that the state court has "expropriated" its investors' funds and that therefore American taxpayers must pay the cost of the settlement plus other financial setbacks it claims the court verdict caused. Shouldn't they have to wear clown suits when they make such claims?

Now, Kafka meets Orwell. NAFTA also allows the foreign corporation to bypass the legal system of the country it is suing. That's right: *The Loewen case is not subject to U.S. courts.* Instead, the case goes before one of two special "corporate courts" (international trade tribunals) designated by NAFTA. Loewen has chosen the International Center for Settlement of Investment Disputes as its legal forum. ICSID is an arm of the World Bank, which is one of the most elitist, corporate-friendly, antidemocratic institutions in the whole wide world. Going there is like a racketeering mafioso saying, "Instead of letting a federal jury judge me, what say I just keep it in the family by letting my Godfather decide the case?"

And what a setup these tribunals are. For starters, the good people of Mississippi, whose judicial fairness and integrity are under attack by Loewen, are not even allowed to participate in the ICSID proceedings. The Loewen case is being heard and ruled upon by three trade arbiters—*one of which is chosen by Loewen itself*! Allred points out that this tribunal "is a court of Star Chamber in the sense that it is not responsive to any people, any nation, any government, any electorate, and it does not have any organic law, such as our Constitution, that limits the breadth of its powers. It meets in secret, does not allow you to confront witnesses or cross-examine, and does not have to publish its proceedings or findings. . . . We understand [in U.S. courts] that anything that is vague and allows a judge to be a tyrant is unconstitutional. [The tribunal] has an informal procedure that consists of whatever they want it to be." ICSID literally can say, on behalf of Loewen, "Off with their heads," forcing the heads of our national government to pay $725 million to the Canadian corporation. There is no appeal.

Adding to the totalitarian absurdity is the fact that these Chapter 11 NAFTA cases can be filed, adjudicated by a tribunal, and paid out without you and me ever knowing they happened. There is no requirement that either the corporation bringing the claim or the government charged with the "investor-rights" violation has to make the case public. Indeed, the Loewen case only came to light because of the diligence of the watchdog group Public Citizen, which came across a tiny reference to it in a securities filing the company had made elsewhere. This raises questions about how many other cases have been filed—and the Department of Justice isn't talking.

Joan Claybrook, president of Public Citizen, says that a victory for Loewen "would completely undermine the American civil justice system." But even if Loewen loses on the merits of this particular case, the NAFTA Gotcha is still operative and available for other corporations to use. Loewen's lead attorney, James Wilderotter (no snickering, please, that's his real name), says we should just get used to it: "NAFTA is part of the American legal system, and the right to bring the action we have brought is clearly found within NAFTA." Slavery was once part of America's legal system, too, Mr. Wilderotter, but that didn't make it right, and a bloody war was fought to abolish it. I don't think that NAFTA's usurpation of our right to self-government will last long, once people see more foreign corporations using this special "right" to bring such actions against us. Our leaders in Washington might be bamboozled (or bought) by those global elites who are trying to force such an antidemocratic crown of thorns down on America's brow, but the people will not accept it.

Mike Allred says he is a libertarian Republican who supports the idea of free trade, but the kind of globalization games embodied in NAFTA are not at all what he has in mind: "I am extremely concerned for my country. I am concerned that the world seems to be more and more and more governed over by supranational corporations that are answerable to no one, and I am concerned that, in this specific instance, [Loewen] can supersede the Constitution that our fighting men fought and died for, letting a foreign corporation deprive the American people of their rights. . . . It is a surrender of the sovereignty of the United States."

GASOLINE. We are not alone in our concern. Canadian sovereignty already has succumbed to Chapter 11 in a case brought by Ethyl Corporation, based in Virginia. Ethyl is the sole producer of MMT, a gasoline additive used to enhance octane. MMT's primary ingredient is manganese, which is known to be toxic to the human nervous system, so here in America, the EPA is working to ban the additive from our gasoline.

Equally concerned about the health of its citizens, Canadian officials banned imports of MMT in 1997. But here came that Orwellian twist from NAFTA again—while Ethyl had no legal grounds to stop the MMT ban in its home country, it is a *foreign* corporation in Canada, so it was eligible to use Chapter 11 there. It claimed that the Canadian ban was an "expropriation" of its investors' profits, and an expropriation of the "good reputation" of the corporation. Pay us $251 million, demanded Ethyl! (I wonder if it used cutout letters from magazines to spell out this demand, like robbers sometimes do?)

In 1998, the Canadian government meekly submitted to the robbery. Fearing that it would lose the case in the NAFTA tribunal, officials settled by revoking their ban, paying $13 million to Ethyl, and even apologizing for implying that MMT is nasty stuff, even though they know it is. What we have here is a case of the presumed "rights" of corporate investors being given a morally superior legal status to the public's right not to be harmed by a corporation's industrial toxins. The term "absurd" seems completely inadequate here, so you choose: □ asinine □ barmy □ empty-headed □ farcical □ grotesque □ harebrained □ icky □ kooky □ moronic □ perverse □ poppycockish □ so stupid it makes my stomach hurt □ wacky to the max.

Californians, too, are learning about the new corporatocracy that has been sanctioned by trade schemes like NAFTA. Alarmed by the health risks of another gasoline additive (methyl teriaty butyl ether) that is leaking into the state's lakes, wells, and groundwater, Governor Gray Davis stepped forward in March 1999 and ordered a phase-out of MTBE, to be completed by 2002. Fine, California is a big boy, right, so it can do what it wants? Not so fast. Methanex Inc., a Canadian corporation that manufactures an ingredient used in the banned additive, has since trumped the governor's announcement by saying it will sue the United States under Old Mister Chapter 11. Its claim is that there was an eighteen-month "period of MTBE uncertainty" during which the ban was being discussed publicly in the California legislature and in the media, and that this very discussion caused Methanex's stock prices to drop, which is an "expropriation" of money from its shareholders.

I don't know about you, but I'm getting slaphappy from all these creative uses of NAFTA! Now we supposedly sovereign peoples cannot even talk about the possibility of regulating some killer of a product because some company somewhere might take a dipsy-doodle in its stock, which is a NAFTA no-no. Methanex Inc. says the California ban must be lifted and that American taxpayers owe the company $970 million for California's "expropriation" of its stock value and its market share. This nonsense would be hooted out of a U.S. court, but once again the case won't go to our judicial system but into the nether world of another NAFTA tribunal.

TEA PARTIES. Should you, through your local and state government, be allowed to apply moral and political principles when your tax dollars are used to buy computers, uniforms, gasoline, office furniture, trucks, and other goods? Should you, say, be able to decide through your local democratic process that your city hall should give a preference to Made-in-the-USA products, or refuse to buy products that contribute to rain-forest destruction, or say no to purchases from corporations that are involved in sweatshop labor or are doing business with horrendous human-rights violators in China, Nigeria, Burma, and elsewhere? Can you believe I'm even asking these questions? OF COURSE YOU SHOULD BE ABLE TO TAKE A PRINCIPLED STAND WITH HOW YOUR LOCAL GOVERNING BODIES SPEND YOUR TAX DOLLARS. SHEESH, THIS IS AMERICA—IT'S YOUR MONEY AND YOUR SOVEREIGN RIGHT AS A SELF-GOVERNING PEOPLE! Both as individual citizens and as a democratic electorate, we have the right to boycott brands based on our principles. The use of such direct economic action by local folks has been a noble part of the American experiment from the Boston Tea Party of 1773 to the boycott movement against South African apartheid some two hundred years later.

If the corporate globalists get their way, however, Tea-Party democracy in America will formally come to an end. "Stand on principle?" they gasp. "How naive. Stand on *principal* maybe, but principle, forget it. There are bucks to be made, boy, now get out of the way." They are out to slap down such local initiatives, and their first target is the fast-spreading grassroots movement to apply state and local sanctions against the bloody thugs who rule Burma. If there is a single poster boy for global horror, it is not Slobodan Milosevic but the SLORC of Burma. Not since Vlad the Impaler has a ruthless regime been more aptly named—just to say "SLORC" (the State Law and Order Restoration Council) conjures the image of some mutant creature from a 1950s horror flick, but these guys are all too real, and their military dictatorship gives brutality a bad name. During the past decade, the junta has crushed democracy and ruled by terror—routinely raping, torturing, enslaving, and killing the people of Burma. Sadly, its rule has been propped up by hard currency delivered to these thugs by brand-name corporations that have been all too eager to do business with them—producing oil, computers, clothing, and millions of dollars' worth of other goods. As Thomas Jefferson put it, "The selfish spirit of commerce knows no country, and feels no passion or principle but that of gain."

Like Sam Adams and his rowdy boys of 1773, however, groups of Americans have rebelled against these SLORC-made corporate goods and have organized across the country to "throw them overboard." Starting, appropriately enough, in the state of Massachusetts and spreading to more than twenty cities (including Boulder, Chapel Hill, Los Angeles, Madison, Oakland, and Portland), sanctions have been passed that are more than mere resolutions of conscience—these have teeth. These autonomous governments have decided that they will not purchase any products from corporations that do business with the Burmese junta. Some may think, so what if a few cities get uppity? But, as the motto of the Free Burma Coalition puts it, "When spiders unite, they can tie down a lion." If even one city puts its money where its mouth is, it makes a noise that the largest corporations notice. But when a state and a couple of dozen cities speak as one, billions of dollars in purchasing power are represented, and this startles the whole corporate world.

One important person who has heard the roar from the United States and been greatly pleased by it is Aung San Suu

Kyi. She is leader of the Burmese Democracy Movement, a winner of the Nobel Peace Prize, and a prisoner of the SLORC. She has praised the "selective purchasing laws" in the United States as an effective way to defund the thugs and give her movement a chance to restore democracy.

There is no doubt that the laws have been effective—Apple Computer, ARCO, Disney, Hewlett-Packard, J. Crew, Kodak, Motorola, and Pepsi are just a few of the corporations that have withdrawn from Burma since 1996, after Massachusetts and others took action. The laws have been so effective that, beginning in 1997, the global corporate powers launched a massive counterattack, claiming that these laws "interfere" with the global marketplace and, ironically, that they just don't work! Logic aside, they are using the World Trade Organization, the Clinton administration, the federal judiciary, and tons of corporate cash in a coordinated campaign to stomp on your and my right to decide how we spend our local and state tax dollars.

They have zeroed in on the Massachusetts law, presuming that if they kill it, all others will die, too. State representative Byron Rushing might not be a direct descendant of Samuel Adams, but he definitely is an heir to his rebellious spirit. Working with Boston-area businessman and Burma activist Simon Billenness, Representative Rushing sponsored the state's selective purchasing act and got it enacted. These two citizens, backed by thousands of supporters, have stood up to an incredible barrage of political and legal artillery hurled at them during the past two years.

First came Japan, wailing on behalf of Toyota, Mitsubishi, and twenty-eight other Japanese corporations consorting with SLORC that Byron's law was denying them their sacred global right to do business in Burma *and* with the state of Massachusetts, human rights and democracy be damned. The European Union joined in Japan's assault, complaining to Washington that this rogue state was violating a holy global commandment called the "Agreement on Government Procurement," found inscribed in tiny print upon the stone tablets creating the World Trade Organization. In January 1997, six months after Representative Rushing's law took effect, the Europeans sent a "démarche" (a formal diplomatic statement, often delivered by a stuffy guy in striped pants, morning coat, and silk top hat) to our state department, demanding repeal of the Massachusetts law or they would go to the WTO and file an AGP complaint ASAP. Rushing, Billenness, and group rallied the entire congressional delegation of the state to fire back at the EU with this formal statement: "We do not believe it is appropriate for the European Union to involve itself in the internal affairs of Massachusetts. If the EU chooses to place dollars ahead of human rights, it has that sovereign right, but the EU should not attempt to intimidate Massachusetts into changing the standards it has established for doing business with the state government." Alright, Ye Sons of Liberty—take that King George!

Alas, under the rules of the WTO, Massachusetts has no legal standing to defend itself there and had to count on the Clinton administration to protect its interest, which is like hiring Willie Sutton to guard the bank. This is the president, after all, who had pushed, prodded, and prostituted to get the WTO, including its procurement provision, enacted. His undersecretary of state, Stuart Eizenstat, was openly strategizing with the corporate interests to kill the Massachusetts law, and had testified before Congress in 1997 that "efforts by state and local officials around the United States . . . to impose various economic sanctions are inappropriate and counterproductive." Likewise, Commerce Secretary Bill Daley was hard at work trying to undermine the sovereign people of Massachusetts, telling a group called the European Institute in March of '97 that the Clinton team has "the same concerns on this" as the EU does, and assuring the assembled proponents of corporate sovereignty that he and other top officials were working with U.S. companies to put the squeeze on Representative Rushing and other Massachusetts stalwarts: "We've encouraged the business community to make their views known. Local legislators will respond better to local companies."

The business community did more than besiege Rushing with their executives and lobbyists; they filed suit in federal court to kill his law. The National Foreign Trade Council, a corporate lobbying outfit in Washington with some six hundred members, is the complainant in the lawsuit. It has refused to release its membership list, but Simon Billenness and his New England Burma Roundtable rooted some of them out. NFTC's board of directors includes such "local companies" as Allied Signal, Amoco, ARCO, AT&T, BankAmerica, Boeing, Boise Cascade, Caterpillar, Chase Manhattan, Chevron, Chrysler, Citibank, Colgate-Palmolive, Du Pont, Duracell, Ernst & Young, GE, GM, IBM, ITT, Johnson & Johnson, Kodak, Mobil Oil, Monsanto, PepsiCo, Pfizer, Procter & Gamble, Rockwell, Texaco, United Technologies, and Westinghouse.

The Trade Council's legal strategy cleverly shifts the focus from the global corporate interests by pretending that the issue is one of U.S. federal power versus state authority. The claim is simply that the people of Massachusetts are meddling in foreign policy with their Burma law, and foreign policy is the sole prerogative of Washington. Lest anyone doubt, however, that this is about globalism, the European Union took the most unusual step of filing a brief in federal court in support of the NFTC. Also, in solidarity with the U.S. corporate powers bringing the suit, the EU retained the politically connected law firm of Hogan & Hartson (where Clinton's national security adviser Sandy Berger held forth prior to moving to the White House) to represent its interests in the case and, pointedly, to be present during the trial. "We're not trying to intervene in a domestic constitutional issue," an EU official explained to the *Journal of Commerce* as the EU intervened in a domestic constitutional issue. "All we're interested in is the foreign policy powers argument." Hello, Mr. EU-man: The foreign policy powers argument *is* a domestic constitutional issue. Now, go home.

AWOL in this legal battle was the President, who could have had his Justice Department filing briefs and working with the outgunned state attorneys, raising the issue from one of legal technicalities to one of common sense and principle. Clearly, the Massachusetts legislature was not making foreign policy—it has no military force to send to Burma, nor can it tell Toyota or Texaco not to do business there. But it most certainly has the sovereign right to spend its own tax dollars on whom it chooses. But Clinton stayed low, choosing sides by his inaction on the case.

Unfortunately, with the EU and the NFTC locking arms and feeding their herd of silk-suited, Gucci-clad lawyers a steady stream of $1,000 bills, they prevailed with the judge, who sided with the powerful and against the people. He ruled that cities and states cannot use their purchasing power to reflect the local citizenry's moral principles on foreign policy issues. As Byron Rushing said after the verdict, "If a ruling like this had been made ten years ago, Nelson Mandela might still be in jail today." This fight, however, is not ultimately about foreign policy powers or state purchasing preferences, says Rushing: "It's a decision about whether, in a globalized economy, corporations have any accountability at all." He adds that the global corporation "doesn't want popular grassroots democratic actions to affect any of the business they do anytime, anywhere. . . . This is the tyranny of corporate America at work."

But Rushing, Billenness, and all the rest are not about to back down, and the fight goes on. The Massachusetts attorney general has appealed the case to the Supreme Court.

BLUE GOLD. Should we invade Canada? I mean with armed forces! Sure, they're nice people, and they're ever so peaceable. (It's going to be hard, I have to admit, to work up much xenophobic hatred in America toward a country that thinks "jeepers" is an expletive, that has "Be Polite" in its national constitution, and that merrily flies a flag with a friendly maple leaf on it.) But Canadians have something we need, and I don't mean hockey players. "Blue Gold," it's been dubbed by a Canadian newspaper, but it's far more valuable than that implies, since the world can actually do without gold.

Water. That's what Canada has that parts of our country and much of the world might literally kill for.

Hell, you say, water's everywhere, 70 percent of the earth is covered in the stuff. Yes, but as Canada's Maude Barlow points out to anyone who'll listen, less than one-half of 1 percent of all the water on the globe is *fresh* water available for us to drink. An author and agitator for common sense, Ms. Barlow heads the Council of Canadians and is founding chair of Action Canada Network, two grassroots groups working for progressive politics and policies. "Worldwide, the consumption of water is doubling every 20 years," she writes in a stunning report entitled "Blue Gold: The Global Water Crisis." Barlow calculates that in a very short while, *most* of the world's people will face shortages or absolute scarcity. This is not a matter of your having to see more news stories of wretched African children dying in horrible droughts, but of imminent water crises in America (the Southwest, Florida, and California especially), in southern Europe, in India, in England, in China ("the first country in the world that will have to literally restructure its economy to respond to water scarcity," predicts Barlow), and in other nations not usually thought of as facing massive water shortages.

Canada, on the other hand, has a blessing of *agua fresca.* W. C. Fields, who once complained of being stranded in the desert for three days with nothing but water to drink, would have gotten the heebie-jeebies in Canada, for there is water everywhere. Some 20 percent of the world's entire supply of fresh water is in the winding rivers and countless lakes splashed all across the vast land (more lake than land in many regions). This is not a reality that has dawned on Canadians alone. Others are casting their eyes northward, thinking, "There's gold in them thar hills." But it's not countries making invasion plans—it's corporations.

To get their hands on the gold, the corporate grubbers first have to change the way the world's supply of drinking water is managed. Instead of letting countries treat it as a *resource* to be held in common and allocated by the public for the general good, they want it to be considered as just another *commodity* to be held and traded by private investors strictly for their own profit. Like oil or pork bellies . . . only this is your drinking water they want to privatize and commodify. Will it surprise you to learn that those bratty globalization twins, NAFTA and the WTO, contain provisions that advance the commodity concept? Thought not. Both incorporate the bald assertion that "water, including . . . ordinary natural water of all kinds (other than sea water)" are "goods" that are subject to the new rules of global trade.

We're talking here about much more than bottled water—Perrier, Evian, Yellow Snow #5, and your other favorite boutique brands. We're talking about *bulk* sales, including whole lakes and aquifers being bought and mined, the flow of rivers being siphoned off, the Great Lakes themselves being put on the market. Maude Barlow and others report that corporations worldwide are already organized to do the deed, using supertankers, pipelines, canals, the rerouting of rivers, and every other mammoth scheme known to humankind to shift the product from water-rich nations to those markets willing to pay top dollar for it:

- Nordic Water Company now totes H_2O from Norway to thirsty European countries by tugging it across the sea in giant, floating plastic bags, like some surreal scene from the Beatles *Yellow Submarine* movie.
- The aptly named Global Water Corporation, a Canadian firm, has cut a deal with the town of Sitka, Alaska, to take

eighteen billion gallons of water per year from nearby Blue Lake and haul it to China, and it is joining with a Houston maritime outfit to ship more Alaskan water aboard bulk tankers to Singapore—"Water has moved from being an endless commodity that may be taken for granted to a rationed necessity that may be taken by force," GWC says in a chilling statement.

- The GRAND Canal (Great Recycling And Northern Development Canal) is an engineer's wet dream, involving the building of a dike across the huge James Bay (get out your atlas, kiddies!) to capture the water of the twenty rivers that flow into it, converting the bay into a giant freshwater reservoir, then building a network of canals, dams, and locks to move the water four hundred miles south to Georgian Bay, where it would be "flushed through" the Great Lakes into pipelines that would take it to America's Sunbelt for the watering of lawns, sprinkling of golf courses, and other essential needs.

- McCurdy Enterprises of Gander, Newfoundland, plans to "harvest" (you've gotta love their PR firms) some thirteen billion gallons of water a year from one of that province's lakes, pipe it to the coast, pump it into old oil tankers (well scrubbed, I'm sure), and ship it to the Middle East for a hefty profit.

- Monsanto sees a multibillion-dollar business opportunity in the emerging water crisis, with one executive saying bluntly: "Since water is as central to food production as seed is, and without water life is not possible, Monsanto is now trying to establish its control over water. . . . Monsanto [has launched] a new water business, starting with India and Mexico, since both these countries are facing water shortages."

"Canada," barked editor Terrence Corcoran of the *Financial Post* in a 1999 editorial, "is a future OPEC of water," urging that the country begin trading in this rich commodity pronto. Likewise, Dennis Mills, a member of Canada's parliament from the governing Liberal Party (which actually is an arm of the country's financial and corporate elites, à la the Democrats in Washington), is a "Blue Gold" booster and is pushing for assorted water projects and trading schemes, declaring with gusto, "Fortunes are made by those who control the flow of water." Thanks to citizen groups like the two Maude Barlow heads, however, the Great Canadian Water Sale-a-Thon has yet to surge forth, for they have alerted the citizenry and generated a national debate on the wisdom of shouting "y'all come" to every global greedhead with a big bucket. Their vigilance has produced a temporary moratorium across the country on bulk sales. This might be a good place for me to add that Maude, and Canadians generally, certainly are not saying "It's our water and the rest of the world can go suck eggs" (remember, these are *extremely* nice people). To the contrary, they are the ones pushing for a public policy of sharing their bounty to meet the global water crisis, allocating water particularly to help those people in need.

But the pressure is intense to simply turn the water loose and let "the market" decide who needs it. And that little nasty, Chapter 11, is being wielded to break the dam and turn the water loose. Sun Belt Water Inc., based in Santa Monica, California, has filed the first NAFTA water case. It had an agreement with a British Columbia company to take water from this far western province and ship it in huge tankers down the west coast to southern California. But such a public outcry ensued when the scheme became public that the provincial government stepped in to protect its water, nixing the shipment by enacting a moratorium on all water exports. Imagine if Sun Belt had quietly worked a deal to sink a siphon into Lake Tahoe and drain it into Los Angeles, and you'll get a sense of how the people of British Columbia felt about Sun Belt's raid.

"Screw the people" was the reaction of the California corporation. It sued Canada in 1998, claiming that its *future profits* were "expropriated" by British Columbia's export moratorium and that, under the infamous Chapter 11, the nice people of Canada owed it $468 million.

Money isn't enough, though. Sun Belt CEO Jack Lindsay also wants to slap the Canadians around a bit. He has expressed outrage at what he perceives as the stinginess of the Canadians: "California has 33 million people—more than the entire population of Canada. This is expected to double in the next 20 years, and they have been living in a permanent drought condition. In 20 years, the shortfall in California will be four million acre-feet of water [per year]—one percent of what spills into the Pacific Ocean from British Columbia—and they're saying 'Sorry, you can't have it'?" What a humanitarian. Jack just wants a few drops for the poor parched people of California. Next thing you know, he'll have Sally Struthers doing heart-rending ads on the BC telly, pleading in a quavering voice for the people of this watery province to "save the thirsty children of Beverly Hills."

What a crock. For the privateers and commodifiers like Lindsay, bulk water deals have nothing to do with global need and everything to do with global greed. As Barlow tells us, they'll deliver the water to whoever will pay the most to get it—like the water-gobbling high-tech companies of Silicon Valley and the sprawling agribusiness corporations that suck up irrigation water like insatiable sponges. Then there is Lindsay's snide comment that, after all, much of the province's water just "spills into the Pacific Ocean." This is a common refrain from the water corporatizers, who claim that if water isn't being used commercially it is being "wasted"—or, as one forest company exec says, if it's unused it's just part of the "decadent wilderness." Never mind that water running to the sea is an essential part of the ecological cycle, delivering nutrients, sustaining the whole fishing economy, replenishing wetlands, and doing much more useful chores than fattening the wallet of a would-be water baron.

Jack just keeps yakking, though, apparently confusing verbosity with profundity. Why is water any different from any other commodity, he wonders: "Canada chops down its trees so we can build houses in California. . . . But I'm watching this debate [over water exports] where Canada is saying this is hockey, this is apple pie." No, Mr. Lindsay, not apple pie, it's water—the essential of life, the unifying essence of the ecosystem, the invaluable resource that belongs to the whole public.

Also, Lindsay and his California corporation are not just "watching" the debate, they are doing all they can to decide its outcome. While they can't claim to be "naturalized" citizens of Canada, thereby legitimate participants in the debate, they do claim some sort of mutant "NAFTA-ized" citizenship in the country: "Because of NAFTA," Lindsay told the *Montreal Gazette* last year, "we are stakeholders in the national water policy of Canada." Sun Belt Water Inc., Ms. Barlow reports, "is openly courting BC coastal communities to consider water exports and is urging local politicians to lobby the provincial government to reverse its ban on exports."

Dealing with NAFTA is trickier than playing hockey in hell, and, for the Canadians, there is another nasty trick in the trade agreement that makes them vulnerable to an all-out corporate raid. Sun Belt and the other water hustlers only need *one* export deal in any one province to break the dam for *all* of Canada's water. This is because the devils who set up the NAFTA game rigged it with a provision called "proportionality," which means that if one company gets a deal, the country has to treat every other company the same. So when one company exports even a trickle of water out of Canada, that opens the tap for all other export deals, and the tap cannot be turned off—even if it is later proven that the massive outflow is doing horrible damage to the environment, to other businesses (fishing, tourism, etc.), or to the country as a whole. Tough luck—

you made your deal with the devil, even though the vast majority of legislators (much less the people) really didn't have a clue what was in the deal. That's the way the devil plays.

This is why Sun Belt Water Inc. is squeezing so hard in British Columbia. Canada's national government, rather than imposing its own ban on water exports, took the kind of half-assed approach our national politicians would take—they asked each of the ten provinces of Canada to implement their own voluntary moratoriums. This makes the politicians look like they've done something, when in fact all they've done is to create betting pools in offices across the country on which province will be the first to crack. If (or when) one province allows an export deal, all the other provincial moratoriums are immediately null and void—and the "Blue Gold Rush" is on.

YOU SASS

Ralph Lauren, the multi-billionaire fashion baron known for his preppy "Polo" line of clothes and other goods, made a news splash in 1998 when he engaged in a bit of "conspicuous philanthropy." He wrote a $10 million company check to the Smithsonian Institution to go toward the restoration of THE Star-Spangled Banner, the badly deteriorating 187-year-old flag that had inspired Francis Scott Key to write our national anthem, which, let's admit, is unsingable (but it's the thought that counts). Lauren Inc.'s donation produced what is known in public relations lingo as an Op-op—the optimum photo op. Held just after July 4th, it included the President of the United States, the First Lady, a brand-name CEO, the massive and historic flag itself, *and* a really big check—all of our national symbols arrayed for this one media moment. The only thing missing was a football.

The star-spangled ceremony was a promotional coup for Lauren's company, well worth the ten mil, for he received saturation media coverage as he wrapped himself in Old Glory, and he was given both a product endorsement and testimonial to his character by the First Couple. President Clinton: "You know, most of us have—well, maybe not most of us, but a lot us, including Hillary and me—have these great Polo sweaters with the American flag on it." Next the First Lady: "The phrase 'Ralph Lauren' has become an adjective for a certain kind of style. Now it will be a symbol of another aspect of the American way: good citizenship." Then Ralph stepped forward to add just the right touch of billionaire humility, saying that he was giving the money because "I am a product of the American dream, and the flag is its symbol." Nice.

But half a globe away one could get a totally different view of the Polo label and of Mr. Lauren's character. In Shenzhen, China, some 350 young women, eighteen to twenty-five years old, work at the Iris Fashion factory, making the clothing that has made Ralph Lauren so much money that he can live the American dream and still give away $10 million. The factory is a sweatshop. "I begin work daily at 7 A.M. six days a week," says a twenty-year-old who sews collars onto shirts for Lauren. "On a normal day, work ends around 9 P.M. If we are under pressure for a rush delivery, we work until midnight. Right now I average eighty hours per week. . . . I'm paid on a piece-rate basis, two cents per collar."

Every four minutes (*Oh, say can you see*) she has to complete a collar (*By the dawn's early light*), which she does for more than fourteen hours a day (*What so proudly we hailed*), six days a week (*At the twilight's last gleaming*) for an average of 29 cents an hour (*Oh, say, does that star-spangled banner yet wave*), which is a poverty wage even by China's standards (*O'er the land of the free*), and she lives jammed with her co-workers six to a room in a prisonlike factory dorm (*And the home of the brave!*).

Hers is but one of hundreds of thousands of real-life stories that are behind the labels of so many of the goods now sold in

American stores—goods that make philanthropists of the Ralph Laurens of the world, even while they bring the stench of rank exploitation to the Star-Spangled Banner itself. Cynics say the public doesn't give a damn, and the global manufacturers sure do all they can to keep the curtain pulled, hoping to keep the public in the dark about their manufacturing methods. Phil Knight, the Baron of Beaverton, Oregon, who has built his Nike empire and a personal fortune on the backs of sweatshop workers throughout Asia, is dismissive of those who raise sweatshop concerns: "This isn't an issue that should even be on the political agenda. It's just a sound bite of globalization." Now there's a guy who loses IQ every time he opens his mouth.

Cynics who think people don't care haven't met Tico Almeida or Eric Brakken, and if Nike's knight thinks he can keep this issue off the political agenda, he has not met Suzanne Clark or Joe Sexauer. These are but a few of the savvy and determined nineteen- and twenty-year-olds who are raising righteous hell about the immorality of the global sweatshop system and are taking matters into their own hands on college campuses all across America. The establishment media are only beginning to notice, but student activism today is not an oxymoron—it's back in a big way. From an insurgency that sprang up on five campuses in the fall of 1997, the movement (yes, it's already advanced to this lofty status) has spread in barely two years to more than a hundred campuses, from liberal Harvard to conservative Claremont College in Southern California, from rural Cornell to NYU in downtown Manhattan, from Ann Arbor to Tuscon. In the summer of '98, the students created a national umbrella organization so they could work together, naming it United Students Against Sweatshops. USAS is the acronym, but you have to say it the way the students do to get the energy and attitude they're bringing to the cause: "You-sass" is how they say it.

Sass indeed. These kids are smack in the face of their university presidents, are stripping bare the wussiness of the Clinton administration (not a pretty sight) on this basic issue of social justice, are rejecting outright the corporate shuck and jive intended to keep the exploitation going, and, most importantly, *are winning*! Well, they haven't won yet, but, my God, what strides they are making on an issue that few of the political cognoscenti, including the liberals, would have predicted (or wanted) to become "The Cause." How did this happen? Why *this issue*?

Because, first, students today are no different from those of us who rose up in the sixties against the outrage of denying civil rights to black people or against the insanity of the Vietnam War—these are people who have not had their ideals bought off or kicked out of them, and they are unafraid to Question Authority, as the bumper sticker keeps urging. Second, there has been a recent organized effort by unions (especially UNITE, the garment workers union) to expose the ugly truth of sweatshop labor to students, just as CORE, SCLC, and other civil rights groups did on campuses in the sixties, rallying a generation to act on conscience and join in the struggle to assure basic liberties for African Americans. Third, students take the sweatshop issue personally, and they can do something about it right where they are. Their focus is on the $2.5 billion a year that American universities pocket on licensing fees for the sales of sweatshirts, windbreakers, caps, Frisbees, stuffed animals, and other "stuff" that is sold bearing the logo of the Wildcats, Blue Devils, Badgers, Tigers, Tarantulas, Mud-Bugs, and other critters that are the mascots of the schools. University administrators license Nike, Reebok, Sara Lee, and other companies to sell these school-branded products, then the companies go shopping around the globe for subcontractors who will produce the goodies for next to nothing.

It doesn't take a very bright bulb to see the light here—the cheapest goods are sweatshop goods, and the university is profiting from the exploitation, paid for by student dollars.

This reality has struck a nerve with students who don't really want to put on a sweater made by someone as young as they are who is subjected to wage slavery and physical abuse as they stitch Bucky the Badger onto the sweater. "Free Bucky" became a slogan at the University of Wisconsin, where students have rebelled against their mascot being held captive by global sweatshop operators. Eric Brakken, a leader of the anti-sweatshop campaign on the Madison campus, says, "We're seeing a lot of people who've never been involved, because this is such a close issue for them."

So close that they have taken to the streets, protesting, marching, petitioning, and—déjà vu all over again—sitting in! University presidents who thirty-some-odd years ago were schooled on campuses where activists seized the offices of the presidents, now find their own offices occupied, though with some important differences. Like Dustbusters. Apparently, this is a much more polite, or at least a tidier, generation. While we were prone to shout the filthiest words in our vocabularies, write graffiti on the walls, cut phone lines, and generally trash an occupied office, the current crop of campus rebels literally have been known to bring Dustbusters and other cleaning equipment with them to clean up after themselves. They are very focused, very purposeful, and trash is not their objective.

Their objective is nothing less than to stop American universities from participating in the sweatshop system, and they are very clear and firm about what that requires:

1. A code of conduct that Nike and the rest must sign and abide by if they are to get any contracts from the university to sell products bearing the school name, logo, mascot, colors, etc.
2. A code that requires contractors to certify that their products are not made in sweatshops, which means at a minimum that there is no child labor or forced labor involved, that no sexual abuse or other violence is used against the

workers, that factory conditions are safe and healthy, that
fundamental civil liberties are honored, that workers can
exercise the right to form a union, *AND* (this turns out to
be a mighty big "and") that wages are sufficient to cover a
family's food, clothing, and shelter.

3. Agreement by contractors that any and all of their factories
   are open to unannounced inspections by *independent* monitors designated by the university.

4. Full disclosure by contractors of where their factories actually are, by specific addresses, including the location of all
   subcontracted work.

USAS leaders have learned the hard way that it's necessary
to spell all of this out for university administrators, as though
talking to small children—"No, dear, it's not enough to say the
factory is in Asia, because, see, we want the nice inspectors to
be able to go to the factory in person, and to go there means
they need to know the town it's in and have the actual street
address." Greased pigs are not as slippery as university officials get when asked to stand on principle against corporate
power, so the students have had to learn the art of cornering
them. One university president, desperately trying not to have
to deal with the matter of decent wages, tried to slip by with
this statement to students: "I think we can all agree that these
people should be paid more than zero."

The officials, pressured by their corporate donors, were dal-
lying with the activists, making soothing statements of principled concern while doing all they could to make the whole
thing go away. "We cannot tolerate having the sweat and tears
of abused and exploited workers mixed with the fabric of the
products which bear our marks," said the Duke director of
licensing, even as Duke's president was quietly trying to
swing a deal for a code of conduct that would cover up the
sweat and tears without doing anything to stop them. The first
cover-up attempt came in November 1998, through something

called the Collegiate Licensing Company, which is a middle-man broker between about 170 universities and hundreds of companies that make products for them. On the defensive as a result of the spreading campus protests, CLC produced its own code of conduct, which, not surprisingly, did not deal with sweatshop wages or require disclosure of factory locations. Grateful school officials were quick to cling to this thin reed: "Sometimes compromises are necessary," Duke president Nan Keohane lectured a group of students who were chanting "Principles, not politics" in protest of the CLC sham. The code was to be approved by February 1 of the next year, and she said she was planning to sign it. "I'd prefer to have a flawed code than no code at all," she told them, as though these were the two choices available to her.

No sale. The students regrouped during the holiday break, and on January 29, 1999, Tico Almeida and a hardy band of thirty other Blue Devil protesters walked into Nan's office and set up camp—the first ever sit-in over a code of conduct. Zapping a constant stream of e-mail updates to antisweatshop leaders across the country, the Duke action electrified the movement—all the more so when, after thirty-one hours, President Keohane agreed to require full disclosure of plant locations from any manufacturers their school dealt with.

A week later, Georgetown's no-sweat activists spent seventy-two hours in their president's office, also winning a commitment to full disclosure. In Madison, U. of Wisconsin students sat in for ninety-seven hours, with some three hundred students rallying outside the administration building, producing the first guarantee by a university that its products would be made only in factories that pay a living wage.

Reeling from this surge, the garment industry itself teamed with the always pliable Clinton administration to try to dodge the student demands. They have created a typically Clintonesque facade called the Fair Labor Association, which purports to be a "public-private partnership" to regulate the use of

sweatshop labor. Nike and Liz Claiborne, two known sweatshop exploiters, have seats on the FLA board. The association's rules have about as much bite as a Twinkie has
nutrition. Rather than punish, the FLA seeks to reward, by
allowing garment makers to sport a neat, "No Sweat" label on
their goods if their shops aren't of the sweat variety. It surely
would be no sweat for the corporations to get FLA approval,
since they would get to designate which of their factories are
to be inspected and when, they would hire the monitors, and
the "investigative" reports would be made not to a public
agency but to the companies themselves. Also, there would be
no standards for wages and no disclosure of factory addresses.
The FLA asked universities to join in this charade, and seventeen universities announced on March 15, 1999, that they
would do so.

Stand back! Here came the students again:

- March 17, Joe Sexauer and other activists have a camp-out
  in the University of Michigan president's office for fifty-one
  hours, getting him to agree not to join the FLA and to
  require a living wage, full factory-location disclosure, *and* a
  women's rights provision from all of its product licensees.
- April 21, University of North Carolina students visit their
  president for seventy-two hours, televising their Chapel
  Hill sit-in live on the Internet and composing new lyrics to
  the old labor classic "Solidarity Forever":

  We came to the chancellor
  with a list of our demands
  But when we left the room
  he was sitting on his hands
  Not gonna let him sell out Carolina to THE MAN
  For the sit-in makes us strong
  We need full disclosure
  and we need a living wage

But chancellor you're not listening
and it's making us enraged
And we're gonna sit right here
until you sign the page
For the sit-in makes us strong.

Whether he gave in because of the singing or because of the principles being raised is not known for sure, but he did agree to a living wage, full disclosure, women's rights, and no FLA membership.

- April 22, an epic, ten-day sit-in begins at the University of Arizona, during which a recalcitrant president refuses to agree to some key demands and threatens repeatedly to bring in the police, but the students hang in there and, *226 hours* later, he relents, and the students walk away with the full package of agreements won elsewhere.

Another measure of the students' success is that various establishmentarian voices have been rushing out lately to say, tut-tut now, you kids might be well-meaning idealists, but you are way over your heads when meddling with the natural laws and realpolitik of globalization. A *Wall Street Journal* editorialist, drawing deeply on an ideological pipe that seems always fully packed with pomposity, tells us that "we would all do well to recognize that what looks like exploitation in Indiana looks an awful lot like opportunity in Indonesia"—clearly written by someone who's never had the opportunity to do sweatshop labor. *Newsweek* has also stepped forward, employing the tired old canard of "radical chic" to try tarnishing the students, then engaging in a sort of stream-of-consciousness wail that the students' ill-considered demands might actually succeed in raising the wages for sweatshop workers which would be horrible don't you see because this could force the factories to close causing the very people the naive students want to help to lose their jobs not to mention the possibility that elimination of sweatshops could ripple back to our shores in the form of higher prices for a Nike shoe or a Lord & Taylor blouse and the next thing you know you've got a consumer backlash on your hands and economic collapse and social chaos—and all of this because some students got to messing in something that's none of their business anyway.

The students have not won their campus fight yet, since the companies and their apologists will keep doing their damnedest to squirm loose, but they certainly have gained the upper hand, and, in only a couple of years, have both forced the issue into the open and put the debate on their terms. Also, while their campus struggle continues, they've already won a larger victory. By simply standing up and standing firm, they've shown us all that corporate globalization need not be accepted as a given, as a force that is either inevitable or too powerful to resist—in fact, it's a paper tiger, totally vulnerable to an organized and principled opposition. The students are in the forefront of a new politics based on the common needs of people worldwide rather than on the selfish whims of a few private interests. Making a better world means standing up to the bastards. As William Jennings Bryan put it, "Destiny is not a matter of chance, it is a matter of choice; it is not something to be waited for, it is a thing to be achieved."

PART THREE

THIS LAND *IS* YOUR LAND

THIS LAND *IS* YOUR LAND

Woody Guthrie wrote "This Land" in 1940 while living in New York City, penning all six verses in one night while staying in a no-star hotel somewhere around Times Square. The song had been forming in his fertile mind for a long time as "he roamed and rambled" all around America, "walking that ribbon of highway." He wrote it not as a sweet sing-along glorifying the American landscape but as a proudly populist anthem for the hardscrabble people he traveled among. He had already written hundreds of songs that chronicled the lives and struggles of these workaday folks who are the strength of our great land, performing his songs for them on picket lines, in migrant camps, and at rallies, as well as performing on radio and at their dances. His music entertained, even as it encouraged people in their battles against the Pinkertons, politicians, and other authorities who fronted for the refined men with soft hands and hard eyes who ran things from afar.

When he wrote the words "*your* land," Woody was pointedly speaking to the steelworkers in Pittsburgh and dockworkers up and down the Pacific coast, the dust-bowl people (of whom he was one) who had lost their crops to drought and their farms to bankers, the workers who risked their lives to build the Grand Coulee and the itinerant harvesters who cut the wheat and stacked the hay, "trying to make about a dollar a day." Every schoolchild has sung "This Land's" gentle verses about the "endless skyway" and "diamond deserts," but the songbooks carefully excise Woody's verses that provoke ordinary citizens to rethink the established order, to realize their democratic strength, and to rebel against the structures of privilege that lock out the majority. Verses like:

> *Was a big high wall there that tried to stop me*
> *A sign was painted said: "Private Property."*
> *But on the back side it didn't say nothing*
> *This side was made for you and me.*©*

Woody knew that this land is our land only if we make it so, only if we have the stomach to confront the elites and challenge the insidious forces of autocracy that are continually at work to make it exclusively their land, in the sense that they control the economic and political decisions that rule us. The essence of democracy is self-government. Anything less is a fraud. Being connected to the Internet is not democracy, having a choice between Gore and Bush is not democracy, receiving five hundred channels of digital television is not democracy, being awarded a slice of corporate-allocated prosperity is not democracy. Democracy is control. Whatever goals we strive for as a people—racial harmony, peace, economic fairness, privacy, clean water and air—all are dependent on our ability to control the decisions that affect these goals.

Pause for a moment to think of what an incredible treasure it is to have the right to govern ourselves. Precious few people in history have even had the possibility of asserting their common will over the will of the ruling powers, and the vast majority of earth's people today cannot even imagine such a right. But, in the Declaration of 1776, we have it in writing: ". . . governments are instituted among men, deriving their just powers from *the consent of the governed*." We're in charge! Not kings or feudal barons, congresses or presidents, and damned sure not corporations or World Trade Organizations.

Having it on paper, though, doesn't make it so. Indeed, when it was first written, it wasn't so for very many citizens at all. In the first presidential election, 1789, only 4 percent of the American people were allowed to vote. No women voted (they were chattel), no African Americans (they were slaves), no Native Americans (they were considered heathens), and no one who was without land (they were riffraff). A broader sense of self-rule came later, and only with great effort, pain, and suffering. From abolitionists to suffragists, from populists to Wobblies, from sit-down strikes to lunch-counter sit-ins, blood has flowed as generation after generation has battled the Powers That Be for a share of "Life, Liberty, and the Pursuit of Happiness." In the 224 years since Jefferson wrote of these "inalienable rights," thousands upon thousands of Americans have died in the ongoing struggle to democratize the Declaration, to extend the possibility of self-government to more citizens. What a debt we owe to those who have sacrificed so much to bring us this far, and what a gift this right to self-government is.

But will we hold on to it? Progress is never assured and democracy cannot be taken for granted, even in our country. As the previous chapters have spelled out, there has been a radical backsliding of democratic control in the past few years—a majority of Americans now find themselves effectively shut out of economic and political decision making, and even greater threats to our sovereignty loom in the ominous form of the WTO, NAFTA, and other antidemocratic creations of the global corporate powers. Democratic power is never given; it always has to be taken, then aggressively defended, and retaken when it slips from our hands, for the moneyed powers relentlessly press to gain supremacy and assert their private will over the majority. Today, our gift of democracy is endangered not by military might threatening a sudden, explosive coup but by the stealth of corporate lawyers and politicians, seizing a piece of self-government from us here, then another piece from over there, quietly installing an elitist regime issue by issue, law by law, place by place, with many citizens unaware that their people's authority is slipping away.

For the past couple of decades, this has been going on, greatly accelerating in the nineties, as corporate will has been enthroned, increasingly reigning supreme over every aspect of our lives—economics, politics, culture, and nature itself. We American people find ourselves, once again, at one of those "When in the course of human events" moments, when it is our time to face the reality that a despotic force is in our midst. In the name of all American rebels who have gone before, are we going to sit by, unwilling to confront the bully in front of us, which grows more powerful the longer we wait? You and I have the lofty responsibility to follow in the footsteps of those rebels, to oppose the corporate usurpers and fight for our nation's unique and hard-won right to self-government. Progress doesn't come by merely standing on guard but, as George Bernard Shaw said about a hundred years ago, "by attacking, and getting well-hammered yourself."

WHAT THE HELL IS A CORPORATION?

This ubiquitous critter called the corporation—we're stuck with it, right? We've just got to learn to live with it, don't we, kind of like we live with cockroaches? After all, a corporation has a natural right to do business, doesn't it? No, no, and no. First of all, a corporation is not a business. It's nothing but a piece of paper, a bit of legalism that does not create a business but instead creates a protective association for individuals who want to do business yet want special protections for themselves against other people, against the public at large . . . against the very workings of democracy.

You can make widgets, you can farm, you can sell hardware or groceries, you can operate a hotel, you can provide banking services, or be in any other business without being a corporation. Most of the businesses in the world are *unincorporated* enterprises—individuals, sole proprietorships, partnerships, co-ops, or other forms of operation. Taking on corporations is not antibusiness at all—we must have business, but that does not mean we have to have corporations.

Where did we get the corporate structure? From the jolly Brits, who devised a devilish scheme called "joint stock companies" during their colonial phase. Empire and all that, eh what? The corporate entity was (and is) a legal fiction, first invented by the crown to assist the barons, merchant traders, and bankers of the day in plundering the wealth of the Empire's colonies, including those in our fair land. It was a way to amass the large sums of capital they needed to plunder faraway places, collecting money from investors to finance the plundering, then distributing the booty back to those investors. The corporate construct is dangerous not only because it can agglomerate an absolutely domineering amount of financial power but also because it allows the owners of the corporation (the shareholders) to profit from its business activities, yet accept *no responsibility* for any harm done by their company's business activities. All gain, no pain. The corporation is a legal shield, granting its owners an extraordinary protective privilege that no other business owners are allowed. Oh, did my company spill eleven million gallons of oil into Prince William Sound (Exxon), did it kill two thousand people in a chemical explosion in Bhopal, India (Union Carbide), did it defraud thousands of senior citizens who were persuaded to put money into bad securities (Prudential), did it dump cancer-causing PCBs into the Hudson River (General Electric)? So sorry, I'm sure, but that's none of my doing—the *corporation* did it. Yet, the corporation has no ass to be kicked, no scruff of the neck to be grabbed, no body to be tossed unceremoniously into the maximum security lockup, no conscience to make it contrite, and no soul that would allow the religious among us to believe that at least this wretched enterprise will be condemned to eternal hell.

To the built-in irresponsibility of the amorphous corporate entity, add the bottom-line imperative of the CEO and board of directors. Academicians, judges, and corporate executives themselves aver that the sole role of corporate management is to make as much money as possible for the shareholders (a group that prominently includes the managers). The managers have no responsibility—none—to workers, environment, consumers, community, flag, or anything else. To the contrary, the entire incentive is for management to cut corners, to short-change, to exploit. It is not a matter of a CEO's good intentions or bad—it is the bottom line, and it must be served. Put away all hope, ye who go in asking corporations to be "good," "responsible," "accountable." It is not in their self-interest or in their nature—you might as well expect a Rottweiler to meow.

As for corporations having natural rights, forget it. It's no longer taught in civics or history classes, and it's definitely not mentioned in today's politics or media, but corporations have no rights at all. Zero. Not even the right to exist. The state gives them the *privilege* to exist, but this existence can be narrowly defined and controlled by We the People. I realize this goes against the received wisdom, against the carefully nurtured assumption that corporations are somehow or other one of God's creatures with inherent powers that are larger and elevated above the powers of us common citizens. We can all be forgiven for assuming this, for that certainly is how it works in practice today. But it need not and should not work that way, nor was it meant to work that way when our country and most of our states were founded. Each corporation was and is the creature of the *citizenry,* allowed to exist only through receipt of a state charter. *We are the sovereign,* not them. They are supposed to serve us, not vice versa.

Back to the future: the American Revolution. Jane Anne Morris, a thinker, digger, strategist, and agitator on the issue of corporate dominance, writes: "The people who founded this nation didn't fight a war so they could have a couple of 'citizen representatives' sitting in on meetings of the British East India Company. They carried out a revolution in order to be free of oppression: corporate, governmental, or otherwise; and to replace it with democratic self-government." Adams, Jefferson, Paine, and the rest had not had a happy experience with the corporations of the crown and were unabashedly anticorporate at the founding, with Jefferson even speaking of the need "to crush in its birth the aristocracy of our moneyed corporations."

The citizens of early America knew what they were up against: raw economic power. They were rightly wary of the corporate structure itself, knowing that it allowed a few individuals in the society to stockpile a massive amount of money and power, then use this and the corporate shield to pursue their private gain to the harm of the common good. Eighteenth- and nineteenth-century Americans were prescient when it came to these entities—citizens expressed concern that corporations would use their money as bribes to pervert democratic elections and buy both legislators and judges; farmers worried that corporations would use their muscle to monopolize markets and control crop prices; and industrial and craft workers were concerned that corporations would, as historian Louis Hartz has written, turn them into "a commodity," treating them "as much an article of commerce as woolens, cotton or yarn." They knew that the unbridled corporation was antithetical to the democratic principles they espoused and a threat to the very system of self-government they had established. So they made damned sure the corporation was securely bridled.

Anyone so timid as to think that it is radical for citizens today even to consider "interfering" with the private will of corporations is not made of the same stout stuff as the citizens who created our states and our country. In America's first hundred years, applicants could get a corporate charter only by approval of their state legislature, usually requiring a two-thirds vote to win one. Few charters were awarded, and those few corporations that got them were limited in their function, in how much money they could aggregate, in how long they could exist, and in how they could function. Citizens took their hard-won sovereignty seriously, adamantly defending it against the possibility of corporate usurpation. State after state imposed strict terms on the issuance of a charter, leaving no doubt about who was in charge. This is our hidden history of proud and aggressive citizenship, and you're likely to be amazed if you look into how the people of your state have stood up to corporate power in the not-so-distant past. Jane Anne Morris dug into the records of her state of Wisconsin and found that from 1848 to as recently as 1953, the legislature had imposed such charter conditions as these:

- Corporations had to have a clearly stated reason for existing, and if they failed to fulfill that purpose or went beyond it, their charter could be revoked.
- The legislature could revoke the charter for any particular reason or, as the Wisconsin attorney general ruled in 1913, "for no reason at all."
- Corporate management and stockholders could be held liable for corporate acts.
- Directors of the corporation were required to come from among the stockholders.
- If a corporation's principal place of business was Wisconsin, it had to have its headquarters and its meetings there.
- Charters were granted for a specific period of time, like twenty years, rather than "in perpetuity."
- Corporations could not own other corporations.
- Corporations could own real estate only if it was necessary to carry out their specific purpose.
- Corporations were flatly prohibited from making any political contribution, direct or indirect, and it was a felony crime if they did so.

- All corporate records and documents were open to the legislature and to the attorney general.

From Maine to California, Wisconsin to Texas, all states had similar stipulations on their books—and they were enforced! Especially important were the revocation clauses, which allowed state legislatures or courts to yank the operating licenses of corporations that behaved badly. Imagine. The people were in charge, the general welfare was paramount over corporate profit, civic authority prevailed over CEO whim. Richard Grossman and Ward Morehouse, two thoughtful activists who codirect POCLAD (the Program on Corporations, Laws and Democracy), have published an excellent pamphlet worthy of Thomas Paine, entitled "Taking Care of Business: Citizenship and the Charter of Incorporation." It notes that the corporate charter was a sacrosanct oath: "The penalty for abuse or misuse of the charter was not a fine or a slap on the wrist, but revocation of the charter and dissolution of the corporation. Citizens believed it was society's inalienable right to abolish an evil." Charters were routinely revoked, including those of the most powerful—in 1894, the Central Labor Union of New York City cited a pattern of abuses against John D. Rockefeller's Standard Oil Trust of New York, asking the attorney general to request that the state supreme court revoke its charter. The AG did . . . and the court did.

After the Civil War, however, with the rise of the Robber Barons, a full-scale assault was begun by the moneyed interests against these inconvenient rules. Railroad baron Cornelius Vanderbilt issued the war cry of the antidemocratic elites when he thundered, "What do I care about the law? H'ain't I got the power?" For the next hundred years—stipulation by stipulation, state by state, bribe by bribe—the sovereign was steadily reduced to the subjugated. Corporate barons like Vanderbilt hauled sacks of money into state capitols to buy legislators and win charter changes favorable to them. The chief justice of Wisconsin's supreme court spoke as early as 1873 of "a new and dark power" that was looming, warning that "the enterprises of the country are aggregating vast corporate combinations of unexampled capital, marching, not for economical conquests only, but for political power. . . ." The Vanderbilts, Goulds, Rockefellers, and others had more money than hell has brimstone, and they used it to corrupt and dominate the same state legislatures that had been bulwarks of democratic resistance to the corporate empire builders. A Pennsylvania legislator is reported to have said, "Mr. Speaker, I move we adjourn, unless the Pennsylvania Railroad has some more business for us to transact."

Gradually, the bridle has been removed, resulting in what we have today—the runaway corporate autocracy that the founders predicted and feared. Shall we just accept it? Shall we timidly continue into another century with the status quo politics of the pathetic ClintonGoreBradley Democrats, who demand again and again that the people must adjust to the private agenda of a handful of corporate executives and investors?

"This is an exciting time to be an American," a Californian wrote to me several months ago. "We are in a crisis. We are on the brink of the failure of our old democratic processes—swamped, subverted, perverted, and filibustered by the corporate feudal system and its totalitarian dominance of our lives. We have the opportunity and the duty to overcome all that," he wrote.

Bingo! In one succinct paragraph, this citizen has nailed it, and he is but one of a growing majority who know that "consent of the governed" is a mockery today, supplanted by a crude bribery system of corporate governance that is becoming as autocratic as anything imagined by King George III and his royally chartered British East India Company, Hudson's Bay Company, and the crown charters that ruled American colonies. Just a few examples: High-handed CEOs can, by fiat, off several thousand workers from the payroll, thereby jacking up the company's stock price and enriching themselves with tens of millions in stock gains, while the workers and their families are allowed no redress for their grievances; your bank, insurance company, credit-card firm, HMO, and other corporations can secretly collect the most intimate details of your private life, then use or sell this information in any way they see fit, without even informing you; imperious biotech corporations can mess dangerously with the very DNA of our food supply for no purpose except to enhance their profits, then force families to be the guinea pigs of their Frankenfood experiments, since there is no labeling of thousands of supermarket items (including baby food) already containing these genetically altered organisms; conniving corporations routinely extract millions from townspeople as the price of building a factory or sports stadium in their town, then can renege on any pledge of job creation and, on whim, pull up stakes and abandon the town altogether; haughty HMOs can make decisions that kill you, yet Congress protects them from legal liability and punishment for your death; "speech" has been perverted to mean money, authorizing corporations and their executives to buy control of the entire political process; a chemical company can callously pollute our air, water, and food, leading to thousands of deaths, birth defects, and other horrors, yet continue doing business and continue polluting, with no punishment beyond, perhaps, a fine, which it easily absorbs and, in some cases, can deduct from its income taxes as a "cost of doing business"; a handful of media giants have attained absolute control over the content of news and the range of ideas that are broadcast on the *public's* airwaves, arbitrarily shrinking the democratic debate; the democratic decisions of a city council, state legislature, or other sovereign government can be arrogantly annulled by corporate action through antidemocratic entities established by NAFTA and the WTO.

Who the hell are these people? Who elected them to run our world? Why are we putting up with this crap? As the bumper sticker puts it: LEMMINGS OF THE WORLD UNITE! YOU HAVE NOTHING TO LOSE BUT YOUR PLACE IN LINE!

We need to crank up a political fight that has some guts to it, some fire-breathing democratic passion in it, some of the revolutionary spirit of 1776 behind it. This is not a fight about regulations or really even about corporations—it's about control, sovereignty, self-government, *democracy*. Let's force the issue and put it as starkly as it is: Are corporations going to rule, or are we? From time to time, I hear veterans of the civil rights and antiwar battles of the sixties bemoan the lack of a "Big Battle" today, one that can unite a majority across traditional political lines, one that is about justice for all, is loaded with citizen outrage, has the spark of genuine passion within it, and is worthy of bloody heads. Well, here it is: The self-evident battle of our era is to defeat corporate autocracy and establish citizen rule over our government, our economy, and our environment.

WHEN YOU FIGHT THE DEVIL, FIGHT TO WIN

Practically every progressive struggle—campaign finance reform, rain forest destruction and global warming, sweatshops, family farms, fair trade, health care for all, unionization, military spending and arms sales, tax reform, alternative energy, healthy food, media access, hazardous waste dumps, redlining, alternative medicine, you name it—is being fought against one cluster of corporations or another. But it is not that corporation over there or this one over here that is the enemy, it is not one industry's contamination of our drinking water or another's perversion of the lawmaking process that is the problem—rather it is the corporation itself that must be addressed if we are to be a free people.

In his powerful pamphlet *Common Sense,* Thomas Paine touched the heart of the American Revolution when he wrote:

"Ye that dare oppose not only tyranny but the tyrant, stand forth." We can all object to consequences and seek remedial action, but will we finally face the tyrant itself? That is the question for progressives as we step into 2000. We can continue fighting the beast as we have been, through scattershot, uncoordinated efforts—a lawsuit here, an investigation there, some legislation, more regulations, prayer, and the always useful sacrificial goat. Occasionally, these approaches succeed. But, as Grossman and Morehouse have written, "Tactically, [this approach] means limiting ourselves to resisting harms one corporate site at a time, one corporate chemical or biotechnology product at a time; to correcting imperfections of the market; to working for yet more permitting and disclosure laws; to initiating procedural lawsuits and attempts to win compensation after corporate harm has been done; to battling regulatory and administrative agencies; to begging leaders of global corporations to please cause a little less harm."

In 1998, Britain's House of Lords dealt with the weighty matter of changing the official costume worn by the Lord Chancellor, that body's top official. The outfit included a long powdered wig, breeches, tights, buckled shoes, white gloves, and black stockings. The incumbent wanted very much not to look, as one reporter described him, like "the frog footman in 'Alice in Wonderland,'" so he proposed a switch to modern business attire. Traditionalists, however, opposed any change in the seventeenth-century garb. Lord Wattington put the case for tradition forcefully, summing up by declaring, "I can see no advantage to the Queen or the public if the Lord Chancellor removes his tights."

At the national level, inside the Beltway, too many of our progressive energies and resources are spent on fights that amount to removing the Lord Chancellor's tights. The piecemeal approach to fighting corporate abuses keeps us spread thin, separated from each other, on the defensive, riveted on the minutiae, and fighting on their terms (literally over the language of *their* laws and regulations, and in *their* courts and legislatures). More often than not, regulatory agencies are shams, working to sustain the business-as-usual tactics of corporations rather than to inhibit them, and the deck is stacked against the public interest anytime we find ourselves within these legalistic meat grinders. This is nothing new—historian Howard Zinn writes about the creation of the Interstate Commerce Commission in 1887, a "reform" pushed by President Grover Cleveland, ostensibly to regulate railroads. But railroad executives were told not to worry by Richard Olney, a railroad lawyer who was soon to be Cleveland's attorney general: "The Commission . . . is or can be made, of great use to the railroads. It satisfies the popular clamor for a government supervision of railroads, at the same time that its supervision is almost entirely nominal. . . . The part of wisdom is not to destroy the Commission, but to utilize it."

Piecemeal battles must certainly continue, for there is real and immediate corporate harm to be addressed for people and communities. But it's time for our strategic emphasis to shift to the offensive, raising what I believe to be the central political issue for the new century: *Who the hell is in charge here?*

It is an open question, despite the appearance that corporations have things pretty tightly locked down. Yes, they have the money, the media, the government, the two major parties, the police and military, and the deadening power of conventional wisdom. But so did King George III. We've been here before, we've done this, and we can do it again.

We've got a couple of things going for our side in this historic struggle. For one thing, our constitutional assertion of citizen control of corporations is still there, as is much of the language in the state codes that formally subjugates corporations to us. As Richard Grossman has found in his years of digging, "We still have the authority to *define* the corporations through their charters; we still have the authority to *amend* the charters; we still have the authority to *revoke* the

charters—the language is still there. We still have the authority to *rewrite the state corporation codes* in order to *order* corporate executives to do what the sovereign people want to
do." We have legal language and authority, a constitutional
claim, a moral position firmly rooted in justice, and a powerful historic precedent that flows from the revolutionary patri-
ots themselves.

We also have the common sense and revolutionary chutzpah of grassroots American agitators going for us. The com-
monsense side says: There are laws in our country that
proclaim to human criminals "three strikes and you're out"—
why not for corporations? Each year, hundreds of doctors,
lawyers, accountants, and other professionals have their
licenses to practice permanently revoked by the states—why
not corporations? The Supreme Court has ruled that the corporation is a "person" under the law; people who murder are
removed from society—why not corporations?

The chutzpah side says: Let's go get 'em. And they are! The
national media have been practically mum about it, but there
already is an important movement among the citizenry to
begin reestablishing citizen control over charters. In Wayne,
Pennsylvania, the locals passed a 1998 ordinance that prohibits any corporation from doing business there if it has a history of consistently violating laws to protect workers,
consumers, the environment, and so forth. In Jay, Maine, a
town of paperworkers, the people were fed up with the
repeated pollution of their water and air by the recalcitrant
International Paper Company, so they enacted the "Jay Environmental and Improvement Ordinance," which gives the
town of Jay the authority to monitor and regulate pollution by
IP's Androscoggin paper mill—the townspeople have their
own full-time environmental administrator with full authority
to fine and shut down the mill for violations. In 1998, the people of South Dakota just said "no" to corporate hog factories in
their state, voting by a sixty-to-forty margin for a constitutional

amendment to prohibit corporations from owning livestock. Also in 1998, New York attorney general Dennis Vacco, a Republican, showed that the Council for Tobacco Research had acted fraudulently and illegally in pretending to do objective research when in fact it was nothing but a lobbyist and a front for the tobacco industry, leading to a settlement in which the council surrendered its corporate charter. The state's new attorney general, Democrat Elliott Spitzer, is expanding Vacco's initiative, considering all corporate charters fair game: "When a corporation is convicted of repeated felonies that harm or endanger the lives of human beings or destroy the environment, the corporation should be put to death, its corporate existence ended, and its assets taken and sold at public auction." He has hired a highly regarded public-interest attorney to oversee this effort.

Meanwhile, in the small coastal town of Arcata, California, there has been a remarkable two-year effort to put the issue of corporate usurpation of democratic authority into the public debate again. It began with Paul Cienfuegos, Gary Houser, and a few others, who organized Democracy Unlimited of Humboldt County, which in 1998 launched a citizens campaign to get on the ballot a local initiative called Measure F: Advisory Measure on Democracy and Corporations. After a few straightforward whereases about the sovereign power of people to govern themselves, the Measure resolved that "the people of Arcata support the amending of the California Constitution so as to clearly declare the authority of citizens over all corporations." The proposition then included a couple of practical steps that, very smartly, took a slow and minimalist approach toward advancing citizen sovereignty in Arcata, establishing a process for democratic discussion in town that could move people along, but not before they were ready to move. First was a simple provision that, if Measure F passed, the city council would sponsor two town hall meetings on this topic: "Can we have democracy when large corporations wield so much power and wealth under law?" Second was for the city government to create an official committee to develop policies and programs to assert democratic control over corporations doing business in Arcata.

The citizens campaign hit the streets, and in just twenty-six days got the signatures needed to put the measure on the ballot. They gained key endorsements from Arcata mayor Jim Test and groups like the central labor council and students at Humboldt State University, and they delivered materials to the doors of nearly every household and business in this town of about seventeen thousand people. In the November 1998 election, their effort paid off: Measure F passed with nearly 60 percent of the vote. Since then, this town has been having what every town, city, neighborhood, and village green needs—a heart-to-heart airing out of the basic question of "Who's in charge?" Ralph Nader visited in 1999 in support of citizen control, likening Arcata's democracy dialogue to the ride of Paul Revere. On the other side, Kenneth Fisher, a *Forbes* magazine columnist and a financial speculator, gave a lecture entitled "Societal Ethics Are Always Unethical," bemoaning Measure F as an example of the "tyranny of democracy." Then came the town hall meetings in April and May of 1999, which produced a turnout of more than six hundred people, far surpassing expectations. The opposition had been active, too, working hard to turn out a pro-corporatist crowd, led by a couple of very vocal officials with the Yakima Corporation, which is based in the area but manufactures at a Mexican border factory. The proceedings were structured so both sides made two presentations of eight minutes each—then the floor was open to the people. The freewheeling discussions went long past the set time, putting the lie to conventional wisdom that insists people are too busy, too satisfied, too uninformed, too unconcerned, too prosperous, too conservative, too short, too stupid, too whatever to get involved with something as "boring" as their own democracy.

Overwhelmingly, participants favored Measure F, and the town's people are now at work on developing the policies and programs for city hall that will put the well-being of the community above corporate whim on issues ranging from chain stores bankrupting local businesses to industry polluting the town's air and water.

Whatever the outcome at city hall, the effort already has accomplished something extraordinarily important: It has launched a citywide democratic conversation on a subject that hasn't been discussed in public for a century. Cienfuegos notes that thousands of local residents are now conversant with corporate rule and how it impacts their lives. It's a conversation that has become common in the cafés, Laundromats, in line at the post office, and elsewhere—literally taking root in the culture of the community. The groundbreaking work in Arcata continues, and it is spreading to other California towns, and to places like Olympia, Washington.

The experts, of course, predict that these citizen uprisings won't succeed, but the experts have a long history of being spectacularly wrong. Christopher Cerf and Victor Navasky have documented this in wonderful detail in their fun book, *The Experts Speak,* which includes these glorious samples of missed predictions:

> *"Just so-so in center field."*
> —*New York Daily News,* May 26, 1951,
> after the major-league debut of Willie Mays

> *"Displays no trace of imagination, good taste or ingenuity.*
> *I say it's a stinkeroo."*
> —*New Yorker* film critic, 1939, reviewing *The Wizard of Oz*

> *"The singer will have to go."*
> —The new manager of the Rolling Stones, 1963, referring to
> Mick Jagger

A great thing about the American people is that we are an optimistic, can-do bunch that will not be deterred by being told something cannot be achieved. Robert Benson is a good example of this spirited stubbornness: "I came to the conclusion sometime ago that things happen when someone does the work, so the point is to just do the work." He's a professor at Loyola Law School in Los Angeles, and he has been a driving force (along with Ronnie Dugger, who cochairs the grassroots Alliance for Democracy organization) behind a national effort to revoke the charter of Unocal—the Union Oil Company of California. Benson has done a lot of work and made a lot of happen by compiling a long rap sheet on this notorious and recidivist corporate reprobate.

Benson's dossier on Unocal includes a pattern and practice of polluting the locations where it operates (the company itself notes that it is named as a potentially responsible party in eighty-two Superfund or similar toxic sites in this country alone), the mistreatment of its employees (it has been cited for hundreds of workplace safety and health violations just in the past decade), and complicity in gross human-rights violations through its operations and working relationship with the repressive totalitarian regimes in Afghanistan and Burma (although pressure from this charter revocation effort and others has since forced Unocal to withdraw from Afghanistan). Prepared with the help of the National Lawyers Guild, the Unocal petition was not a political tract but a serious legal filing, alleging ten separate counts, citing twenty-four state and federal laws, forty-five cases, forty international laws, fourteen scholarly legal writings, and dozens of other relevant materials.

Unocal announced in 1996 that it "no longer considers itself as a U.S. company." But it is chartered in California, it operates here, and its major market is the good ol' USA, so a broad coalition of some 150 people and organizations (from the Feminist Majority Foundation to the Surfers Environmental Alliance, from pastors to professors, from the Green Party to Greenpeace, from business to labor, from city council members to state legislators) have joined the effort, asking the California attorney general to use the statutory authority that has long lain ignored in his desk drawer—the authority "to procure a judgment [from state court] dissolving the corporation."

The very filing of the citizens' petition in September 1998 scared the constipation out of Dan Lungren, the Republican AG who was running for governor at the time. Benson reports that "Lungren's office went into a comical panic," calling the California Highway Patrol the night before the coalition was to hold a press conference at the attorney general's branch office in Los Angeles. He had the state police warn Benson, Dugger, and group not to appear because a permit was needed to have a press conference on state property. That was about as effective as calling "time-out" in a cattle stampede. Undeterred, the group held its press conference. Lungren's spokeswoman immediately responded that the AG had no authority to revoke charters. But—oops!—it was pointed out to her that section 803 of the code of civil procedure not only allows him to act but says he "must bring action" whenever he has "reason to believe" a corporation has violated the law. Well, she said, we'll need several months to study it, which conveniently would put the matter on the shelf until well past Lungren's election fight. But that couldn't have pleased Unocal executives, who would have wanted this dicey bit of legal unpleasantness bludgeoned to death with a sledgehammer on the spot. Sure enough, three business days later, Lungren suddenly dispatched a four-sentence letter to the coalition, the operative phrase of which was: "We decline to institute legal proceedings." He didn't bother offering an explanation. In response, the petitioners lambasted him far and wide for being "selectively soft" on crime.

But wait a minute, here came the Lone Stranger riding to the rescue! Bill Lockyer, a Democrat, was elected attorney general six weeks later to replace Lungren (who also had his gubernatorial ambitions thwarted by the voters). After taking office, Lockyer declared that he wanted to be known as a "Teddy Roosevelt" in taking on corporate criminals. So Benson and the coalition saddled up as Rough Riders and resubmitted their Unocal petition to "Teddy" Lockyer. Last May, the Democrat bested the Republican AG by rejecting the petition in only *three* sentences, including the exact same phrase used by the Republican: "We decline to institute legal proceedings." Again, no explanation. Benson called the AG's office and learned that the professional staff that normally analyzes such requests for action had never seen the coalition's filing against Unocal. Pressed by the coalition (which includes some prominent Democratic officeholders), Lockyer finally tried to explain his reasoning in an August letter that showed a breathtaking ignorance of the petition, of the issues raised, and, most shockingly, of his authority and responsibility under California law. The letter is three paragraphs of blah-blah-blah, punctuated by this courageous stand on policing corporate charters: "It's simply not my job." Who needs Republican enemies when we've got such Democratic "friends"?

The coalition continues to organize, using the Unocal petition to teach more citizens not only about this scofflaw company but more importantly about their own right to control all corporations. The legal process also continues, as does the political—public meetings will be held, with Lockyer invited, to educate the AG about his "job," and billboards are planned bearing the new attorney general's mug and the cutline: "Lockyer. Soft on Corporate Crime." Patronizing politicians like him make a mistake if they think they're getting away with anything or that this democracy movement will go away. Pols who misread the seriousness, preparedness, cleverness, and fighting spirit of people like Benson and Dugger remind me of Gen. John Sedgwick, the Union commander whose last words at the battle of Spotsylvania Court House in 1864 were: "They couldn't hit an elephant at this dist—"

RUN RIGHT AT THE BASTARDS

When I first ran for political office in Texas, I was campaigning out near Abilene and came upon a fellow who bent my ear for a while, telling me a story about how he had really been furious with the local sheriff, who he felt was incompetent, crooked, or both. "I wrote letters to the editor about the guy, I called him up personally to protest his actions, I filed formal complaints," he told me. "But that was two years ago, and now I'm no longer mad at the sheriff. That's because I filed against the son of a bitch and beat him, so now I *am* the sheriff!"

Nothing gets the attention of the system quite like running against it. This is the most radical aspect of America's democratic experiment—not merely that you can vote for whatever choices the system throws up (literally throws up, it so often seems), but that we can generate our own choices! It's the difference between being a passive *consumer* of the process and being a *citizen*, a forceful participant in the democracy. When all is said and done, the gods don't give us candidates . . . we have to create them.

The place to start is not in the presidential race. That's like trying to build a house by putting the roof on first. Poor carpentry. Yet, there's an unfortunate tendency among leaders of national progressive organizations and among progressive funders to focus on the quadrennial run for the White House or for control of Congress, ignoring the races for state rep, county commissioner, city council, and others at the ground level. This is where we should be—building a solid foundation for a genuine progressive political movement, framing the issues that can rally the workaday majority of people, developing political skills and talent, and steadily moving on up to that roof project in 2008 or 2012.

These are offices that can be won with people power, where we are less likely to be swamped by a tsunami of money power. Equally important to winning, we can put these offices to work for ordinary folks, siding with them against the corporate interests that are running roughshod over them, earning credibility with today's disenchanted voters, bringing them back into the process, and gaining the voter strength it takes to maintain the movement, lifting it ever higher. The key is to get back to the honest, painstaking, grunt-level work of party building, working continually in the communities, homes, churches, beauty parlors, saloons, and elsewhere to touch people, involve them, and demonstrate that we're there to stay, sticking with them for the long haul, not just for Election Day.

Happily, this is not a process we can only wish would happen—it's already under way. The Greens in New Mexico, for example, have won city council seats and have already become a force to be reckoned with in congressional and statewide races there. In California the Green Party has been running for a myriad of offices, most recently having elected their first state assembly member from Oakland. Audie Elizabeth Bock, a single mom and small business woman whose last campaign was for high school class secretary, ran as a Green in an April 1999 election on a platform that featured universal health care and plugging corporate tax loopholes. She defeated a well-known former Oakland mayor who had been a Democratic Party officeholder for two decades and had outspent Bock twenty to one. "There's a change going on," said Bock. "People are not satisfied by what the two major parties have to offer." A spokeswoman for the California Greens noted: "I think you're going to see a lot more Greens running for office in the year 2000. We think [Bock's election] proves the people will vote for a Green Party candidate when there's hope the Green Party candidate will win."

Exactly. Give the people a sense that their vote matters, that it can produce a change, and they'll be there. This is the importance of building locally before thinking you're a national phenom. The Greens are hardly alone—the Labor

Party, the New Party, the Reform Party (hey, it's not your same old Ross Perot Oldsmobile anymore) are offering serious progressive opportunities.

No group is doing it better than the New Party. A coalition of labor, low-income advocates like ACORN, minorities, Democratic Party dissidents, tax reformers, anticorporatists, seniors, gays and lesbians, and people simply fed up with business-as-usual politics, this grassroots political party has been winning offices from the Big Apple to Little Rock. In the last election, New Party endorsees won thirty-two of the thirty-nine elections they entered, and for the past decade, the party has won two-thirds of the elections it has contested. More important than winning, however, it has been building the progressive foundation. To see it in practice, let me take you to Missoula, Montana.

When you think of hotbeds of progressive activism, the mind jerks to Berkeley, Greenwich Village, Ann Arbor, Cambridge, Madison . . . but Missoula? Situated along the Clark Fork River, this small city is home to the University of Montana, but it really can't be described as a college town—more like a working-class town with a university in it. It's certainly a picturesque and pleasant place, with a population of about fifty thousand (and rapidly growing), and its downtown boasts agreeable touches of upscale urbanity, including cappuccino shops, restored buildings, and a good microbrewery. Just minutes away, though, are acres of trailer parks and low-income neighborhoods, home to Missoulians who think of coffee as a regular cup-a-joe rather than a two-dollar cappuccino. These are families who are employed at the nearby paper mill, casinos, and tourist businesses, working hard and poorly paid.

Out of this mix of modern American life way out in the Rockies has come some of the most vibrant, progressive politics in our country today, thanks to the Missoula New Party (MNP), which has energized and mobilized people who had given up on a political process that has long been controlled by the business-as-usual Democrat-Republican power structure. What we have in Missoula is a snapshot of what can happen when progressives get their act together, get to organizing, and go head-on at that power structure. I'm not talking about protesting but about vying for political power—running for office and *winning*. In only seven years of existence, New Party members in Missoula have gone from ground zero to being a power player, with its members now holding four of the twelve city council seats and two state legislative seats. How did they get there? Not luck, but potluck.

The MNP is known as the "Party that likes to Party." From its start, it has organized around the great American tradition of the neighborhood potluck—folks gathering in homes around good food and drink, talking about local matters and how things could be made better. Secky Fascione, about as feisty an organizer as you'd ever hope to meet, told me about the potluck she hosted early in 1993, when Dan Cantor was coming to town. Dan, the national director of the New Party, lives in New York City and was in Montana for a speech in Billings. A mutual friend had suggested that he should know the progressives working in Missoula, so he offered to stop by while he was in the state. "I guess people back east don't know it's a six-hour drive between Billings and Missoula," Secky shrugged, but Cantor came. "We told a couple of friends to come over and meet the guy and, to our surprise, about thirty-five folks showed up. That early crew was representative of much of the base of the New Party today: the women's community, our low- and moderate-income organization, environmental activists, senior citizens, and a few of us progressive labor leaders."

What Cantor did that night was to offer a structural framework (the New Party) for what these folks already were wanting to do—build an effective progressive movement—and to focus them on electoral politics. The Missoulians took it from there. They went door to door, neighborhood to neighborhood, talking with people long ignored by the existing political structure about the opportunity of having their own party, talking with them about the issues they could raise together. The issues were the need for living wages, affordable housing, stopping pollution, making growth work for people rather than vice versa, and other kitchen-table matters that neither established party was addressing. People signed up, more potlucks were organized in more homes, and more people got involved.

MNP also hit the ground running, literally. In their first year of existence, the group backed three unabashedly progressive candidates for city council, putting its burgeoning grassroots network behind them. The results were stunning, even to MNP members—all three of their candidates won sweeping victories in the September '93 Democratic primary, and two went on to win council seats in that year's general election (the third lost by only six votes). Among the brand-new New Party activists who worked in this first electoral go-round was Ren Essene. "I was twenty-three, fresh out of college, and although having been involved with an unorganized group of college Democrats previously, was pretty disenchanted with politics, as was most of my generation. I thought of politics as entrenched and elite. I got involved with the New Party but was cynical about what changes we could effect. Then we won! We had a voice, we were framing a different debate at the city level. We elected candidates that gave voice to the everyday person concerns." Ren later became cochair of MNP and now serves on the national New Party executive committee.

Here's a key to New Party strategy: It's not concerned merely with electing candidates but with implementing policy. Jim "Flash" Fleischmann, chair of the election committee, tells me that you don't get MNP backing by being smooth, winking at the committee members, and promising to support "good government." You have to promise to join the party if you're not already a member, to acknowledge publicly your MNP endorsement, to attend meetings where the rank and file can get you by the short hairs, and to demonstrate on a regular basis that you are pushing the policies that you pledged to support. The people hold the politicians accountable for doing what they said they were going to do. Outrageous.

Another key element of the MNP's success is that it doesn't disappear between elections. Instead, it actually establishes a relationship with voters (something the two major parties reserve for platinum-level contributors). The monthly meetings are not sterile, *Robert's Rules of Order*-type affairs, but lively, debate-filled, consensus-run sessions held in someone's home with children running about, potluck dishes to savor, and often some of that microbrew available to help lubricate the little gray cells. As Ren says, "You've got to build FUN into the Party, because you need to be able to keep coming back to do the work. We have great cooks—being a community, we socialize with each other and that keeps us together." This sense of community extends to helping anyone who wants to be better at doing the work of citizenship—training to be leaders in a campaign or even to run for office, learning more about an issue, getting public-speaking lessons, and so forth. It's more than politics, too—people active in MNP have worked through other organizations to launch a day-care co-op, a recycling program, and other community projects.

The party also is pragmatic rather than dogmatic—it agrees to disagree on divisive issues within the party, focusing on the common issues that unite them, and it doesn't lose itself in meaningless ideological nattering about being "pure" as a third party, instead working happily with and even endorsing Democrats or other candidates willing to support the party's progressive policies. A good example of this is Peter Talbot. He wasn't involved in local politics until about a decade ago when Missoula's rampant growth became a concern to him. He went to the Democratic Party in town, but found the leaders there an "uninspiring bunch of good ol' boys with few ideas."

He heard of the New Party that was just starting up, went to a meeting, and "found they were sharp and well-informed people who wanted to change things to be more responsive to regular folks." He's been a New Party member ever since—but now he's also chairman of the Missoula Democratic Party. The very presence of this new, grassroots, *successful* political player has altered the whole electoral landscape—the MNP's current four council members can often count on one or two other Democratic council members and occasionally on the Democratic mayor to stand with them.

Jim McGrath, an early New Party member who is now on the city council (and who is so effective there that the chamber of commerce has declared that its highest priority is to "take him out") is particularly supportive of worrying less about structural purity than getting the job done: "Let's not forget what the real work is. For me, the real work is empowering the citizens (particularly those least powerful, such as low-income and minorities), creating the framework for people to have significant control over their lives and communities, and the ability to create a sustainable society."

Who are these people? "We've been vilified as coming from Moscow or—worse—New York City," says council member McGrath, who actually is a longtime Missoula resident. He and his wife, Julie, have two adopted sons who have Down's syndrome, she's a writer, and he's director of the Community Gardens program in town. Other MNP members presently running for council seats include a small business man who raises llamas and takes people into the mountains on pack trips, a retired schoolteacher active on senior issues, a fellow who works for the Missoula Children's Theater, and a young mother who got into politics because of a proposal to close her child's neighborhood school. Not a lawyer, a lobbyist, a banker, or a millionaire among them.

Not that the party wins all of its elections—indeed, in '97 the old Democrat-Republican clique teamed up with the chamber-of-commerce crowd and a load of money from out-of-town developers to form a front group called Citizens for Common Sense Government, putting up a slate of candidates to wipe out these upstarts. A CCSG fund-raiser was held, appropriately enough, at the Linda Vista Country Club, and an unprecedented amount of money suddenly flowed into Missoula politics. In the Ward 1 race, for example, New Party candidate Dave Harmon was outspent two to one, with his CCSG opponent getting three-fourths of her war chest from developers, contractors, real estate brokers, bankers, and others determined to get a developer-friendly city hall. Harmon's money, by contrast, came from a logger, a few artists, teachers, some nurses, U. of M. professors, and a poet, among others, with his largest check being $150.

Harmon won anyway, but two New Party incumbents on the council narrowly lost, cutting their margin from five seats to four. But the spirit of MNP members only rose—as Ren Essene says, "Having an opposition means you're doing something right. We're proud of bucking the system, and we won't back down from progressive stances." Is this bunch fun, or what?! Showing a maturity and confidence rooted in a solid base of support and good political organizing, MNP withstood the onslaught of money and has since redoubled its grassroots efforts. It retains, with a couple of liberal Democrats, a working majority on the council, it won two seats in the state legislature in the '98 election, it supported a winner for county commissioner that same year, it has put a living-wage initiative on the ballot in '99, and it has strong candidates for the next council election, with a chance to pick up two additional seats, including one in a ward the party's not run in before. More important than the specific wins, however, is MNP's overall victory—it has changed politics for the good in Missoula, reframing the debate around people's issues, putting corporate power on the defensive, and energizing ordinary folks to take charge of their own destiny.

I've been to Missoula and met these people, just as I've met similar folks in Little Rock, Milwaukee, Seattle, Tucson, Minneapolis, Colorado Springs, Chicago, western Oklahoma, Durham, and elsewhere—ordinary Americans who are doing the extraordinary by fighting back against the established order, winning, and taking power themselves. Pessimists can say, "Yeah, yeah, Hightower, but these are localized victories, we need a national movement." Hello? Did the American Revolution begin in Philadelphia in 1776 with the approval of the Declaration of Independence, or had there been years of local rebellion that got the movement to that point? Did the populist movement, which completely altered American politics at the end of the nineteenth century, spring forth full-grown as a national movement, or did it begin in a farm kitchen near Lampasas, Texas, later spreading across the South, up the Plains, and into the upper Midwest? Did the civil rights movement begin with Martin Luther King Jr.'s 1963 speech at the Lincoln Memorial, or had it been built in hundreds of backwater southern churches by thousands of people who bled and died to get King to that majestic moment? The New Party's strategic motto is: "Start local. Think long term." That's the ticket, and that's what thousands of good people all across our country are doing.

They are beautiful to behold. There's a sparkle in their eyes, a bounce in their step, a sense of joy that they are doing political work that matters, organizing a new politics that cuts across the theoretical lines of right to left, realizing that the real political spectrum for Americans is top to bottom. Right to left is theory, and it divides us falsely. Top to bottom is experience; it's where people actually live and work—and the vast majority of people today know that they're no longer in shouting distance of the Wall Street–Washington, Republican-Democrat powers at the top. Here is the constituency for something big. As Jim McGrath of Missoula says, "We see a huge opportunity for a mass, democratic movement developing in America. With the continued decline for most Americans, and the lack of any coherent governmental response, the demand for a politics that imposes values (other than just profit) over the economy and pushes for real democratic reform will only grow."

People are ready for a politics that challenges the ongoing corporate grabfest. A recent series of focus-group sessions with middle-class folks (most of whom made in the range of $20,000–$60,000 a year) produced results that cannot be comforting to the Keepers of the Established Order:

- 68 percent of the people viewed corporate greed as an "equally important" or "more important" cause of working families' economic woes than big government—nearly half say corporations are the "more important" cause.
- 70 percent believe that such actions as massive downsizings, cutbacks on worker benefits, and sending U.S. jobs overseas are not motivated by the corporate need to be competitive and efficient, but by greed.
- 79 percent of Democrats in the groups, 67 percent of Republicans, and 74 percent of ticket splitters say the economic and human impacts of these corporate behaviors are serious enough to warrant purposeful government intervention.

I realize that this goes counter to the constant message from those on high who keep telling us that we Americans are a conservative people, but I find the regular folks of this country to be a gutsy bunch who, at their core, have an ingrained commitment to the ideal of democracy, a deep (and hard-earned) distrust of concentrations of economic and political power, and a fighting spirit that doesn't need much kindling to flare. People are not "conservative," certainly not in the corporate sense, nor are they "liberal," in the sense of believing that more social programs and nitpicking regulations are going to clean up the messes that are being made by global corporate greed. People are antiestablishment mavericks, and they know (as any mother or kindergarten teacher can tell you) that the better plan is not to keep trying to clean up the messes but to get control over the brutes that are making the messes.

If the progressive movement is going to matter, going to make any difference at all in twenty-first-century politics, it has to understand and act on the latent radicalism (à la 1776) and maverick spirit of the true majority. The term "maverick" even has revolutionary roots—a member of the Maverick family was one of the five "liberty boys" killed at the "Boston Massacre" in 1770. But the term as we use it today actually came from another member of this same family. Samuel Maverick was his name, a pioneer Texas rancher who had fought in the 1836 revolution against the Mexican authorities. A thoroughly independent sort, Sam refused to brand his cattle. So, out on the range, any unbranded calf or steer one came across was said to be a maverick.

Go into the coffee shops and bars where middle-class, workaday America hangs out, chat with cab drivers and grocery clerks, visit working-class churches and neighborhood block parties, talk with nurses, janitors, mechanics, clerks, and restaurant workers while they're on break, shoot the breeze with the regulars at the barber shops or in the feed-and-seed stores. Here's where you'll find the maverick majority for the progressive politics I'm talking about, a constituency willing to run right at corporate power. This is where the progressive future is—not in Washington, fidgeting with policy on the fringes of power, quibbling over which of the namby-pamby corporate suck-ups running for president will do the most for "the cause."

Hey, let's gut it up, decamp from Washington, put our resources into the countryside, slug the corporate bastards right in the snout, and get it on with a grassroots politics that gives regular folks a reason to be excited and to get involved.

Why not start the new century and millennium with a political crusade that is worthy of all of our energies and capabilities, a fight that is big enough, important enough, and bold enough to rally the workaday majority? It's the fight to take our government back, take our economy back, take our environment back by taking our sovereignty back—taking back our constitutional right as a people to *be in charge* of our own destinies.

"I may not get there with you," said a prophetic Martin Luther King Jr. in a sermon on the eve of his assassination, but "I've seen the promised land." The land that Reverend King saw is the same land that Jim McGrath sees from Missoula, that Woody Guthrie sang about in his cross-country rambles, and that I see today as I travel. It's *our* land, an extraordinary land where ordinary people are the strength, a place with awesome *possibility* to implement the democratic ideals of the people themselves. Through the generations, Americans have taken historic stands to hold on to and advance those ideals. Now is our time, our chance, and our duty to make real the promise of democracy—if not for ourselves, then for our grandchildren.

This *is* an exciting time to be an American.

CONNECTIONS

"Agitator" is a word that the Powers That Be have tried to turn into a pejorative, as in "Those damn agitators have stirred people up." But being an agitator is what America is all about—if it was not for the agitators of circa 1776, we'd all be wearing white powdered wigs and still be singing "God Save the Queen." Agitation at the grassroots level is what it has always taken to produce progressive advances in our society. Think of it like this: the agitator is the center post in the washing machine that gets the dirt out.

The following is a list of some of the groups that not only are premier agitators themselves, but also connect up citizen agitators with solid information, with organizing assistance, with action steps . . . and with each other. There are many, many more groups than I list here, but these are ones from which I drew much of the information that's in this book. I pass the list along to assist readers who want more detail on particular issues I've raised here—and to urge you to connect up with them and other groups to agitate, agitate, agitate.

ACORN
Living Wage Resource Center
739 8th Street, SE
Washington, DC 20003
202-547-2500
www.acorn.org

Agribusiness Examiner
Corporate Agribusiness Research
    Project
P.O. Box 2201
Everett, WA 98203–0201
avkrebs@earthlink.net

Alliance for Democracy
681 Main Street, 2–16
Waltham, MA 02451
781-894-1179
http://afd.online.org

Campaign for America's Future
1101 14th Street, NW, Suite 600
Washington, DC 20005
202-955-5665
www.ourfuture.org

Center on Budget and Policy
  Priorities
820 First Street, NE, Suite 510
Washington, DC 20002
202-408-1080
www.cbpp.org

Center for Community Change
1000 Wisconsin Ave., NW
Washington, DC 20007
202-342-0519
www.communitychange.org

Center for Public Integrity
910 17th Street, NW, 7th Floor
Washington, DC 20006
202-466-1300
www.publicintegrity.org

Center for Responsive Politics
1320 19th Street, NW
Washington, DC 20036
202-857-0044
www.opensecrets.org

Ralph Nader
Center for Study of Responsive Law
P.O. Box 19405
Washington, DC 20036
202-387-8030
www.essential.org

Citizens for Tax Justice
1311 L Street, NW
Washington, DC 20005
202-626-3780
www.ctj.org

Committee for the Study of the
  American Electorate
421 New Jersey Avenue, SE
Washington, DC 20003
202-546-3221

Common Cause
1250 Connecticut Avenue, NW
Washington, D.C. 20036
202-833-1200
www.commoncause.org

Council of Canadians
502–151 Slater Street
Ottawa, ON, Canada K1P 5H3
613-233-2773
www.canadians.org

Economic Policy Institute
1660 L Street, NW, Suite 1200
Washington, DC 20036
202-775-8810
www.epinet.org

Fairness and Accuracy in
  Reporting (FAIR)
130 West 25th Street, 8th Floor
New York, NY 10001
212-633-6700
www.fair.org

Farm Aid
334 Broadway, Suite 5
Cambridge, MA 02139
617-354-2922
www.farmaid.org

Financial Markets Center
P.O. Box 334
Philomont, VA 22131
540-338-7754
www.fmcenter.org

Global Exchange
2017 Mission Street, #303
San Francisco, CA 94110
415-255-7296
www.globalexchange.org

Global Trade Watch
215 Pennsylvania Avenue, SE
Washington, DC 20003
202-546-4996
www.citizen.org

Granny D
P.O. Box 1492
Dublin, NH 03444
www.grannyd.com

Greens/Green Party USA
P.O. Box 100
Blodgett Mills, NY 13738
978-682-4353
www.greenparties.org

Independent Media Institute
77 Federal Street
San Francisco, CA 94107
415-284-1420
www.alternet.org

Institute for Agriculture and
    Trade Policy
2105 First Avenue South
Minneapolis, MN 55404
612-870-0453
www.iatp.org

Institute of Policy Studies
1601 Connecticut, NW, Room 500
Washington, DC 20009
202-234-9382
www.ips-dc.org

The International Law Project
    for Human, Ecological and
    Environmental Defense (HEED)
8124 W. 3rd Street, Suite 201
Los Angeles, CA 90048
213-736-1000
www.heed.net

Jobs With Justice
501 Third Street, NW
Washington, DC 20001
202-434-1106
www.jwj.org

Labor Party
P.O. Box 53177
Washington, DC 20009
20-234-5190
www.labornet.org/lpa

Multinational Monitor
P.O. Box 19405
Washington, DC 20036
202-387-8034
www.essential.org/monitor

National Farmers Union
400 Virginia Avenue, SW,
    Suite 710
Washington, DC 20024
202-554-1600
www.nfu.org

National Labor Committee
275 7th Avenue, 16th floor
New York, NY 10001
212-242-3002
www.nlcnet.org

National Low Income Housing
    Coalition
1012 14th Street, NW, #1200
Washington, DC 20005
202-662-1530
www.nlihc.org

National Priorities Project
Sullivan Square, 3rd Floor
17 New South Street
Northhampton, MA 01060
413-584-9556
www.natprior.org

New England Burma Roundtable
    Trillium Asset Management
711 Atlantic Avenue
Boston, MA 02111
800-548-5684
www.trilliuminvest.com

New Party
88 Third Avenue
Brooklyn, NY 11217
800-200-1294
www.newparty.org

The Preamble Center for Public
    Policy
1737 21st Street
Washington, DC 20009
202-265-3263
www.preamble.org

The Program On Corporations,
    Law & Democracy (POCLAD)
P.O. Box 806
Cambridge, MA 02140
508-398-1145
www.poclad.org

Public Campaign
1320 19th Street, NW, Suite M1
Washington, DC 20036
202-293-0222
www.publicampaign.org

Public Citizen
1600 20th Street, NW
Washington, DC 20009
202-588-1000
www.citizen.org

Reform Party
P.O. Box 9
Dallas, TX 75221
www.reformparty.org

Rocky Mountain Media Watch
P.O. Box 18858
Denver, CO 80218
303-832-7558
www.bigmedia.org

Shadow Bureau of Government
    Statistics
P.O. Box 348
Hawthorne, NJ 07507

Sindlinger Fax
405 Osborne Lane
Wallingford, PA 19086

TomPaine.com
1636 Connecticut Avenue, NW,
    Suite 30
Washington, DC 20009
202-332-2881
www.tompaine.com

United for a Fair Economy
37 Temple Place, 5th Floor
Boston, MA 02111
617-423-2148
www.stw.org

United Students Against Sweatshops
1413 K Street, NW, 9th Floor
Washington, DC 20005
202-NO SWEAT
www.umich.edu/"sole/usassy1/
    or by 2000, try: www.usass.org

US Public Interest Research
Group (PIRG)
218 D Street, SE
Washington,DC 20003
202-546-9707
www.pirg.org

INDEX